TO

FROM

DATE

3-Minute Devotions
for Women

CHOOSE
joy

FOR
MORNING &
EVENING

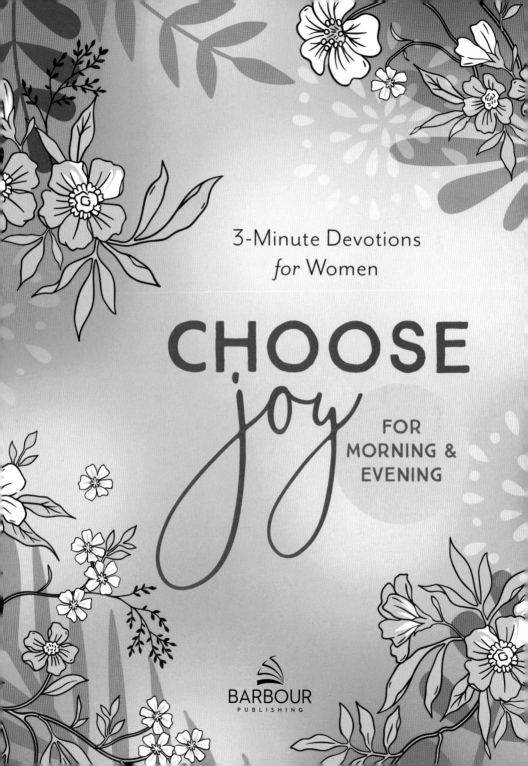

BARBOUR
PUBLISHING

MORNING AND EVENING. . .
joy for your soul

I'm thanking you, GOD, from a full heart,
I'm writing the book on your wonders.
I'm whistling, laughing, and jumping for joy;
I'm singing your song, High God.
PSALM 9:1–2 MSG

This delightful *Choose Joy for Morning and Evening* devotional collection
will help you discover an abundance of comfort and inspiration in daily,
just-right-sized morning and evening readings that will help you grow
ever closer to the Joy-Giver Himself. Each day's reading will meet you
right where you are and is a simple and practical way to begin a lifelong
habit of daily quiet time in the heavenly Father's presence.

Be blessed!

JOY IN THE *morning* MORNING

All who seek the LORD will praise him.
Their hearts will rejoice with everlasting joy.
PSALM 22:26 NLT

Every day, God provides us with beauty all around to cheer and help us. It may come through the beauty of flowers or the bright blue sky—or maybe the white snow covering the trees of a glorious winter wonderland. It may be through the smile of a child or the grateful face of the one we care for. Each and every day, the Lord has a special gift to remind us of whose we are and to generate the joy we need to succeed.

Lord God, I thank You for Your joy; I thank You for providing it
every day to sustain me. I will be joyful in You. Amen.

HE ENJOYS *evening* YOU

"The LORD your God is in your midst, a mighty one who will
save; he will rejoice over you with gladness; he will quiet you
by his love; he will exult over you with loud singing."
ZEPHANIAH 3:17 ESV

Zephaniah's words remind us that God is our loving parent. Our mighty Savior offers us a personal relationship, loving and rejoicing over us, His children, glad that we live and move in Him. He is the Lord of the universe, and yet He will quiet our restless hearts and minds with His tender love. He delights in our lives and celebrates our union with Him. We can rest in His affirmation and love, no matter what circumstances surround us.

Lord, help me remember that You are always with me
and that You delight in me. Remind me that I am Your
child and that You enjoy our relationship. Amen.

morning
SWEET AROMA

The heartfelt counsel of a friend is as sweet as perfume and incense.
PROVERBS 27:9 NLT

Whether it's over coffee, dessert, or even on the phone, a cherished friend can offer the encouragement and God-directed counsel we all need from time to time. Friendships that have Christ as their center are wonderful relationships blessed by the Father. Through the timely, godly advice these friends offer, God speaks to us, showering us with comfort that is as sweet as perfume and incense. So what are you waiting for? Make a date with a friend and share the sweet aroma of Jesus!

Jesus, Your friendship means the world to me. I value the close friendships You've blessed me with too! Thank You for the special women in my life. Show me every day how to be a blessing to them, just as they are to me. Amen.

evening
THE NEW ME

Therefore, if anyone is in Christ, the new creation has come: The old has gone, the new is here!
2 CORINTHIANS 5:17 NIV

Are you in Christ? Is He consistently Lord of your life? Then you are a new creation. *Everything* is new. What's history is done and over—and Jesus has replaced your old with His new: new peace, new joy, new love, new strength. Since God Himself sees us as a new creation, how can we do any less? We need to choose to see ourselves as a new creation too. And we can, through God's grace. Be glad. Give thanks. Live each day as the new creation you have become through Jesus.

Father, I'm so thankful that You are a God of grace—and I thank You that I am a new creation. Please give me the spiritual eyes to see myself as a new creation, looking past the guilt of yesterday's choices. Amen.

morning
SET FREE

The Spirit you received does not make you slaves, so that you live in fear again; rather, the Spirit you received brought about your adoption to sonship. And by him we cry, "Abba, Father."
ROMANS 8:15 NIV

Do you struggle with fear? Do you feel it binding you with its invisible chains? If so, then there's good news. Through Jesus, you have received the Spirit of sonship. A son (or daughter) of the Most High God has nothing to fear. Knowing you've been set free is enough to make you cry, "Abba, Father!" in praise. Today, acknowledge your fears to the Lord. He will loose your chains and set you free.

Lord, thank You that You are the great chain breaker! I don't have to live in fear. I am Your child, Your daughter, and You are my Daddy-God! Amen.

evening
PEOPLE PLEASER VS. GOD PLEASER

We are not trying to please people but God, who tests our hearts.
1 THESSALONIANS 2:4 NIV

When we allow ourselves to be real before God, it doesn't matter what others think. If the God of the universe has accepted us, then who cares about someone else's opinion? It is impossible to please both God and man. We must make a choice. Man looks at the outward appearance, but God looks at the heart. Align your heart with His. Let go of impression management that focuses on outward appearance. Receive God's unconditional love, and enjoy the freedom to be yourself before Him!

Dear Lord, may I live for You alone. Help me transition from a people pleaser to a God pleaser. Amen.

morning
HE WILL SEND HELP

*"The waves of death swirled about me; the torrents of destruction
overwhelmed me. . . . In my distress I called to the LORD. . . .
From his temple he heard my voice; my cry came to his ears."*
2 SAMUEL 22:5, 7 NIV

God never asked us to do life alone. When the waves of death swirl around us, and the pounding rain of destruction threatens to overwhelm us, we can cry out to our heavenly Father, knowing that He will not let us drown. He will hear our voice, and He will send help. So, next time you feel that you can't put one foot in front of the other, ask God to send you His strength and energy. He will help you to live out your purpose in this chaotic world.

*Lord, thank You for strengthening me when the "dailyness" of life,
and its various trials, threatens to overwhelm me. Amen.*

evening
SHAKE IT UP!

*The LORD had said to Abram, "Leave your native country, your
relatives, and your father's family, and go to the land that I will show
you. . . . I will bless you. . .and you will be a blessing to others."*
GENESIS 12:1–2 NLT

In God's wisdom, He likes to shake us up a little, stretch us out of our comfort zone, push us out on a limb. Yet we resist the change, cling to what's known, and try to change His mind with fat, sloppy tears. Are you facing a big change? God wants us to be willing to embrace change that He brings into our lives. Even unbidden change. You may feel as if you're out on a limb, but don't forget that God is the tree trunk. He's not going to let you fall.

*Holy, loving Father, in every area of my life,
teach me to trust You more deeply. Amen.*

morning
RELEASE THE MUSIC WITHIN

Those who are wise will find a time and a way to do what is right.
ECCLESIASTES 8:5 NLT

It has been said that many people go to their graves with their music still in them. Do you carry a song within your heart, waiting to be heard?

Whether we are eight or eighty, it is never too late to surrender our hopes and dreams to God. A wise woman trusts that God will help her find the time and manner in which to use her talents for His glory as she seeks His direction. Let the music begin.

Dear Lord, my music is fading against the constant beat of a busy pace. I surrender my gifts to You and pray for the time and manner in which I can use those gifts to touch my world. Amen.

evening
SIMPLY SILLY

A cheerful disposition is good for your health.
PROVERBS 17:22 MSG

Imagine the effect we could have on our world today if our countenance reflected the joy of the Lord all the time: at work, at home, at play. Jesus said, "I have told you this so that my joy may be in you and that your joy may be complete" (John 15:11 NIV). Is your cup of joy full? Have you laughed today? Not a small smile, but laughter. Maybe it's time we looked for something to laugh about and tasted joy. Jesus suggested it.

Lord, help me find joy this day. Let me laugh and give praises to the King. Amen.

morning
ANXIOUS ANTICIPATIONS

*I am not saying this because I am in need, for I have
learned to be content whatever the circumstances.*

PHILIPPIANS 4:11 NIV

Have you ever been so eager for the future that you forgot to be thankful for the present day?

Humans have a tendency to complain about the problems and irritations of life. It's much less natural to appreciate the good things we have—until they're gone. While it's fine to look forward to the future, let's remember to reflect on all of *today's* blessings—the large and the small—and appreciate all that we do have.

*Thank You, Lord, for the beauty of today. Please remind me when I become
preoccupied with the future and forget to enjoy the present. Amen.*

evening
REFRESHING GIFT

*For we have great joy and consolation in your love, because the
hearts of the saints have been refreshed by you, brother.*

PHILEMON 1:7 NKJV

Jesus always took the time for those who reached out to Him. In a crowd of people, He stopped to help a woman who touched Him. His quiet love extended to everyone who asked, whether verbally or with unspoken need. God brings people into our path who need our encouragement. We must consider those around us. Smile and thank the waiter, the cashier, the people who help in small ways. Cheering others can have the effect of an energizing drink of water so that they will be able to finish the race with a smile.

*Jesus, thank You for being an example of how to encourage and refresh
others. Help me to see their need and to be willing to reach out. Amen.*

morning
INFINITE AND PERSONAL

*Am I a God at hand, saith the LORD, and not a God
afar off? . . . Do not I fill heaven and earth?*
JEREMIAH 23:23–24 KJV

God says that He is both close at hand and over all there is. Whether your day is crumbling around you or is the best day you have ever had, do you see God in it? If the "sky is falling" or the sun is shining, do you still recognize the One who orders all the planets and all your days? Whether we see Him or not, God tells us He is there. And He's here too—in the good times and bad.

*Lord, empower me to trust You when it's hard to remember that You are
near. And help me to live thankfully when times are good. Amen.*

evening
CHOSEN

*"Before I formed you in the womb I knew you [and approved of you as
My chosen instrument], and before you were born I consecrated you."*
JEREMIAH 1:5 AMP

God said that before He formed Jeremiah in his mother's womb, He knew him. God separated him from everyone else to perform a specific task, and He consecrated him for that purpose. We can be sure that if God did that for Jeremiah, He did it for each one of us. Nothing about us or our circumstances surprises God. He knew about everything before we were born. And He ordained that we should walk in those ways because we are uniquely qualified by Him to do so. What an awesome God we serve!

*Father, the thought that You chose me before the foundation of the
world and set me apart for a specific calling is humbling. You are
so good. May I go forward with a renewed purpose in life. Amen.*

GOD IN THE *morning* DETAILS

*"When we heard of it, our hearts melted in fear and
everyone's courage failed because of you, for the LORD your
God is God in heaven above and on the earth below."*

JOSHUA 2:11 NIV

Sometimes, when our lives seem to be under siege from the demands of work, bills, family, whatever, finding the work of God amid the strife can be difficult. Even though we acknowledge His power, we may overlook the gentle touches, the small ways in which He makes every day a little easier. Just as the Lord cares for the tiniest bird (Matthew 10:29–31), so He seeks to be a part of every detail in your life. Look for Him there.

*Father God, I know You are by my side every day, good or bad,
and that You love and care for me. Help me to see Your work in
my life and in the lives of my friends and family. Amen.*

PRACTICALITY VS *evening* PASSION

*Leaving her water jar, the woman went back to the
town and said to the people, "Come, see a man who told
me everything I ever did. Could this be the Messiah?"*

JOHN 4:28–29 NIV

Practicality gave way to passion the day the woman at the well abandoned her task, laid down her jar, and ran into town. Everything changed the day she met a man at the well and He asked her for a drink of water. Although they had never met before, He told her everything she had ever done, and then He offered her living water that would never run dry. Do you live with such passion, or do you cling to your water jar? Has an encounter with Christ made an impact that cannot be denied in your life?

*Lord, help me to lay down anything that stifles my passion
for sharing the Good News with others. Amen.*

morning
MARVELOUS PLANS

*Lord, you are my God; I will exalt you and praise
your name, for in perfect faithfulness you have done
wonderful things, things planned long ago.*

ISAIAH 25:1 NIV

God has a "promised land" for us all—a marvelous plan for our lives. Recount and record His faithfulness in your life in the past, because God has already demonstrated His marvelous plans to you in so many ways. Then prayerfully anticipate the future journey with Him. Keep a record of God's marvelous plans in a journal as He unfolds them day by day. You will find God to be faithful in the smallest aspects of your life and oh so worthy of your trust.

*O Lord, help me to recount Your faithfulness, record Your faithfulness,
and trust Your faithfulness in the future. For You are my God, and
You have done marvelous things, planned long ago. Amen.*

evening
LIFE PRESERVERS

*My comfort in my suffering is this:
Your promise preserves my life.*

PSALM 119:50 NIV

In the difficulties of life, God is our life preserver. When we are battered by the waves of trouble, we can expect God to understand and to comfort us in our distress. His Word, like a buoyant life preserver, holds us up in the bad times. But the life preserver only works if you put it on *before* your boat sinks. God will surround you with His love and protection—even if you're unconscious of His presence. He promises to keep our heads above water in the storms of living.

*Preserving God, I cling to You as my life preserver. Keep my head above the
turbulent waters so I don't drown. Bring me safely to the shore. Amen.*

A SHADOW OF THE PAST
morning

*"Only Rahab the prostitute and all who are with her in her
house shall be spared, because she hid the spies we sent."*
JOSHUA 6:17 NIV

Rahab wasn't trapped by her past. It didn't hold her back. She was used by God. Her name has come down to us centuries later because of her bold faith. We all have to deal with a past. But God is able to bring good from a painful past. By the grace and power of God, we can make choices in the present that can affect our future. There is transforming power with God. We have hope, no matter what lies behind us.

*Holy Spirit, You are always at work. Don't ever stop! Show me a
new way, Lord. Help me to make healthier choices for myself and my
family. Thank You for Your renewing presence in my life. Amen.*

CHARM BRACELET
evening

*But the fruit of the Spirit is love, joy, peace, patience, kindness, goodness,
faithfulness, gentleness, self-control; against such things there is no law.*
GALATIANS 5:22–23 NASB

A charm bracelet is a beautiful way to commemorate milestones or special events. Consider your spiritual charm bracelet. If you had a charm to represent your growth in each of the traits from Galatians 5, how many would you feel comfortable attaching to your bracelet in representation of that achievement? Ask your Father which areas in your Christian walk need the most growth. Do you need to develop those traits more before you feel comfortable donning your bracelet?

*Lord, please show me which milestones of Christian living I need to focus
on in order to have the full markings of the Holy Spirit in my life. Please
help me to grow into the Christian woman You call me to be. Amen.*

morning
BOARD GOD'S BOAT

*Then, because so many people were coming and going that they
did not even have a chance to eat, he said to them, "Come with
me by yourselves to a quiet place and get some rest."*

MARK 6:31 NIV

The apostles ministered tirelessly—so much so, they had little time to eat. The Lord noticed that they had neglected to take time for themselves. Sensitive to their needs, the Savior instructed them to retreat by boat with Him to a solitary place of rest where He was able to minister to them. Often we allow the hectic pace of daily life to drain us physically and spiritually, and in the process, we deny ourselves time alone to pray and read God's Word. Meanwhile, God patiently waits. So perhaps it's time to board God's boat to a quieter place!

*Heavenly Father, in my hectic life I've neglected time apart
with You. Help me to board Your boat and stay afloat through
spending time in Your Word and in prayer. Amen.*

evening
A CHILD IN NEED

*"For all those things My hand has made, and all those things exist,"
says the LORD. "But on this one will I look: on him who is poor
and of a contrite spirit, and who trembles at My word."*

ISAIAH 66:2 NKJV

A humble child of God with a need catches His eye. Though He is always watching over all of us, He is drawn to a child who needs Him. We may need forgiveness, wisdom, courage, endurance, patience, health, protection, or even love. God promises to come to our aid when He sees us with a hand up, reaching for His assistance. What needs do you have in your life today? Raise your hand in prayer to God. He'll take care of your needs, and then some—blessing your life in ways you can't even imagine!

*Father, thank You for caring about the needs of Your children.
Help me to remember to always seek You first. Amen.*

THE SECRET OF *morning* SERENDIPITY

A happy heart makes the face cheerful.

PROVERBS 15:13 NIV

Can you remember the last time you laughed in wild abandon? Better yet, when was the last time you did something fun, outrageous, or out of the ordinary? Perhaps it is an activity you haven't done since you were a child, like slip down a waterslide, strap on a pair of ice skates, or pitch a tent and camp overnight. A happy heart turns life's situations into opportunities for fun. When we seek innocent pleasures, we glean the benefits of a happy heart. So try a bit of whimsy just for fun. And rediscover the secret of serendipity.

*Dear Lord, because of You, I have a happy heart. Lead me
to do something fun and spontaneous today! Amen.*

A VERY IMPORTANT *evening* PHRASE

And it came to pass. . .

FOUND MORE THAN 400 TIMES IN THE KING JAMES BIBLE

There are times in life when we think we can't bear one more day, one more hour, one more minute. But no matter how bad things seem at the time, they are temporary. What's really important is how we handle the opportunities before us today, whether we let our trials defeat us or look for the hand of God in everything. Every day, week, and year are made up of things that "come to pass"—so even if we fail, we needn't be disheartened. Other opportunities—better days—will come. Let's look past those hard things today and glorify the name of the Lord.

*Lord Jesus, how awesome it is that You send or allow these
little things that will pass. May we recognize Your hand
in them today and praise You for them. Amen.*

morning
THE WHITE KNIGHT

Then I will rejoice in the LORD. I will be glad because he rescues me.
PSALM 35:9 NLT

We're all waiting for someone to rescue us. We wait and wait and wait. . . The truth is, God doesn't want you to exist in a perpetual state of waiting. Live your life—your whole life—by seeking daily joy in the Savior of your soul, Jesus Christ. And here's the best news of all: He's already done the rescuing by dying on the cross for our sins! He's the *true* white knight who secured your eternity in heaven. Stop waiting; seek His face today!

Jesus, I praise You because You are the rescuer of my soul. Remind me of this fact when I'm looking for relief in other people and places. You take care of my present and eternal needs, and for that I am grateful. Amen.

evening
IS ANYONE LISTENING?

"And I will ask the Father, and He will give you another Helper (Comforter, Advocate, Intercessor—Counselor, Strengthener, Standby), to be with you forever."
JOHN 14:16 AMP

Our heavenly Father wants to hear from us. He cares so much that He sent the Holy Spirit to be our Counselor, our Comforter. When we pray—when we tell God our needs and give Him praise—He listens. Then He directs the Spirit within us to speak to our hearts and give us reassurance. Our world is filled with noise and distractions. Look for a place where you can be undisturbed for a few minutes. Take a deep breath, lift your prayers, and listen. God will speak—and your heart will hear.

Dear Lord, I thank You for Your care. Help me to recognize Your voice and to listen well. Amen.

A COMFORTABLE PLACE
morning

Don't you realize that your body is the temple of the Holy Spirit, who lives in you and was given to you by God? You do not belong to yourself.
1 Corinthians 6:19 nlt

We take the time to make our homes comfortable and beautiful when we know visitors are coming. In the same way, we ought to prepare our hearts for the Holy Spirit who lives inside of us. We should daily ask God to help us clean up the junk in our hearts. We should take special care to tune up our bodies through exercise, eating healthful foods, and dressing attractively and modestly. Our bodies belong to God. Taking care of ourselves shows others that we honor God enough to respect and use wisely what He has given us.

Dear Lord, thank You for letting me belong to You.
May my body be a comfortable place for You. Amen.

ONE THING IS NEEDED
evening

"Martha, Martha," the Lord answered, "you are worried and upset about many things, but few things are needed—or indeed only one."
Luke 10:41–42 niv

We are each given twenty-four hours in a day. Einstein and Edison were given no more than Joseph and Jeremiah of the Old Testament. Since God has blessed each of us with twenty-four hours, let's seek His direction on how to spend this invaluable commodity wisely—giving more to people than things, spending more time on relationships than the rat race. In Luke, our Lord reminded dear, dogged, drained Martha that only one thing is needed—Him.

Father God, I often get caught up in the minutiae of life. The piled laundry
can appear more important than the people around me. Help me to use
my time wisely. Open my eyes to see what is truly important. Amen.

morning
WHO HELPS THE HELPER?

The LORD is my strength and my shield; my heart trusted in him, and I am helped:
therefore my heart greatly rejoiceth; and with my song will I praise him.
PSALM 28:7 KJV

Helping can be exhausting. The needs of young children, teens, grandchildren, aging parents, our neighbors and fellow church members—the list is never ending—can stretch us until we're ready to snap. And then we find that *we* need help. Who helps the helper? The Lord does. When we are weak, He is strong. When we are vulnerable, He is our shield. When we can no longer trust in our own resources, we can trust in Him. He is always there, ready to help. Rejoice in Him, praise His name, and you will find the strength to go on.

Father, I'm worn out. I can't care for all the people and needs
You bring into my life by myself. I need Your strength.
Thank You for being my Helper and my Shield. Amen.

evening
MAGNIFYING LIFE

My soul makes its boast in the LORD; let the humble hear and be glad.
Oh, magnify the LORD with me, and let us exalt his name together!
PSALM 34:2–3 ESV

Mary knew she was the object of God's favor and mercy. That knowledge produced humility. Try as we might, we can't produce this humility in ourselves. It is our natural tendency to be self-promoters. . .to better our own reputations. We need the help of the Spirit to remind us that God has favored each of us with His presence. He did not have to come to us in Christ, but He did. He has chosen to set His love on us. His life *redeemed* ours, and He sanctifies us. We are recipients of the action of His grace.

Christ Jesus, help me remember what You have done for me
and to desire for others to see and know You. Amen.

morning
NO MORE STING

O death, where is thy sting? O grave, where is thy victory?
1 CORINTHIANS 15:55 KJV

We have a choice to make. We can either live life in fear or live life by faith. Fear and faith cannot coexist. Jesus Christ has conquered our greatest fear—death. He rose victorious and has given us eternal life through faith. Knowing this truth enables us to courageously face our fears. There is no fear that cannot be conquered by faith. Let's not panic but trust the Lord instead. Let's live by faith and experience the victory that has been given to us through Jesus Christ, our Lord.

Lord, You alone know my fears. Help me to trust You more.
May I walk in the victory that You have purchased for me. Amen.

evening
WELL WATERED

"The LORD will guide you always; he will satisfy your needs in a
sun-scorched land and will strengthen your frame. You will be like
a well-watered garden, like a spring whose waters never fail."
ISAIAH 58:11 NIV

We need a downpour of God's Word and the Holy Spirit's presence in our parched spirits. Not an occasional sprinkle, but a soul-soaking to replenish our frazzled bodies and weary minds. We know this soaking comes from consistent Bible study, the necessary pruning of confessed sin, and prayer time. These produce a well-watered garden, fruitful and lush, mirroring God's beauty, creating a life to which others are drawn to come and linger in His refreshing presence.

Eternal Father, strengthen my frame, guide my paths, and
satisfy my needs as only You can. Make my life a well-watered
garden, fruitful for You and Your purposes. Amen.

morning
A BETTER OFFER

"So in everything, do to others what you would have them do to you."
MATTHEW 7:12 NIV

Jesus took responsibilities, commitments, and obligations seriously. In fact, Jesus said, "All you need to say is simply 'Yes' or 'No'; anything beyond this comes from the evil one" (Matthew 5:37 NIV). Satan desires for us to be stressed out, overcommitted, and not able to do anything well. Satan delights when we treat others in an unkind, offensive manner. However, God, upon request, will help us prioritize our commitments so that our "yes" is "yes" and our "no" is "no." Then in everything we do, we are liberated to do to others as we would have them do to us.

Lord, please prioritize my commitments to enable me in everything to do to others as I would desire for them to do to me. Amen.

evening
PUT ON A HAPPY FACE

He restoreth my soul: he leadeth me in the
paths of righteousness for his name's sake.
PSALM 23:3 KJV

Our God is not a God of negativity but of possibility. He will guide us through our difficulties and beyond them. Today we should turn our thoughts and prayers toward Him. Focus on a hymn or a praise song and play it in your mind. Praise chases away the doldrums and tips our lips up in a smile. With a renewed spirit of optimism and hope, we can thank the Giver of all things good. Thankfulness to the Father can turn our plastic smiles into real ones, and as the psalm states, our souls will be restored.

Father, I'm down in the dumps today. You are my unending source of strength. Gather me in Your arms for always. Amen.

morning ONE STEP AT A TIME

*With your help I can advance against a troop;
with my God I can scale a wall.*
PSALM 18:29 NIV

We often become discouraged when we face a mountain-size task. Whether it's weight loss or a graduate degree or our income taxes, some things just seem impossible. And they often *can't* be done—not all at once. Tasks like these are best faced one step at a time. One pound at a time. Chipping away instead of moving the whole mountain at once. With patience, perseverance, and God's help, your goals may be more attainable than you think.

Dear Father, the task before me seems impossible. However, I know I can do it with Your help. I pray that I will trust You every step of the way. Amen.

evening MIRROR IMAGE

Behold, thou art fair, my love; behold, thou art fair; thou hast doves' eyes.
SONG OF SOLOMON 1:15 KJV

No matter how hard we try, when the focus is on self, we see shortcomings. Our only hope is to see ourselves through a different mirror. We must remember that as we grow as Christians, we take on the characteristics of Christ. The more we become like Him, the more beautiful we are in our own eyes and to those around us. God loves to behold us when we are covered in Christ. The mirror image He sees has none of the blemishes or imperfections, only the beauty.

*O God, thank You for beholding me as being fair and valuable.
Help me to see myself through Your eyes. Amen.*

morning
STOP AND CONSIDER

*"Listen to this, Job; stop and consider God's wonders. Do you know how
God controls the clouds and makes his lightning flash? Do you know how the
clouds hang poised, those wonders of him who has perfect knowledge?"*

JOB 37:14–16 NIV

"Stop and consider My wonders," God told Job. Then He pointed to ordinary observations of the natural world surrounding Job—the clouds that hung poised in the sky, the flashes of lightning. "Not so very ordinary" was God's lesson. Maybe He was trying to remind us that there is no such thing as ordinary. Let's open our eyes and see the wonders around us.

*O Father, teach me to stop and consider the ordinary moments
of my life as reminders of You. Help me not to overlook Your
daily care and provisions that surround my day. Amen.*

evening
REJOICING WITH FRIENDS

*"Then he calls his friends and neighbors together and says,
'Rejoice with me; I have found my lost sheep.'"*

LUKE 15:6 NIV

Think of all the reasons you have to celebrate. Are you in good health? Have you overcome a tough obstacle? Are you handling your finances without much grief? Doing well at your job? Bonding with friends or family? If so, then throw yourself a party and invite a friend. Better yet, call your friends and neighbors together, as the scripture indicates. Share your praises with people who will truly appreciate all that the Lord is doing in your life. Let the party begin!

*Lord, thank You that I'm created in the image of a God who knows
how to celebrate. I have so many reasons to rejoice today. Thank
You for Your many blessings. And today I especially want to thank
You for giving me friends to share my joys and sorrows. Amen.*

morning
WHY ME?

*I am Alpha and Omega, the beginning and the ending, saith the Lord,
which is, and which was, and which is to come, the Almighty.*
REVELATION 1:8 KJV

When God spoke our world into existence, He called into being a certain reality, knowing then everything that ever was to happen—and everyone who ever was to be. That you exist now is cause for rejoicing! God made *you* to fellowship with Him! If that fellowship demands trials for a season, rejoice that God thinks you worthy to share in the sufferings of Christ—and, eventually, in His glory. Praise His holy name!

*Father, I thank You for giving me this difficult time in my life. Shine
through all my trials today. I want You to get the glory. Amen.*

evening
FAITH, THE EMOTIONAL BALANCER

*No man is justified by the law in the sight of God,
it is evident: for, The just shall live by faith.*
GALATIANS 3:11 KJV

Emotions mislead us. One day shines with promise as we bounce out of bed in song, while the next day dims in despair and we'd prefer to hide under the bedcovers. It has been said that faith is the bird that feels the light and sings to greet the dawn while it is still dark. The Bible instructs us to live by faith—not by feelings. Faith assures us that daylight will dawn in our darkest moments, affirming God's presence so that even when we fail to pray and positive feelings fade, our moods surrender to song.

*Heavenly Father, I desire for my faith, not my emotions, to
dictate my life. I pray for balance in my hide-under-the-cover
days so that I might surrender to You in song. Amen.*

morning
CHOOSE LIFE

*"The thief comes only to steal and kill and destroy; I have
come that they may have life, and have it to the full."*
JOHN 10:10 NIV

God's Word shows us the lie—and the "liar"—behind defeating thoughts. We have an enemy who delights in our believing negative things, an enemy who wants only destruction for our souls. But Jesus came to give us life! We only have to choose it, as an act of the will blended with faith. When we rely on Him alone, He'll enable us to not only survive but *thrive* in our daily routine. Each day, let's make a conscious decision to take hold of what Christ offers us—life, to the full.

*Loving Lord, help me daily to choose You and the life
You want to give me. Give me the eyes of faith to trust
that You will enable me to serve lovingly. Amen.*

evening
FOLLOW THE LORD'S FOOTSTEPS

Then He said to them, "Follow Me, and I will make you fishers of men."
MATTHEW 4:19 NKJV

Jesus asked His disciples to follow Him, and He asks us to do the same. Following Jesus requires staying right on His heels. We need to be close enough to hear His whisper. Stay close to His heart by opening the Bible daily. Allow His Word to speak to your heart and give you direction. Throughout the day, offer up prayers for guidance and wisdom. Keep in step with Him, and His close presence will bless you beyond measure.

*Dear Lord, grant me the desire to follow You.
Help me not to run ahead or lag behind. Amen.*

morning
ANNUAL OR PERENNIAL?

*They are like trees planted along the riverbank, bearing fruit each
season. Their leaves never wither, and they prosper in all they do.*
PSALM 1:3 NLT

Annuals or perennials? Each has its advantages. Annuals are inexpensive, provide instant gratification, and keep boredom from setting in. Perennials require an initial investment but, when properly tended, faithfully provide beauty year after year—long after the annuals have dried up and withered away. Perennials are designed for the long haul—not just short-term enjoyment, but long-term beauty. The application to our lives is twofold. First, be a perennial—long lasting, enduring, slow growing, steady, and faithful. Second, don't be discouraged by your inevitable dormant seasons. Tend to your soul, and it will reward you with years of lush blossoms.

Father, be the gardener of my soul. Amen.

evening
HAVE YOU LOOKED UP?

*The heavens proclaim the glory of God. The skies display his craftsmanship.
Day after day they continue to speak; night after night they make him known.*
PSALM 19:1–2 NLT

God has placed glimpses of creation's majesty—evidence of His love—throughout our world. Sunsets, seashells, flowers, snowflakes, changing seasons, moonlit shadows. Such glories are right in front of us every single day! But we must develop eyes to see these reminders in our daily life and not let the cares and busyness of our lives keep our heads turned down. Have you looked up today?

*Lord, open my eyes! Unstuff my ears! Teach me to see the wonders
of Your creation every day and to point them out to others. Amen.*

morning
FAULTLESS

*To him who is able to keep you from stumbling and to present you
before his glorious presence without fault and with great joy. . .*
JUDE 1:24 NIV

Jesus loves us so much despite our shortcomings. He is the One who can keep us from falling—who can present us faultless before the Father. Because of this, we can have our joy restored no matter what. Whether we have done wrong and denied it or have been falsely accused, we can come into His presence to be restored and lifted up. Let us keep our eyes on Him instead of on our need to justify ourselves to God or others.

*Thank You, Jesus, for Your cleansing love and for
the joy we can find in Your presence. Amen.*

evening
REFLECTING GOD IN OUR WORK

*Whatever you do, work at it with all your heart,
as working for the Lord, not for human masters.*
COLOSSIANS 3:23 NIV

As believers, we are God's children. No one is perfect, and for this there is grace. However, we may be the only reflection of our heavenly Father that some will ever see. Our attitudes and actions on the job speak volumes to those around us. Although it may be tempting to do just enough to get by, we put forth our best effort when we remember we represent God to the world. A Christian's character on the job should be a positive reflection of the Lord.

*Father, help me to represent You well through
my work. I want to reflect Your love in all I do. Amen.*

morning
JUST HALF A CUP

"I am coming to you now, but I say these things while I am still in the world, so that they may have the full measure of my joy within them."
JOHN 17:13 NIV

Our heavenly Father longs to bestow His richest blessings and wisdom on us. He loves us, so He desires to fill our cup to overflowing with the things that He knows will bring us pleasure and growth. Do you tell Him to stop pouring when your cup is only half full? You may not even realize it, but perhaps your actions dictate that your cup remain half empty. Seek a full cup, and enjoy the full measure of the joy of the Lord.

Dear Jesus, forgive me for not accepting the fullness of Your blessings and Your joy. Help me to see the ways that I prevent my cup from being filled to overflowing. Thank You for wanting me to have the fullness of Your joy. Amen.

evening
HIDE AND SEEK

"And do you seek great things for yourself? Seek them not, for behold, I am bringing disaster upon all flesh, declares the LORD."
JEREMIAH 45:5 ESV

God warns us: *"Don't seek great things."* The more we seek them, the more elusive they become. As soon as we think we have them in our grasp, they disappear. If we commit to more activities than we can realistically handle, the best result is that we can't follow through. Worse, we might make them our god. Jesus tells us what we should seek: the kingdom of God and His righteousness (Matthew 6:33). When we seek the right things, He'll give us every good and perfect gift (James 1:17). And that will be more than we can ask or dream.

Lord, please teach me to seek not greatness, but You. May You be the all in all of my life. Amen.

morning
LOCATION, LOCATION, LOCATION

Those who live in the shelter of the Most High will find rest in the shadow of the Almighty. This I declare about the Lord: He alone is my refuge, my place of safety; he is my God, and I trust him.
PSALM 91:1–2 NLT

If something is getting you down in life, check your location. Where are your thoughts? Let what the world has conditioned you to think go in one ear and out the other. Stand on the truth, the promises of God's Word. Say of the Lord, "God is my refuge! I am hidden in Christ! Nothing can harm me. In Him I trust!" Say it loud. Say it often. Say it over and over until it becomes your reality. And you will find yourself dwelling in that secret place every moment of the day.

God, You are my refuge. When I abide in You, nothing can harm me. Your Word is the truth on which I rely. Fill me with Your light and the peace of Your love. It's You and me, Lord, all the way! Amen.

evening
LIGHT MY PATH

Your word is a lamp for my feet, a light on my path.
PSALM 119:105 NIV

God's Word is like a streetlamp. Often, we *think* we know where we're going and where the stumbling blocks are. We believe we can avoid pitfalls and maneuver the path successfully on our own. But the truth is that without God's Word, we are walking in darkness, stumbling and tripping. When we sincerely begin to search God's Word, we find the path becomes clear. God's light allows us to live our lives in the most fulfilling way possible, a way planned out from the very beginning by God Himself.

Jesus, shine Your light upon my path. I have spent too long wandering through the darkness, looking for my way. As I search Your Word, I ask You to make it a lamp to my feet so that I can avoid the pitfalls of the world and walk safely along the path You have created specifically for me. Amen.

DAY 26

morning POWER UP

The Spirit of God, who raised Jesus from the dead, lives in you.
ROMANS 8:11 NLT

God is the same yesterday, today, and forever. His strength does not diminish over time. That same mountain-moving power you read about in the lives of people from the Old and New Testaments still exists today. We don't have to go it alone. Our heavenly Father wants to help. All we have to do is ask. He has already made His power available to His children. Whatever we face, wherever we go, whatever dreams we have for our lives, take courage and know that anything is possible when we draw on the power of God.

Father, help me to remember that You are always with
me, ready to help me do all things. Amen.

evening COMFORT FOOD

For whatever things were written before were written for our learning, that
we through the patience and comfort of the Scriptures might have hope.
ROMANS 15:4 NKJV

Romans 15:4 tells us that the scriptures are comfort food for the soul. They were written and given so that, through our learning, we would be comforted with the truths of God. Worldly pleasures bring a temporary comfort, but the problem still remains when the pleasure or comfort fades. However, the words of God are soothing and provide permanent hope and peace. Through God's Word, you will be changed, and your troubles will dim in the bright light of Christ. So the next time you are sad, lonely, or disappointed, turn to the Word of God as your source of comfort.

Thank You, Father, for the rich comfort Your Word provides.
Help me to remember to find my comfort in scripture rather than
through earthly things that will ultimately fail me. Amen.

morning
POWER OF THE WORD

*"The Spirit gives life; the flesh counts for nothing. The words I
have spoken to you—they are full of the Spirit and life."*
JOHN 6:63 NIV

Jesus told His followers that His words were Spirit and life. When we hear His Word, meditate on it, pray it, memorize it, and ask for faith to believe it, He comes to us in it and transforms our lives through it. Once the Word is in our mind or before our eyes and ears, the Holy Spirit can work it into our hearts and our consciences. Jesus told us to abide in His Word. . .putting ourselves in a place to hear and receive the Word. The rest is the beautiful and mysterious work of the Spirit.

*Thank You, Jesus, the Living Word, who changes my heart
and my mind through the power of Your Word. Amen.*

evening
CAN GOD INTERRUPT YOU?

In their hearts humans plan their course, but the LORD establishes their steps.
PROVERBS 16:9 NIV

Have you ever considered that perhaps God has ordained our interruptions? Perhaps, just perhaps, God may be trying to get your attention. There is nothing wrong with planning our day. However, we have such limited vision. God sees the big picture. Be open. Be flexible. Allow God to change your plans in order to accomplish His divine purposes. Instead of becoming frustrated, look for ways the Lord might be working. Be willing to join Him. When we do, interruptions become blessings.

*Dear Lord, forgive me when I am so rigidly locked into my own
agenda that I miss Yours. Give me Your eternal perspective
so that I may be open to divine interruptions. Amen.*

morning
MARVELOUS THUNDER

"God's voice thunders in marvelous ways;
he does great things beyond our understanding."

JOB 37:5 NIV

Have you ever reflected deeply on the power that God is? Not that He *has*, but that He is.

Consider this: The One who controls nature also holds every one of our tears in His hand. He is our Father, and He works on our behalf. He is more than enough to meet our needs; He does things far beyond what our human minds can understand. This One who is power loves you. He looks at you and says, *"I delight in you, My daughter."* Wow! His ways are marvelous and beyond understanding.

Lord God, You are power. You hold all things in Your hand, and You choose to love me. You see my actions, hear my thoughts, watch my heartbreak. . .and You still love me. Please help me trust in Your power, never my own. Amen.

evening
EYE CARE

For thus says the LORD of hosts. . ."he who
touches you touches the apple of His eye."

ZECHARIAH 2:8 NKJV

To think that we are the apple of God's eye is incredible. Consider the care He must take for us. He will go to great lengths to protect us from harm. When something or someone does attack us, God feels our pain. He is instantly aware of our discomfort, for it is His own. When the storms of life come, we must remember how God feels each twinge of suffering. Despite the adversity, we can praise God, for He is sheltering us.

Thank You, God, that You are so aware of what is happening
to me. Thank You for Your protection. Amen.

morning
GOD'S MOUNTAIN SANCTUARY

*And seeing the multitudes, he went up into a mountain. . .and. . .his
disciples came unto him: and he opened his mouth, and taught them.*
MATTHEW 5:1–2 KJV

Jesus often retreated to a mountain to pray. There He called His disciples to depart
from the multitudes so that He could teach them valuable truths—the lessons we learn
from nature. Do you yearn for a place where problems evaporate like the morning
dew? Do you need a place of solace? God is wherever you are—behind a bedroom
door, nestled alongside you in your favorite chair, or even standing at a sink full
of dirty dishes. Come apart and enter God's mountain sanctuary.

*Heavenly Father, I long to hear Your voice and to flow in the path You clear
before me. Help me to find sanctuary in Your abiding presence. Amen.*

evening
A FRAGRANT OFFERING

*Follow God's example, therefore, as dearly loved children and
walk in the way of love, just as Christ loved us and gave himself
up for us as a fragrant offering and sacrifice to God.*
EPHESIANS 5:1–2 NIV

If we carry the scent of Christ in our daily walk, people will be drawn to us and want
to "stay for a while." But how do we give off that amazing, inviting fragrance? There's
really only one way—by imitating God. By loving others fully. By seeing them through
His eyes. By looking with great compassion on those who are hurting, as Jesus did when
He went about healing the sick and pouring out His life for those in need. As we live a
life of love in front of those we care for, we exude the sweetest fragrance of all—Christ.

*Dear Lord, I long to live a life that points people to You. As I care
for those in need, may the sweet-smelling aroma of You and
Your love be an invitation for people to draw near. Amen.*

morning
MASTERPIECE

*You made all the delicate, inner parts of my body
and knit me together in my mother's womb.*
PSALM 139:13 NLT

At the moment of your conception, roughly three million decisions were made about you. Everything—from your eye color and the number of your wisdom teeth to the shape of your nose and the swirl of your fingerprints—was determined in the blink of an eye. God is a big God. Unfathomable. Incomparable. Frankly, words just don't do Him justice. And He made *you*. You were knit together by a one-of-a-kind, amazing God who is absolutely, undeniably, head-over-heels crazy-in-love with you. Try to wrap your brain around that.

*Heavenly Father and Creator, thank You for the amazing
gift of life, for my uniqueness and individuality. Help me
to use my life as a gift of praise to You. Amen.*

evening
HOW ABOUT SOME FUN?

*A twinkle in the eye means joy in the heart,
and good news makes you feel fit as a fiddle.*
PROVERBS 15:30 MSG

God does not want His kids to be worn out and stressed out. A little relaxation, recreation, and—yes—*fun* are essential components of a balanced life. Even Jesus and His disciples found it necessary to get away from the crowds and pressures of ministry to rest. There's a lot of fun to be had out there—playing tennis or golf, jogging, swimming, painting, knitting, playing a musical instrument, visiting an art gallery, playing a board game, or going to a movie, a play, or a football game. Have you had any fun this week?

*Lord, You are the One who gives balance to my life. Help me to find
time today for a little relaxation, recreation, and even fun. Amen.*

morning
LADIES IN WAITING

I will wait for the LORD. . . . I will put my trust in him.
ISAIAH 8:17 NIV

Do we want joy without accepting heartache? Peace without living through the stress? Patience without facing demands? God sees things differently. He's giving us the opportunity to learn through these delays, irritations, and struggles. Like Isaiah, we need to learn the art of waiting on God. He will come through every time—but in *His* time, not ours. The wait may be hours or days, or it could be years. But God is always faithful to provide for us. It is when we learn to wait on Him that we will find joy, peace, and patience through the struggle.

Father, You know what I need, so I will wait. Help me be patient, knowing that You control my situation and that all good things come in Your time. Amen.

evening
WHEN I THINK OF THE HEAVENS

When I consider your heavens, the work of your fingers, the moon and the stars, which you have set in place, what is mankind that you are mindful of them, human beings that you care for them?
PSALM 8:3–4 NIV

Daughter of God, you are important to your heavenly Father, more important than the sun, the moon, and the stars. You are created in the image of God, and He cares for you. In fact, He cares so much that He sent His Son, Jesus, to offer His life as a sacrifice for your sins. The next time you look up at the heavens, the next time you *ooh* and *aah* over a majestic mountain or emerald waves crashing against the shoreline, remember that those things, in all their splendor, don't even come close to you—God's greatest creation.

O Father, when I look at everything You have created, I'm so overwhelmed with who You are. Who am I that You would think twice about me? And yet You do. You love me, and for that I'm eternally grateful! Amen.

morning
THE DREAM MAKER

"What no eye has seen, what no ear has heard, and what no human mind
has conceived"—the things God has prepared for those who love him.

1 CORINTHIANS 2:9 NIV

Dreams, goals, and expectations are part of our daily lives. We have an idea of what we want and how we're going to achieve it. Disappointment can raise its ugly head when what we wanted—what we expected—doesn't happen like we thought it should or doesn't happen as fast as we planned. God knows the dreams He has placed inside of you. He created you and knows what you can do—even better than you know yourself. Maintain your focus—not on the dream but on the Dream Maker—and together you will achieve your dream.

God, thank You for putting dreams in my heart. I refuse to quit. I'm
looking to You to show me how to reach my dreams. Amen.

evening
A HEAVENLY PARTY

"I tell you that in the same way there will be more rejoicing
in heaven over one sinner who repents than over ninety-
nine righteous persons who do not need to repent."

LUKE 15:7 NIV

The Father threw your very own party at the moment you accepted His Son as your Savior. Did you experience a taste of that party from the response of your spiritual mentors here on earth? As Christians, we should celebrate with our new brothers and sisters in Christ every chance we get. If you haven't yet taken that step in your faith, don't wait! Heaven's party planners are eager to get your celebration started.

Father, I am so grateful that You rejoice in new Christians. Strengthen
my desire to reach the lost while I am here on earth. Then, when I
reach heaven, the heavenly parties will be all the sweeter! Amen.

morning
CHOOSING WISELY

Our mouths were filled with laughter.
PSALM 126:2 NIV

We women often plan perfect family events, only to find out how imperfectly things can turn out. The soufflé falls, the cat leaps onto the counter and licks the cheese ball, little Johnny drops Aunt Martha's crystal gravy dish (full of gravy, of course). The Bible says that Sarah laughed at the most unexpected, traumatic time of her life—when God announced that she would have a baby at the age of ninety (Genesis 18:12). At this unforeseen turn of events, she could either laugh, cry, or run away screaming. She chose to laugh.

Lord, give us an extra dollop of grace and peace to laugh about unexpected dilemmas that pop up. And to remember that our reaction is a choice. Amen.

evening
ANXIETY CHECK!

Do not be anxious about anything, but in every situation, by prayer and petition, with thanksgiving, present your requests to God.
PHILIPPIANS 4:6 NIV

Checking to make sure we've locked the door, turned off the stove, and unplugged the curling iron just comes naturally. So why do we forget some of the bigger checks in life? Take anxiety, for instance. When was the last time you did an anxiety check? Days? Weeks? Months? Chances are, you're due for another. After all, we're instructed not to be anxious about anything. Instead, we're to present our requests to God with thanksgiving in our hearts. We're to turn to Him in prayer so that He can take our burdens. Once they've lifted, it's bye-bye anxiety!

Father, I get anxious sometimes. And I don't always remember to turn to You with my anxiety. In fact, I forget to check for anxiety at all. Today I hand my anxieties to You. Thank You that I can present my requests to You. Amen.

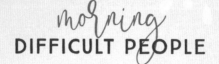

morning
DIFFICULT PEOPLE

*Do not turn your freedom into an opportunity for the
flesh, but serve one another through love.*
GALATIANS 5:13 NASB

Sometimes, like David, we need to turn our skirmishes with others over to the Lord. Then, by using our weapons—God's Word and a steadfast faith—we need to love and forgive others as God loves and forgives us. Although we may not like to admit it, we have all said and done some pretty awful things ourselves, making the lives of others difficult. Yet God has forgiven us *and* continues to love us. So do the right thing. Pull your feet out of the mire of unforgiveness, sidestep verbal retaliation, and stand tall in the freedom of love and forgiveness.

*The words and deeds of others have left me wounded and bleeding.
Forgiveness and love seem to be the last thing on my mind. Change my heart,
Lord. Help me to love and forgive others as You love and forgive me. Amen.*

evening
A STRONG HEART

*Whom have I in heaven but you? And earth has nothing I
desire besides you. My flesh and my heart may fail, but God
is the strength of my heart and my portion forever.*
PSALM 73:25–26 NIV

You don't have to be strong. In your weakness, God's strength shines through. And His strength surpasses anything you could produce, even on your best day. It's the same strength that spoke the heavens and the earth into existence. The same strength that parted the Red Sea. And it's the same strength that made the journey up the hill to the cross. So how do you tap into that strength? There's really only one way. Come into His presence. Spend some quiet time with Him. Allow His strong arms to encompass you. God is all you will ever need.

*Father, I feel so weak at times. It's hard just to put one
foot in front of the other. But I know You are my strength.
Invigorate me with that strength today, Lord. Amen.*

morning
KING FOREVER

You, O God, are my king from ages past, bringing salvation to the earth.
PSALM 74:12 NLT

Sometimes it seems like every part of our lives is affected by change. Nothing ever seems to stay the same. These changes can leave us feeling unsteady in the present and uncertain about the future. It's different in God's kingdom. He's the King now, just as He was in the days of Abraham. His reign will continue until the day His Son returns to earth, and then on into eternity. We can rely—absolutely depend on—His unchanging nature. Take comfort in the stability of the King—He's our leader now and forever!

Almighty King, You are my rock. When my world is in turmoil and changes swirl around me, You are my anchor and my center of balance. Thank You for never changing. Amen.

evening
GOING ABOVE AND BEYOND

Now to him who is able to do immeasurably more than all we ask or imagine, according to his power that is at work within us, to him be glory in the church and in Christ Jesus throughout all generations, for ever and ever!
EPHESIANS 3:20–21 NIV

Think for a moment. What have you asked for? What have you imagined? It's amazing to think that God, in His infinite power and wisdom, can do immeasurably more than all that! How? According to the power that is at work within us. It's not our power, thankfully. We don't have enough power to scrape the surface of what we'd like to see done in our lives. But His power in us gets the job done. . .*and more*. Praise the Lord! Praise Him in the church and throughout all generations! He's an immeasurable God.

Heavenly Father, I feel pretty powerless at times. It's amazing to realize You have more power in Your little finger than all of mankind has put together. Today I praise You for being a God who goes above and beyond all I could ask or imagine. Amen.

morning PUT ON LOVE

*And over all these virtues put on love, which binds
them all together in perfect unity.*

COLOSSIANS 3:14 NIV

There is one accessory that always fits, always looks right, always is appropriate, and always makes us more attractive to others. When we wear it, we are beautiful. When we wear it, we become more popular, more sought-after, more admired. What is that accessory, you ask, and where can you buy it? It's love, and you can't buy it anywhere. But it's free, and it's always available through the Holy Spirit. When we call on Him to help us love others, He cloaks us in a beautiful covering that draws people to us and makes us perfectly lovely in every way.

*Dear Father, as I get dressed each day, help me to remember
the most important accessory I can wear is Your love. Amen.*

evening CARTWHEELS OF JOY

*I'm singing joyful praise to GOD. I'm turning cartwheels of joy to my
Savior God. Counting on GOD's Rule to prevail, I take heart and gain
strength. I run like a deer. I feel like I'm king of the mountain!*

HABAKKUK 3:18–19 MSG

What would happen if we followed the advice of the psalmist and turned a cartwheel of joy in our hearts—regardless of the circumstances—then leaned into and trusted His rule to prevail? Think of the happiness and peace that could be ours with a total surrender to God's care. Taking a giant step, armed with scriptures and praise and joy, we can surmount any obstacle put before us, running like a deer, climbing the tall mountains. With God at our side, it's possible to be king of the mountain.

*Dear Lord, I need Your help. Gently guide me so I might learn
to lean on You and become confident in Your care. Amen.*

morning
TRIALS AND WISDOM

*Consider it pure joy, my brothers and sisters, whenever you face trials of many
kinds, because you know that the testing of your faith produces perseverance.
Let perseverance finish its work so that you may be mature and complete,
not lacking anything. If any of you lacks wisdom, you should ask God, who
gives generously to all without finding fault, and it will be given to you.*

JAMES 1:2–5 NIV

Things won't be easy and simple until we get to heaven. So how can we lift our chins
and head into tomorrow without succumbing to discouragement? We remember that
God is good. We trust His faithfulness. We ask for His presence and peace during each
moment. We pray for wisdom and believe that the God who holds the universe in His
hands is working every single trial and triumph together for our good and for His glory.
This passage in James tells us that when we lack wisdom we should simply ask God for
it! Be encouraged that the Lord will give you wisdom generously without finding fault!

*Lord Jesus, please give me wisdom. So many troubles are weighing me down.
Help me give You all my burdens and increase my faith and trust in You. Amen.*

evening
STEP BY STEP

*For we walk by faith, not by sight [living our lives in a manner
consistent with our confident belief in God's promises].*

2 CORINTHIANS 5:7 AMP

The experiences and circumstances of our lives can often lead us to lose heart. The
apostle Paul exhorts us to look away from this present world and rely on God by faith.
Webster's dictionary defines *faith* as a firm belief and complete trust. Trusting, even
when our faith is small, is not an easy task. Today, grasp hold of God's Word and feel His
presence. Hold tightly and don't let your steps falter. He is beside you and will lead you.

*Dear heavenly Father, today I choose to clutch Your hand and feel Your
presence as I trudge the pathways of my life. I trust You are by my side. Amen.*

morning
RAISE THE ROOF

Come, let's shout praises to GOD, raise the roof for the Rock who saved us!
Let's march into his presence singing praises, lifting the rafters with our hymns!
PSALM 95:1–2 MSG

Not many had it rougher than King David, who curled up in caves to hide from his enemies, or Paul in a dark dungeon cell—yet they still praised God despite the circumstances. And our God extended His grace to them as they acclaimed Him in their suffering. The Lord wants to hear our shouts of joy and see us march into the courtyard rejoicing. He hears our faltering songs and turns them into a symphony for His ears. So lift up your voice and join in the praise to our Creator and Lord.

Dear heavenly Father, I praise Your holy name. Bless You, Lord.
Thank You for Your grace and mercy toward me. Amen.

evening
BIBLICAL ENCOURAGEMENT
FOR YOUR HEART

Don't be concerned about the outward beauty of fancy hairstyles,
expensive jewelry, or beautiful clothes. You should clothe yourselves
instead with the beauty that comes from within, the unfading beauty
of a gentle and quiet spirit, which is so precious to God.
1 PETER 3:3–4 NLT

God is concerned with what is on the inside. He listens to how you respond to others and watches the facial expressions you choose to exhibit. He sees your heart. The Lord desires that you clothe yourself with a gentle and quiet spirit. He declares this as unfading beauty, the inner beauty of the heart. Focus on this, and no one will even notice whether your jewelry shines. Your face will be radiant with the joy of the Lord, and your heart will overflow with grace and peace.

Lord, grant me a quiet and gentle spirit. I ask this in Jesus' name. Amen.

THE GIFT OF *morning* PRAYER

*First of all, then, I urge that petitions (specific requests), prayers,
intercessions (prayers for others) and thanksgivings be offered
on behalf of all people. . . . This [kind of praying] is good and
acceptable and pleasing in the sight of God our Savior.*

1 TIMOTHY 2:1, 3 AMP

There is such joy in giving gifts. Seeing the delight on someone's face to receive something unexpected is exciting. Perhaps the absolute greatest gift one person can give to another doesn't come in a box. It can't be wrapped or presented formally; instead, it is the words spoken to God for someone—the gift of prayer. When we pray for others, we ask God to intervene and to make Himself known to them. We can pray for God's plan and purpose in their lives. We can ask God to bless them or protect them. Who would God have you give the gift of prayer to today?

*Lord, thank You for bringing people to my heart and mind who need prayer.
Help me to pray the things that they need from You in their lives. Show me
how to give the gift of prayer to those You would have me pray for. Amen.*

evening ENCOURAGE ONE ANOTHER

*Therefore encourage one another and build
each other up, just as in fact you are doing.*

1 THESSALONIANS 5:11 NIV

Encouragement is more than words. It is also valuing, being tolerant of, serving, and praying for one another. It is looking for what is good and strong in a person and celebrating it. Encouragement means sincerely forgiving and asking for forgiveness, recognizing someone's weaknesses and holding out a helping hand, giving humbly while building someone up, helping others to hope in the Lord, and praying that God will encourage them in ways that you cannot. Will you encourage someone today? Get in the habit of encouraging others. It will bless them and you.

*Heavenly Father, open my eyes to those who need
encouragement. Show me how I can help. Amen.*

morning JOYOUS LIGHT

Whom having not seen, ye love; in whom, though now ye see him not, yet believing, ye rejoice with joy unspeakable and full of glory.

1 PETER 1:8 KJV

Jesus is the Light of the World. When we accept Him, the light is poured into us. The Holy Spirit comes to reside within, bringing His light. A glorious gift graciously given to us. When we realize the importance of the gift and the blessings that result from a life led by the Father, we can't contain our happiness. The joy and hope that fill our hearts wells up. Joy uncontained comes when Jesus becomes our Lord. Through Him, through faith, we have hope for the future. What joy! So let it spill forth in love.

Lord, help me to be a light unto the world, shining forth Your goodness. Amen.

evening HE CARRIES US

In his love and mercy he redeemed them. He lifted them up and carried them through all the years.

ISAIAH 63:9 NLT

Are you feeling broken today? Depressed? Defeated? Run to Jesus and not away from Him. He will carry us—no matter what pain we have to endure. No matter what happens to us. God sent Jesus to be our Redeemer. He knew the world would hate, malign, and kill Jesus. Yet He allowed His very flesh to writhe in agony on the cross—so that we could also become His sons and daughters. He loved me—and you—that much.

Lord Jesus, thank You for coming to us—for not abandoning us when we are broken. Thank You for Your work on the cross, for Your grace, mercy, and love. Help me to seek You even when I can't feel You, to love You even when I don't know all the answers. Amen.

LINKING HEARTS *morning* WITH GOD

*"You will receive power when the Holy Spirit comes on you;
and you will be my witnesses. . .to the ends of the earth."*
ACTS 1:8 NIV

God knows our hearts. He knows what we need to make it through a day. So in His kindness, He gave us a gift in the form of the Holy Spirit. As a Counselor, a Comforter, and a Friend, the Holy Spirit acts as our inner compass. He upholds us when times are hard and helps us hear God's directions. When the path of obedience grows dark, the Spirit floods it with light. What revelation! He lives within us. Therefore, our prayers are lifted to the Father, to the very throne of God!

*Father God, how blessed I am to come into Your presence.
Help me, Father, when I am weak. Guide me this day. Amen.*

YOU ARE A WOMAN *evening* OF WORTH

*A wife of noble character who can find? She is worth far more than
rubies. Her husband has full confidence in her and lacks nothing of
value. She brings him good, not harm, all the days of her life.*
PROVERBS 31:10–12 NIV

Are you the woman of worth that Jesus intends you to be? We often don't think we are. Between running a household, rushing to work, taking care of the children, volunteering for worthwhile activities, and still being a role model for our families, we think we've failed miserably. Sometimes we don't fully realize that learning to be a noble woman of character takes time. Our experiences can be offered to another generation seeking wisdom from others who have "been there." You are a woman of worth. God said so!

*Father God, thank You for equipping me to be a woman of noble character.
You tell me that I am more precious than jewels, and I claim and believe
that wholeheartedly. I love You, Lord, and I will continue to put You first
in my life. Help me to be the woman You created me to be! Amen.*

morning
LIKE LITTLE CHILDREN

Some people brought their little children to Jesus so he could touch them, but his followers told them to stop. When Jesus saw this, he was upset and said to them, "Let the little children come to me. Don't stop them, because the kingdom of God belongs to people who are like these children. I tell you the truth, you must accept the kingdom of God as if you were a little child, or you will never enter it."
MARK 10:13–15 NCV

This passage in Mark tells us that no matter how old we are, God wants us to come to Him with the faith of a child. He wants us to be open and honest about our feelings. He wants us to trust Him wholeheartedly, just like little kids do. As adults, we sometimes play games with God. We tell God what we think He wants to hear, forgetting that He already knows our hearts! God is big enough to handle your honesty. Tell Him how you really feel.

Father, help me come to You as a little child and be more open and honest with You in prayer. Amen.

evening
LOVING SISTERS

But Ruth replied, "Don't urge me to leave you or to turn back from you. Where you go I will go, and where you stay I will stay. Your people will be my people and your God my God."
RUTH 1:16 NIV

The story of Ruth and Naomi is inspiring on many levels. Both women realized that their commitment, friendship, and love for each other surpassed any of their differences. They were a blessing to each other. Do you have girlfriends who would do almost anything for you? A true friendship is a gift from God. Those relationships provide us with love, companionship, encouragement, loyalty, honesty, understanding, and more! Lasting friendships are essential to living a balanced life.

Father God, may I be the blessing to my girlfriends that they are to me. Please help me to always encourage and love them well. I praise You for my loving sisters! Amen.

morning
BREATH OF LIFE

He heals the brokenhearted and binds up their wounds
[healing their pain and comforting their sorrow].
PSALM 147:3 AMP

When your life brings disappointment, hurt, and pain that are almost unbearable, remember that you serve the One who heals hearts. He knows you best and loves you most. When the wind is knocked out of you and you feel like there is no oxygen left in the room, let God provide you with the air you need to breathe. Breathe out a prayer to Him, and breathe in His peace and comfort today.

Lord, be my breath of life, today and always. Amen.

evening
HIGH EXPECTATIONS

"They found grace out in the desert. . . . Israel, out looking for a place
to rest, met God out looking for them!" GOD told them, "I've never
quit loving you and never will. Expect love, love, and more love!"
JEREMIAH 31:2–3 MSG

Despite their transgressions, God told the Israelites He never quit loving them. That is true for you today. Look beyond any circumstances, and you will discover God looking at you, His eyes filled with love. Scripture promises an overwhelming, unexpected river of love that will pour out when we trust the Lord our God. Rest today in His Word. Expect God's love, love, and more love to fill that empty place in your life.

Father, I read these words and choose this day
to believe in Your unfailing love. Amen.

morning
A CONTINUAL FEAST

The cheerful heart has a continual feast.
PROVERBS 15:15 NIV

Our choice of companions has much to do with our outlook. Negativity and positivity are both contagious. The writer of Proverbs says that a cheerful heart has a continual feast. So it's safe to assume that a grumpy heart will feel hungry and lacking, instead of full. While God calls us to minister to those who are hurting, we can do so with discernment. Next time someone complains, ask them to pray with you about their concerns. Tell them a story of how you overcame negativity or repaired a relationship. You might help turn their day around!

God, help me be a positive influence on my friends and family.
Give me wisdom and the unwavering hope that comes from
Christ, that I may share Your joy with others. Amen.

evening
A GOOD MORSEL

Taste and see that the LORD is good; blessed is the one who takes refuge in him.
PSALM 34:8 NIV

The world gives the idea to nonbelievers that God isn't worth a taste. The world emphasizes a self-focus, while the Lord says to put others before self, and God before all. In reality, walking and talking with God is the best thing you can do for yourself. Like so many foods that are good for us, all it requires is that first taste, a tiny morsel, which whets the appetite for more of Him. Then you can be open to all the goodness, all the fullness of the Lord.

Lord, fill my cup to overflowing with Your love so that it pours
out of me in a way that makes others want what I have. Amen.

morning
BE HAPPY!

Blessed are those who act justly, who always do what is right.
PSALM 106:3 NIV

In the world that we live in today, some might think that a bank error or a mistake on a bill in their favor would be justification for keeping the money without a word. But a true Christ follower would not look at these kinds of situations as good or fortunate events. Our happiness is being honest, doing what is right, because that happiness is the promised spiritual reward. Because we want to be blessed by God, we will seek to always do what is right.

Gracious and heavenly Father, thank You for Your blessings each and every day. I am thankful to be Your follower. When I am tempted to do something that would displease You, remind me that You will bless me if I act justly. My happiness will be a much better reward. In Your name, amen.

evening
YOUR HEAVENLY FATHER

The LORD's love never ends; his mercies never stop.
They are new every morning; LORD, your loyalty is great.
LAMENTATIONS 3:22–23 NCV

Regardless of your relationship with your earthly father, your heavenly Father loves you with an *unfailing love.* He is faithful to walk with you through the ups and downs of life. Remember that every day is a day to honor your heavenly Father. Begin and end today praising Him for who He is. Express thanksgiving. Present your requests to Him. Tell Him how much you love Him. God longs to be your Abba Father, a loving Daddy to you, His daughter!

Father, thank You for being a loving God,
my Abba Father, my Redeemer. Amen.

START YOUR DAY *morning* WITH GOD

*In the morning, LORD, you hear my voice; in the morning
I lay my requests before you and wait expectantly.*

PSALM 5:3 NIV

As you wake up in the morning, thank the Lord for a new day. Ask Him to control your thoughts and attitude as you make the bed. Thank Him for providing for you as you toast your bagel. Ask that your self-image be based on your relationship with Christ as you get dressed and brush your teeth. Continue to pray as you drive to work or school. Spend time in His Word throughout the day. Then end your day by thanking Him for His love and faithfulness.

*Dear Lord, thank You for the gift of a new day. Help me
be aware of Your constant presence in my life. Amen.*

LISTENING CLOSELY *evening*

I will listen to what God the LORD says.

PSALM 85:8 NIV

Listening is a learned art, too often forgotten in the busyness of a day. The alarm clock buzzes; we hit the floor running, toss out a prayer or maybe sing a song of praise, grab our car keys, and are out the door. If only we'd slow down and let the heavenly Father's words sink into our spirits, what a difference we might see in our prayer life. Right now, stop. Listen. See what God has in store for you.

*Lord, how I want to surrender and seek Your will.
Please still my spirit and speak to me. Amen.*

morning
PRAY ABOUT EVERYTHING

The LORD directs the steps of the godly. He delights in every detail of their lives.
PSALM 37:23 NLT

The Bible says that the Lord delights in every detail of His children's lives. Adult prayers don't have to be well ordered and formal. God loves hearing His children's voices, and no detail is too little or dull to pray about. Tell God that you hope the coffeehouse will have your favorite pumpkin spice latte on their menu. Ask Him to give you patience as you wait in line. Thank Him for how wonderful that coffee tastes! Get into the habit of talking with Him all day long, because He loves you and delights in all facets of your life.

Dear God, teach me to pray about everything
with childlike innocence and faith. Amen.

evening
A JOYFUL HEART

Sarah said, "God has brought me laughter,
and everyone who hears about this will laugh with me."
GENESIS 21:6 NIV

In the Bible, King Solomon said, "Every day is hard for those who suffer, but a happy heart is like a continual feast" (Proverbs 15:15 NCV). Are you or someone you know unhappy? A little laughter might help. Begin with a smile. When you hear laughter, move toward it and try to join in. Seek the company of happy friends, and invite humor into your conversations. Most of all, praise God. Praise is the best way to heal a hurting soul. Praise God joyfully for His many blessings.

Lord, whenever my heart is heavy, encourage me to heal it with joy. Amen.

FIX YOUR THOUGHTS ON TRUTH
morning

*And now, dear brothers and sisters, one final thing. Fix your thoughts
on what is true, and honorable, and right, and pure, and lovely, and
admirable. Think about things that are excellent and worthy of praise.*

PHILIPPIANS 4:8 NLT

Dig through the scriptures and find truths from God's Word to combat any false messages that you may be struggling with. Write them down and memorize them. Here are a few to get started:

God looks at my heart, not my outward appearance. (1 Samuel 16:7)

I am free in Christ. (1 Corinthians 1:30)

I am a new creation. My old self is gone! (2 Corinthians 5:17)

The next time you feel negativity and false messages slip into your thinking, fix your thoughts on what you know to be true. Pray for the Lord to replace the doubts and negativity with His words of truth.

*Lord God, please control my thoughts, and help
me set my mind and heart on You alone. Amen.*

THE SIMPLE THINGS
evening

In him our hearts rejoice, for we trust in his holy name.

PSALM 33:21 NIV

God knows all the simple pleasures you enjoy—and He created them for your delight. When the simple things that can come only by His hand fill you with contentment, He is pleased. He takes pleasure in you. You are His delight. Giving you peace, comfort, and a sense of knowing that you belong to Him is a simple thing for Him. Take a moment today and step away from the busyness of life. Take notice and fully experience some of those things you enjoy most. Then share that special joy with Him.

*Lord, thank You for the simple things that bring pleasure
to my day. I enjoy each gift You've given me. I invite
You to share those moments with me today. Amen.*

morning
ENCOURAGE OTHERS

Worry weighs a person down; an encouraging word cheers a person up.
PROVERBS 12:25 NLT

There is so much sorrow in this world. At any given time, there are many people within your sphere of influence who are hurting. Worry weighs them down as they face disappointment, loss, and other trials. Think about how much it means to you when someone takes the time to encourage you. Do the same for others. Be the voice of encouragement. There is blessing to be found in lifting up those around you.

Father, as I go through this week, make me an encourager. Provide opportunities for me to encourage those around me. I truly desire to cheer up the hearts of those who are worried. Amen.

evening
WHISPERS IN THE WIND

Then Jesus told him, "Because you have seen me, you have believed; blessed are those who have not seen and yet have believed."
JOHN 20:29 NIV

We can't see God. We can't take Him by the hand or even converse with Him face-to-face like we do a friend. But we still know He is present in our lives because we can experience the effects. God moves among His people, and we can see it. God speaks to His people, and we can hear the still, small voice. And, just like we can feel the wind across our cheeks, we can feel God's presence. We don't need to physically see God to know that He exists and that He's working.

You are like the wind, Lord. Powerful and fast moving, soft and gentle. We may not see You, but we can sense You. Help us to believe, even when we can't see. Amen.

morning
LOVING THE UNLOVABLE

"You have heard the law that says, 'Love your neighbor' and hate your enemy. But I say, love your enemies! Pray for those who persecute you! In that way, you will be acting as true children of your Father in heaven."
MATTHEW 5:43–45 NLT

Sometimes running into a difficult person can actually be a "divine appointment"! Maybe you're the only person they'll see all week who wears a smile on her face. When you happen upon a difficult person whom you'd rather not talk to, take the time to pray for your attitude and then pray for that person. Greet them with a smile and look them in the eye. There is no reason to fear difficult people if you trust in God. He will show you what to do and say as you listen to His promptings (Luke 12:12).

Heavenly Father, I pray that You would help me not to shy away from the people You have allowed to cross my path. Help me speak Your truth and share Your love boldly. Amen.

evening
STANDING IN THE LIGHT

Though I have fallen, I will rise. Though I sit in darkness, the LORD will be my light.
MICAH 7:8 NIV

We may fall down, but God will lift us up. We may feel surrounded by darkness on every side, but He will be our light, guiding the way, showing us which step to take next. No matter where we are, what we've done, or what we're facing, God is our Rescuer, our Savior, and our Friend.

Satan wants to convince us that we have no hope, no future. But God's children always have a future and a hope. . .we are cherished, and we belong to Him.

Dear Father, thank You for giving me confidence in a future filled with good things. When I'm feeling down, remind me to trust in Your love. Thank You for lifting me out of darkness to stand in Your light. Amen.

PRAYING THE *morning* MIND OF CHRIST

We demolish arguments and every pretension that sets
itself up against the knowledge of God, and we take
captive every thought to make it obedient to Christ.
2 Corinthians 10:5 niv

By reading and praying scripture and using positive statements in our prayers that claim what God has already said He will do for us, the mind of Christ is being activated in us. By taking captive every thought, we learn to know what thought is of God, what belongs to us, and what is of the enemy. Recognize, take captive, and bind up the thoughts that are of the enemy and throw them out! The more we commune with God, fellowship with Him, and learn from Him, the more we cultivate the mind of Christ.

Lord, help me identify the thoughts that are not Your
thoughts and purge them. In this way, I will hear You more
clearly so I may be an obedient disciple. Amen!

REFRESHMENT IN *evening* DRY TIMES

"The grass withers and the flowers fall, but the word of our God endures forever."
Isaiah 40:8 niv

Sometimes our lives feel just like the grass—dry and listless. Maybe we're in a season where things seem to stand still, and we've tried everything to change our circumstances for the better to no avail. It is during those times that we need to remember the faithfulness of God and the permanence of His Word. His promises to us are many and true! God will never leave us or forsake us; and He will provide for, love, and protect us. And, just like the drought, eventually our personal dry times will give way to a time of growth, refreshment, and beauty.

Dear Lord, even though it's sometimes hard to hear Your voice or
be patient during hard times, please remind me of Your many
promises, and remind me to stand firmly on them. You are
everything I need and the refreshment I seek. Amen.

morning
THE END OF YOUR ROPE

Do not be far from me, for trouble is near and there is no one to help.
PSALM 22:11 NIV

Jesus reaches down and wraps you in His loving arms when you call to Him for help. The Bible tells us that He is close to the brokenhearted (Psalm 34:18). We may not have the answers we are looking for here in this life, but we can be sure of this: God sees your pain and loves you desperately. Call to Him in times of trouble. If you feel that you're at the end of your rope, look up! His mighty hand is reaching toward you.

Heavenly Father, I feel alone and afraid. Surround me with Your love, and give me peace and joy. Amen.

evening
JUNGLE OF LIFE

God's word is alive and working and is sharper than a double-edged sword. It cuts all the way into us, where the soul and the spirit are joined, to the center of our joints and bones. And it judges the thoughts and feelings in our hearts.
HEBREWS 4:12 NCV

When you take the Bible and live according to God's plans, His Word cuts like a machete through the entanglements of life. When you choose to use the Sword of Truth, it clears a path and can free you from the weights of the world that try to entrap and ensnare you. No matter what the challenges of life are saying to you today, take His Word and speak His plans into your life. Choose His words of encouragement and peace instead of the negative things life's circumstances are telling you.

God, I want to live in Your truth. I want to believe what You say about me in the Bible. Help me to speak Your words today. Help me believe. Amen.

morning
O THE DEEP, DEEP LOVE OF JESUS

I pray that out of his glorious riches he may strengthen you with power through his Spirit in your inner being, so that Christ may dwell in your hearts through faith. And I pray that you, being rooted and established in love, may have power, together with all the Lord's holy people, to grasp how wide and long and high and deep is the love of Christ.
EPHESIANS 3:16–18 NIV

What an amazing picture. That Christ should care for us in such a way is almost incomprehensible. Despite our shortcomings, our sin, He loves us. It takes a measure of faith to believe in His love. When we feel a nagging thought of unworthiness, of being unlovable, trust in the Word and sing a new song. For His love is deep and wide.

Lord, thank You for loving me, even when I'm unlovable. Amen.

evening
THE ULTIMATE ACT OF LOVE

Bring joy to your servant, Lord, for I put my trust in you. You, Lord, are forgiving and good, abounding in love to all who call to you.
PSALM 86:4–5 NIV

Forgiveness doesn't require that the person who did the hurting apologize or acknowledge what they've done. It's not about making the score even. It doesn't even require forgetting about the incident. But it is about admitting that the one who hurt us is human, just like we are. We surrender our right for revenge and, like God, let go and give the wrongdoer mercy, therefore blessing them.

Gracious and loving Father, thank You that You love me and have forgiven me of my sins. May I be more like You in forgiving others. Although I may not be able to forgive as easily as You do, please encourage me to take those small steps. In forgiving others, Father, I am that much closer to being like You. Amen.

morning
I GROW WEARY

*But those who wait for the LORD [who expect, look for, and hope in Him]
will gain new strength and renew their power; they will lift up their wings
[and rise up close to God] like eagles [rising toward the sun]; they will
run and not become weary, they will walk and not grow tired.*

ISAIAH 40:31 AMP

As long as we are warring inside, we will not find rest. We must find out what Jesus wants for our lives and then obey. Feasting on His Word and learning more about Him will give us the direction we need and the ability to trust. It is only when we understand our salvation and surrender that we can come to Him, unencumbered by guilt or fear, and lay our head on His chest. Safe within His embrace, we can rest. We will be as a well-watered garden, refreshed and blessed by our loving Creator.

*Father, I am weary and need Your refreshing
Spirit to guide me. I trust in You. Amen.*

evening
REAP IN JOY!

*Remember this: Whoever sows sparingly will also reap sparingly,
and whoever sows generously will also reap generously.*

2 CORINTHIANS 9:6 NIV

Each of us wants to feel appreciated, and we like to deal with a friendly person. Have you ever worked with a person who seemed to have a perpetually bad attitude? You probably didn't feel particularly encouraged after an encounter with this coworker. Yes, sometimes things go wrong, but your attitude in the thick of it is determined by your expectations. If you expect things to turn out well, you'll generally have a positive mental attitude. Treat everyone with genuine kindness, courtesy, and respect, and that is what will be reflected back to you.

*Heavenly Father, help me plant the seeds of patience, love,
compassion, and courtesy in all those I come in contact with.
I want to joyfully reap a rich harvest for Your kingdom. Amen!*

morning
WHY PRAISE GOD?

Though he slay me, yet will I trust in him.
JOB 13:15 KJV

It's difficult to praise God when problems press in harder than a crowd exiting a burning building. But that's the time to praise Him the most. We wait for our circumstances to change, while God desires to change us despite them. Praise coupled with prayer in our darkest moments is what moves the mighty hand of God to work in our hearts and lives. How can we pray and praise God when everything goes wrong? The bigger question might be: How can we not?

Jesus, help me to pray and praise You, despite my circumstances. Amen.

evening
EVERLASTING LIGHT

In him was life, and that life was the light of all mankind. The light shines in the darkness, and the darkness has not overcome it.
JOHN 1:4–5 NIV

Focus on the fact that Jesus is the Light of the World who holds out wonderful hope for us. Set your prayer life to start with praise and adoration of the King of kings. Lift your voice in song, or read out loud from the Word. The Light will eliminate the darkness every time. Keep your heart and mind set on Him as you walk through the day. Praise Him for every little thing; nothing is too small for God. A grateful heart and constant praise will bring the Light into your day.

*Dear Lord, how we love You. We trust in You this day
to lead us on the right path lit with Your light. Amen.*

THE WORD FOR *morning* EVERY DAY

*As for God, his way is perfect; the word of the LORD
is tried: he is a buckler to all them that trust in him.*

2 SAMUEL 22:31 KJV

God's Word is such an incredible gift, one that goes hand in hand with prayer. It's amazing, really, that the Creator of the universe gave us the scriptures as His personal Word to us. When we're faithful to pick up the Word, He is faithful to use it to encourage us. Reading and praying through scripture is one of the keys to finding and keeping our sanity, peace, and joy.

*God, thank You for Your gifts of the holy scriptures and
sweet communion with You through prayer. Amen.*

THE RIGHT *evening* FOCUS

*Turning your ear to wisdom and applying your heart to understanding—
indeed, if you call out for insight and cry aloud for understanding, and if
you look for it as for silver and search for it as for hidden treasure, then you
will understand the fear of the LORD and find the knowledge of God.*

PROVERBS 2:2–5 NIV

Frustration and stress can keep us from clearly seeing the things that God puts before us. Time spent in prayer and meditation on God's Word can often wash away the dirt and grime of the day-to-day and provide a clear picture of God's intentions for our lives. Step outside the pressure and into His presence, and get the right focus for whatever you're facing today.

Lord, help me to avoid distractions and keep my eyes on You. Amen.

PASS IT ON!

After the usual readings from the books of Moses and the prophets, those in charge of the service sent them this message: "Brothers, if you have any word of encouragement for the people, come and give it."

ACTS 13:15 NLT

Encouragement brings hope. Have you ever received a word from someone that instantly lifted your spirit? Did you receive a bit of good news or something that diminished your negative outlook? Perhaps a particular conversation helped to bring your problems into perspective. Paul passed on encouragement and many benefited. So the next time you're encouraged, pass it on! You may never know how your words or actions benefited someone else.

Lord, thank You for the wellspring of encouragement through Your holy Word. Amen.

SEEK GOD

"I love all who love me. Those who search will surely find me."

PROVERBS 8:17 NLT

Scripture tells us that God loves those who love Him and that if we search for Him, we will surely find Him. One translation of the Bible says it this way: "Those who seek me early and diligently will find me" (AMP). Seek God in all things and in all ways. Search for Him in each moment of every day you are blessed to walk on this earth. He is found easily in His creation and in His Word. He is with you. Just look for Him. He wants to be found!

Father in heaven, thank You for Your unfailing love for me. Help me to search for You diligently. I know that when I seek, I will find You. Amen.

WHEN YOU GIVE YOUR LIFE AWAY
morning

*Which of you, intending to build a tower, sitteth not down first,
and counteth the cost, whether he have sufficient to finish it?*
LUKE 14:28 KJV

Every person has the same amount of time each day. What matters is how you spend it. It's easy to waste your day doing insignificant things, leaving little time for God. The most important things in life are eternal endeavors. Spending time in prayer to God for others. Giving your life to building a relationship with God by reading His Word and growing in faith. Sharing Christ with others and giving them the opportunity to know Him. These are things that will last. What are you spending your life on?

Heavenly Father, my life is full. I ask that You give me wisdom and instruction to give my life to the things that matter most. The time I have is precious and valuable. Help me to invest it wisely in eternal things. Amen.

THANKFUL, THANKFUL HEART
evening

I will praise you, LORD, with all my heart. I will tell all the miracles you have done.
PSALM 9:1 NCV

When you choose to approach life from the positive side, you can find thankfulness in most of life's circumstances. It completely changes your outlook, your attitude, and your countenance. When you are tempted to feel sorry for yourself or to blame others or God for difficulties, push PAUSE. Take a moment and rewind your life. Look back and count the blessings God has given you. As you remind yourself of all He has done for you and in you, it will bring change to your attitude and give you hope in the situation you're facing. Count your blessings today.

Lord, I am thankful for my life and all You have done for me. When life happens, help me to respond to it in a healthy, positive way. Remind me to look to You and trust You to carry me through life's challenges. Amen.

morning
LOVE YOUR ENEMIES

*"Love your enemies, do good to them, and lend to them without
expecting to get anything back. Then your reward will be great."*
LUKE 6:35 NIV

God calls us to a love so brave, so intense that it defies logic and turns the world on its side. He calls us to love like He loves. That means we must show patience where others have been short. We must show kindness where others have been cruel. We must look for ways to bless when others have cursed. God promises great rewards for those who do this. Oh, the rewards may not be immediate. But when God promises great rewards, we can know without doubt that any present struggle will be repaid with goodness and blessing, many times over.

*Dear Father, help me to love those who hate me, bless
those who curse me, and show kindness to those who have
been cruel. Help me to love like You love. Amen.*

evening
REJOICE!

Rejoice in the Lord always. I will say it again: Rejoice!
PHILIPPIANS 4:4 NIV

When God is the source of our joy, we will never lose that joy. Circumstances may frustrate us and break our hearts. But God is able to supply all our needs. He is able to restore broken relationships. He can give us a new job or help us to succeed at our current job. Through it all, *despite* it all, we can rejoice in knowing that we are God's and He loves us.

*Dear Father, thank You for loving me. Help me
to make You the source of my joy. Amen.*

morning
UNSHAKABLE LOVE

"For even if the mountains walk away and the hills fall to pieces, my love won't walk away from you, my covenant commitment of peace won't fall apart." The GOD who has compassion on you says so.
ISAIAH 54:10 MSG

We must rest in God's wild, unbending love for us. He promises in Isaiah that no matter what happens, He will never remove Himself from us. When we believe Him wholeheartedly and rest in His love, we will be filled with fear-busting peace and adventurous faith. That faith allows us to dream big dreams and conquer the worries that keep us chained.

Lord, thank You for Your love, which never leaves me.
Help me to rest in Your love above all else. Amen.

evening
UNFAILING LOVE

I will instruct you and teach you in the way you should go; I will counsel you with my loving eye on you. . . . Many are the woes of the wicked, but the LORD's unfailing love surrounds the one who trusts in him.
PSALM 32:8, 10 NIV

God's love surrounds us always—if we trust in Him. Have you put your complete trust in the Lord? If not, open your heart to Him and ask Him to become the Lord of your life. Jesus is standing at the door of your heart, ready to come in when you respond (Revelation 3:20). Or maybe you've already accepted Christ as your Savior, but you're not really sure if He can be trusted. Know that He has been faithful to His children through all generations and that He is working out every circumstance in your life for your own good (Romans 8:28).

Father God, I praise You for Your unfailing love. Continue to counsel me and lead me in the way I should go. Thank You for watching over me. Help me trust You completely. Amen.

morning
LOOK UP!

Your love, Lord, reaches to the heavens, your faithfulness to the skies.
PSALM 36:5 NIV

In Bible times, people often studied the sky. Looking up at the heavens reminded them of God and His mighty wonders. A rainbow was God's sign to Noah that a flood would never again destroy the earth. God used a myriad of stars to foretell Abraham's abundant family, and a single star heralded Christ's birth. This immense space that we call "sky" is a reflection of God's infinite love and faithfulness. So take time today. Look up at the heavens, and thank God for His endless love.

Heavenly Father, remind me to stop and appreciate Your wonderful creations. And as I look upward, fill me with Your infinite love. Amen.

evening
THOU SHALT NOT WORRY!

"Do not worry about tomorrow, for tomorrow will worry about itself. Each day has enough trouble of its own."
MATTHEW 6:34 NIV

What if the Lord had written an eleventh commandment: "Thou shalt not worry." In a sense, He did! He commands us in various scriptures not to fret. So cast your anxieties on the Lord. Give them up! Let them go! Don't let worries zap your strength and your joy. Today is a gift from the Lord. Don't sacrifice it to fears and frustrations! Let them go. . .and watch God work!

Father God, lift all anxiety from my heart and make my spirit light again. I know that I can't do it on my own. But with You, I can let go. . .and watch You work! I praise You, God! Amen.

JOR *morning*
JOY. . .MINUTE BY MINUTE

*Keep your eyes focused on what is right,
and look straight ahead to what is good.*
PROVERBS 4:25 NCV

Ever wonder how you can be perfectly happy one minute and upset the next? If joy is a choice, then it's one you have to make. . .continually. We are often ruled by our emotions, which is why it's so important to stay focused, especially when you're having a tough day. Don't let frustration steal even sixty seconds from you. Instead, choose joy!

*Dear heavenly Father, please help me to keep my emotions in check
today—and every day. If I keep my focus on You. . .and because
of Your goodness, God, I can always choose joy. Amen.*

evening
AN OFFERING OF JOY

*Then my head will be exalted above the enemies who surround me;
at his sacred tent I will sacrifice with shouts of joy;
I will sing and make music to the LORD.*
PSALM 27:6 NIV

It's one thing to offer a sacrifice of joy when things are going your way and people are treating you fairly. But when you've been through a terrible betrayal, it's often hard to recapture that feeling of joy. As you face hurts and betrayals, remember that God is the lifter of your head. Sing praises and continue to offer a sacrifice of joy!

*Lord, lift my head. Wrap me in Your warm embrace. Help me to
remember that even though I've experienced betrayal, I can still
praise You and offer a sacrifice of joy. I love You, Father! Amen.*

morning
A JOYOUS TREASURE

*"The kingdom of heaven is like treasure hidden in a field.
When a man found it, he hid it again, and then in his joy
went and sold all he had and bought that field."*
MATTHEW 13:44 NIV

Have you ever stumbled across a rare treasure—one so priceless that you would be willing to trade everything you own to have it? If you've given your heart to Christ, if you've accepted His work on Calvary, then you have already obtained the greatest treasure of all. . .new life in Him. Oh, what immeasurable joy comes from knowing He's placed that treasure in your heart for all eternity!

*Father, thank You for the gift of Your Son. Because of Your
loving sacrifice, I can forever have joy in my heart. . .knowing
that I will spend eternity in heaven with You. Amen.*

evening
JOY IN THE BATTLE

*Then they returned, every man of Judah and Jerusalem, and
Jehoshaphat in the forefront of them, to go again to Jerusalem with
joy; for the LORD had made them to rejoice over their enemies.*
2 CHRONICLES 20:27 KJV

Enemy forces were just around the bend. Jehoshaphat, king of Judah, called his people together. After much prayer, he sent the worshippers (the Levites) to the front lines, singing joyful praises as they went. The battle was won! When you face your next battle, praise your way through it! Strength and joy will rise up within you! Prepare for victory!

*No matter what kind of hardship I face, Father God, I want to praise my
way through it and come through even stronger than I was before. Thank
You for helping me to win life's battles, both large and small. Amen.*

morning
ETERNAL JOY!

And the ransomed of the LORD shall return, and come to Zion with songs and everlasting joy upon their heads: they shall obtain joy and gladness, and sorrow and sighing shall flee away.

ISAIAH 35:10 KJV

Have you ever pondered eternity? Forever and ever and ever. . . ? Our finite minds can't grasp the concept, and yet one thing we understand from scripture—we will enter eternity in a state of everlasting joy and gladness. No more tears! No sorrow! An eternal joyfest awaits us! Now that's something to celebrate!

When life becomes difficult, help me to keep things in perspective, Father. The hardships I face in the day-to-day are but blips in time compared to the eternal joy I will experience in heaven. Thank You for joy that lasts forever. Amen.

evening
JOYOUS FREEDOM

Blessed is he whose transgression is forgiven, whose sin is covered.

PSALM 32:1 KJV

What if you were locked up in a prison cell for years on end? You waited for the day when the jailer would turn that key in the lock—releasing you once and for all. In a sense, experiencing God's forgiveness is like being set free from prison. Can you fathom the joy? Walking into the sunshine for the first time in years? Oh, praise Him for His forgiveness today!

Sweet freedom, Lord. . . It's a beautiful feeling to have experienced the joy of Your complete and utter forgiveness. Thank You for setting my spirit free! Amen.

morning
PRESSED DOWN, RUNNING OVER

*Give, and it shall be given unto you; good measure, pressed down,
and shaken together, and running over, shall men give into your bosom.*
LUKE 6:38 KJV

"Give, and it shall be given unto you." Likely, if you've been walking with the Lord for any length of time, you've heard this dozens of times. Do we give so that we can get? No, we give out of a grateful heart, and the Lord—in His generosity—meets our needs. Today, pause and thank Him for the many gifts He has given you. Do you feel the joy running over?

*Lord, help me to always give from a grateful heart and never
because I plan to get something in return. You have given me abundant
blessings, Father. Thank You for always meeting my needs. Amen.*

evening
WHO EXALTS?

*No one from the east or the west or from the desert can exalt themselves.
It is God who judges: He brings one down, he exalts another.*
PSALM 75:6–7 NIV

Sometimes we grumble when others are exalted. We feel left out. Why do others prosper when everything around us seems to be falling apart? We can't celebrate their victories. We aren't joyful for them. Shame on us! God chooses whom to exalt. . . and when. We can't pretend to know His thoughts. But we can submit to His will and celebrate with those who are walking through seasons of great favor.

*God, it's so hard to be happy for others when I feel like I haven't
been blessed in the same way. Please help me to rejoice when
others experience Your favor, while I continue to trust that You
have a plan for my life—and that Your plan is good! Amen.*

A SACRIFICE OF *morning* PRAISE

Is any among you afflicted? let him pray.
Is any merry? let him sing psalms.

JAMES 5:13 KJV

It's tough to praise when you're not feeling well, isn't it? But that's exactly what God calls us to do. If you're struggling today, reach way down deep. . . . Out of your pain, your weakness, offer God a sacrifice of praise. Spend serious time in prayer. Lift up a song of joy—even if it's a weak song! You'll be surprised how He energizes you with His great joy!

I'm struggling today, God. But that's no surprise to You,
is it? You know just how I feel. Please energize my sluggish
spirit. I want to sing praises to You! Amen.

JOYFUL IN *evening* GLORY

Let the saints be joyful in glory: let them sing aloud upon their beds.

PSALM 149:5 KJV

When do you like to spend time alone with the Lord? In the morning, as the stillness of the day sweeps over you? At night, when you rest your head upon the pillow? Start your conversation with praise. Let your favorite worship song or hymn pour forth! Tell Him how blessed you are to be His child. This private praise time will strengthen you and will fill your heart with joy!

As I enter into this conversation with You, Father, I praise You.
Thank You for being Lord—and leader—of my life. Amen.

morning
FINISHING WITH JOY

*But none of these things move me, neither count I my life dear
unto myself, so that I might finish my course with joy.*
ACTS 20:24 KJV

The Christian life is a journey, isn't it? We move from point A to point B, and then on from there—all the while growing in our faith. Instead of focusing on the ups and downs of the journey, we should be looking ahead to the finish line. We want to be people who finish well. Today, set your sights on that unseen line that lies ahead. What joy will come when you cross it!

*Father God, help me to keep my eyes on the finish line
so I can finish my journey with joy. Amen.*

evening
EVERYDAY JOY

For in him we live, and move, and have our being.
ACTS 17:28 KJV

Every breath we breathe comes from God. Every step we take is a gift from our Creator. We can do nothing apart from Him. In the same sense, every joy, every sorrow. . . God goes through each one with us. His heart is for us. We can experience joy in our everyday lives, even when things aren't going our way. We simply have to remember that He is in control. We have our being. . .in Him!

*Thank You for being in control of all things, God. I would rather
have You by my side than anyone else in the world—through
every up, down, and in between, You are there! Amen.*

morning
MERCY MULTIPLIED

Mercy unto you, and peace, and love, be multiplied.
JUDE 1:2 KJV

Have you ever done the math on God's mercy? If so, you've probably figured out that it just keeps multiplying itself out, over and over again. We mess up; He extends mercy. We mess up again; He pours out mercy once again. In the same way, peace, love, and joy are multiplied back to us. Praise the Lord! God's mathematics work in our favor.

Father God, I am so thankful that Your math
works differently than mine! Amen.

evening
GO OUT WITH JOY

For ye shall go out with joy, and be led forth with peace: the
mountains and the hills shall break forth before you into singing,
and all the trees of the field shall clap their hands.
ISAIAH 55:12 KJV

God reveals Himself in a million different ways, but perhaps the most breathtaking is through nature. The next time you're in a mountainous spot, pause and listen. Can you hear the sound of God's eternal song? Does joy radiate through your being? Aren't you filled with wonder and with peace? The Lord has, through the beauty of nature, given us a rare and glorious gift.

When I view the wonders of Your marvelous creation,
Lord, my heart fills with absolute joy! Amen.

morning
SECOND CHANCES

*For his anger lasts only a moment, but his favor lasts a lifetime;
weeping may stay for the night, but rejoicing comes in the morning.*
PSALM 30:5 NIV

Don't you love second chances? New beginnings? If only we could go back and redo some of our past mistakes. . .what better choices we'd make the second time around. Life in Jesus is all about the rebirth experience—the opportunity to start over. Each day is a new day, in fact. Praise God! The sorrows and trials of yesterday are behind us. With each new morning, joy dawns!

*I am so glad You allow second chances, Father. Thank You for
each new morning that is an opportunity to start over! Amen.*

evening
JOYOUS TOMORROW

But if we hope for that we see not, then do we with patience wait for it.
ROMANS 8:25 KJV

Are you in a "waiting" season? Is your patience being tested to the breaking point? Take heart! You are not alone. Every godly man and woman from biblical times till now went through seasons of waiting on the Lord. Their secret? They hoped for what they could not see. (They never lost their hope!) And they waited patiently. So, as you're waiting, reflect on the biblical giants and realize. . .you're not alone!

*Father, thank You for Your Word that gives examples of others who
have walked the same path before me. Because of You, I know that I
am not alone—today, tomorrow, or any day after that! Amen.*

morning
ENJOYING LIFE

*Let all who seek You rejoice and be glad in You; and let those
who love Your salvation say continually, "May God be
magnified!". . . . You are my help and my deliverer.*

PSALM 70:4–5 NASB

Sometimes we approach God robotically: "Lord, please do this for me. Lord, please do that." We're convinced we'll be happy, if only God grants our wishes like a genie in a bottle. We're going about this backward! We should start by praising God. Thank Him for life, health, and the many answered prayers. Our joyous praise will remind us just how blessed we already are! Then—out of genuine relationship—we make our requests known.

*Father God, my joy comes from You—and only You. Without You, I could
never experience all of the joys that life has to offer. Thank You! Amen.*

evening
A ROYAL VISION

*Yes, joyful are those who live like this!
Joyful indeed are those whose God is the LORD.*

PSALM 144:15 NLT

How wonderful to realize you're God's child. He loves you and wants nothing but good for you. Doesn't knowing you're His daughter send waves of joy through your soul? How happy we are when we recognize that we are princesses. . .children of the Most High God! Listen closely as He whispers royal secrets in your ear. Your heavenly Father offers you keys to the kingdom. . .and vision for the road ahead.

*Joy floods my soul when I think about how much You love me,
Lord. Thank You for making me Your child. Amen.*

morning
THE KEY TO HAPPINESS

He who heeds the word wisely will find good,
and whoever trusts in the LORD, happy is he.
PROVERBS 16:20 NKJV

Want the key to true happiness? Try wisdom. When others around you are losing their heads, losing their cool, and losing sleep over their decisions, choose to react differently. Step up to the plate. Handle matters wisely. Wise choices always lead to joyous outcomes. And along the way, you will be setting an example for others around you to follow. So c'mon. . .get happy! Get wisdom!

Father, thank You for the wisdom of Your Word, which will always
point me in the right direction when I have a choice to make. Amen.

evening
A NET OF LOVE

No one has ever seen God; but if we love one another,
God lives in us and his love is made complete in us.
1 JOHN 4:12 NIV

It's hard to be a good witness if you've got a sour expression on your face. People aren't usually won to the Lord by grumpy friends and coworkers. If you hope to persuade people that life in Jesus is the ultimate, then you've got to let your enthusiasm shine through. Before you reach for the net, spend some time on your knees, asking for an infusion of joy. Then, go catch some fish!

Dear heavenly Father, I want to be a good witness for You. Help me
remember to exude joy and love. . .so others will be drawn to You. Amen.

morning
NOT WITHHOLDING

*Anything I wanted, I would take. I denied myself no pleasure. I even
found great pleasure in hard work, a reward for all my labors.*
ECCLESIASTES 2:10 NLT

Work beckons. Deadlines loom. You're trying to balance your home life against your work life, and it's overwhelming. Take heart! It is possible to rejoice in your labors—to find pleasure in the day-to-day tasks. At work or at play. . .let the Lord cause a song of joy to rise up in your heart.

*Help me to slow down—every day—and enjoy the moments
as they come, Father God. May I not become so busy
that I miss out on life's simple pleasures. Amen.*

evening
JOY IN YOUR WORK

*Go, eat your food with gladness, and drink your wine with
a joyful heart, for God has already approved what you do.*
ECCLESIASTES 9:7 NIV

Ever feel like nothing you do is good enough? Your boss is frustrated over something you've done wrong. The kids are complaining. Your neighbors are even upset at you. How wonderful to know that God accepts our works, even when we feel lacking. He encourages us to go our way with a merry heart, completely confident that we are accepted in the Beloved.

*When it feels like I'm a complete failure—and that I am letting
others down, Lord—please infuse my soul with confidence. No
matter what, I am Yours. I am accepted. I am loved. Amen.*

morning
HE FIRST LOVED US

*This is how God showed his love among us: He sent his one
and only Son into the world that we might live through him.*
1 JOHN 4:9 NIV

Many things about God are quite a mystery. If there is anything at all that we can understand for sure, though, we can know He loves us. There is nothing we could ever do to make God *stop* loving us, because certainly we did nothing to make Him start. God is concerned about everything we do. He celebrates our victories and cries with us during our difficult times. God proved His love for us long before we were ever born! How could we not love such a God who first loved us so much?

*You have always loved me, God, and You will love me forever. I am so grateful!
Compared to Yours, my love is small, but I love You with all of my heart. Amen.*

evening
SOUL COMFORT

In the multitude of my anxieties within me, Your comforts delight my soul.
PSALM 94:19 NKJV

We don't know for sure who wrote Psalm 94, but we can be certain that the psalmist was annoyed and anxious when he wrote it. He cries out to God, asking Him to "render a reward to the proud" (v. 2 NIV). Then, he goes on with a list of accusations about the evil ones. . . . "In the multitude of my anxieties within me." Does that phrase describe you? When anxiety overwhelms us, we find relief in the words of Psalm 94:19. When we turn our anxious thoughts over to God, He brings contentment to our souls.

*Dear God, on those days when frustration and anxiety overwhelm me,
please come to me, comfort my soul, and remind me to praise You. Amen.*

morning
SHINE ON!

Let the message about Christ, in all its richness, fill your lives. Teach and counsel each other with all the wisdom he gives. Sing psalms and hymns and spiritual songs to God with thankful hearts.

COLOSSIANS 3:16 NLT

We need to live the Word of God every day. It will shine through us! The old song says, "They will know we are Christians by our love." This means reflecting the love of God in everything we do. When we spend time in God's Word, we find peace, wisdom, and contentment that we get from no other place. This is a peace we love to have. This is happiness! Imagine being anything but thankful to God for filling us with His love, peace, and wisdom!

O Lord, my Rock and my Redeemer, may my words and my actions be a reflection of Your Word and pleasing in Your sight. Amen.

evening
VISIBLE REMINDERS

Let the morning bring me word of your unfailing love, for I have put my trust in you.

PSALM 143:8 NIV

We don't know if David was a morning person or a night owl, but he chose to start his day looking for visible reminders of God's unfailing love. It might have been easy to remember God's love for him if he had witnessed a glorious morning sunrise, but if the night had been stormy and he was dealing with spooked sheep in the midst of a downpour, God's unfailing love may have felt a little distant. Whether or not conditions were favorable for faith, David believed in God's unfailing love—even if he couldn't see it in the world around him.

I awake in the morning, and You are there. You are with me all day long and throughout the night. Thank You, heavenly Father, for Your ever-present love. Amen.

morning
LOYAL HEARTS

*"For the eyes of the LORD range throughout the earth to
strengthen those whose hearts are fully committed to him."*
2 CHRONICLES 16:9 NIV

God seeks a relationship with those who have open and receiving hearts. He is not looking to condemn or judge but to find hearts committed to knowing Him and learning His way. He desires people who want to talk and listen to Him and who have a deep thirst to serve and please Him. God looks for us, and the only requirement is for each of us to have a fully devoted heart. We open our hearts and hands to receive Him, and He will find us.

*Find me, Lord; draw me near to You. Open up my heart so that
I may fully receive all that You want to pour into it. Amen.*

evening
GOD'S COMMAND

*So He said, "Come." And when Peter had come down
out of the boat, he walked on the water to go to Jesus.*
MATTHEW 14:29 NKJV

Jesus stayed behind to send the crowds away—and then to pray. Later that evening, the disciples, wrestling their boat against a contrary wind, saw a ghostly figure approaching. Jesus assured them it was Him, and Peter asked the Lord to command him to come. Jesus did—and Peter, briefly, walked on water. What does it take for an ordinary person to walk on water? A command of God. By the power of God, ordinary men and women, responding to God's call, have successfully accomplished difficult, even impossible, tasks.

*You are my strength, O Lord. Whenever I feel like giving up, I will turn
to You believing that You will give me the power to carry on. Amen.*

morning
GOD OF POSSIBLE

*Jesus looked at them and said, "With man
this is impossible, but with God all things are possible."*
MATTHEW 19:26 NIV

No one can be saved by their own efforts! Man's greatest efforts pale in comparison to the requirements of a holy God. But grace, freely offered by God and accepted by individuals, will admit us to heaven. With God, all things *are* possible—especially enabling forgiven sinners to live eternally. Realizing we can do nothing is the key to gaining everything.

*Dear Father, I appreciate Your grace—Your loving-kindness
that I don't deserve. There is nothing I have done to earn it.
Grace is Your gift to me, and I thank You. Amen.*

evening
EVERY STEP OF THE WAY

Never stop praying.
1 THESSALONIANS 5:17 NLT

God wants to be involved in our daily routines. He wants to hear from us and waits for us. God never promised an easy life to Christians. If we will allow Him, though, God will be there with us every step of the way. All we need to do is come to Him in prayer. With those three simple words from 1 Thessalonians 5:17, our lives can be fulfilling as we live to communicate with our Lord.

*Father, when I pray, remind me that prayer is not only about talking to You,
but also about listening to You. Open my heart to Your words. Amen.*

morning
PLANTED DEEP

Fix these words of mine in your hearts and minds; tie them as symbols on your hands and bind them on your foreheads.
DEUTERONOMY 11:18 NIV

Memorizing Bible verses isn't a fashionable trend in today's world, but learning key verses plants the Word of God deeply in our hearts. We draw strength and nourishment in dark times from remembering what God told us in the Bible. In times of crisis, we recall God's promises of hope and comfort. In our everyday moments, repeating well-known verses reminds us that God is always with us—whether it feels like it or not.

What an awesome gift You have given me, God—the Bible! I will fix Your words in my mind and heart and carry them with me wherever I go. Amen.

evening
REVEL IN THE BEAUTY

He has made everything beautiful in its time. He has also set eternity in the human heart; yet no one can fathom what God has done from beginning to end.
ECCLESIASTES 3:11 NIV

No one can completely "fathom what God has done." That's what makes Him God. And yet, still we try. Thankfully, our hearts don't need to understand; neither do they need earthly "fixes." They just need to be set free, to find God and revel in the beauty of His never-ending creation. Believers, stop letting unanswerable questions prevent you from loving Him more completely. And unbelievers, ask yourself, if you had every material thing you could want, wouldn't your heart still be reaching out for eternity?

I have questions, God—so many unanswered questions about life and about You. Increase my trust in You. Help me to set aside my uncertainty and to delight in Your never-ending love. Amen.

KEEP SMILING

*"When they were discouraged, I smiled and that
encouraged them and lightened their spirits."*
JOB 29:24 TLB

Our most authentic forms of communication occur without a word. Rather, they flow from an understanding smile, a compassionate touch, a loving gesture, a gentle presence, or an unspoken prayer. God used Job, an ordinary man with an extraordinary amount of love and wisdom—a man whose only adornment was righteous living and a warm smile. And He wants to use us too. So keep smiling. Someone may just need it.

*Remind me, Jesus, to bless others through my actions. A warm
smile, a simple act of kindness, a loving touch might be just
what someone needs today. Remind me, please. Amen.*

LOVE IS. . .

*And now these three remain: faith, hope and love.
But the greatest of these is love.*
1 CORINTHIANS 13:13 NIV

Who can deny the power of faith? Throughout history, faith has closed the mouths of lions, opened blind eyes, and saved countless lost souls. And the scriptures note that without it, we cannot please God (Hebrews 11:6). Yet as wonderful as these qualities are, it is love that God deems the greatest. Love lasts and never fails. It is patient, kind, unselfish, and honest; it never keeps a record of wrongs or delights in evil. In a word, love is God. And there is no *One* greater.

*Father, I strive to love patiently, kindly, unselfishly, and honestly, because
in doing so I become more perfect in love and more like You! Amen.*

morning
GOD'S HEART

"I will give them an undivided heart and put a new spirit in them; I will remove from them their heart of stone and give them a heart of flesh."
 Ezekiel 11:19 niv

God is willing to give us an undivided heart—a heart that is open and ready to see, hear, and love God. This heart has a single focus: loving God and others with a tenderness that we know comes from Someone beyond us. The good news is we have already had successful surgery, and our donor heart is within us. We received our heart transplant when Jesus died for us, creating new spirits within us. God's heart changes everything and creates us as new people with living hearts.

Thank You, Lord, for giving me a new heart, a heart so perfect in love that it will last me forever. Amen.

evening
NEVER ALONE

"But the Advocate, the Holy Spirit, whom the Father will send in my name, will teach you all things and will remind you of everything I have said to you."
John 14:26 niv

Jesus called the Holy Spirit "the Advocate," a translation of the Greek word *parakletos*: "one called alongside to help." It can also indicate Strengthener, Comforter, Helper, Adviser, Counselor, Intercessor, Ally, and Friend. The Holy Spirit walks with us to help, instruct, comfort, and accomplish God's work on earth. Through His presence inside us, we know the Father. In our deepest time of need, He is there. He comforts and reveals to us the truth of God's Word. Jesus is always with us, because His Spirit lives in our hearts. No Christian ever walks alone!

Strengthener, Comforter, Helper, Adviser, Counselor, Intercessor, Ally, Friend—O Holy Spirit of God! Thank You for dwelling within my heart, guiding me, and drawing me near to the Father. Amen.

morning
GOD-BREATHED

*All Scripture is inspired by God and is useful to teach us what is
true and to make us realize what is wrong in our lives. It corrects
us when we are wrong and teaches us to do what is right.*

2 TIMOTHY 3:16 NLT

God's Word continues to be God-breathed! It is as relevant today as it ever was!
Scripture speaks to us in our current situations just as it did to people a few thousand
years ago. . .just as it will for eternity. Situations and cultures and languages and tech-
nologies have changed all throughout history, but God has been able to speak to people
exactly where they are through His living Word. There is certainly no other book,
collection of books, or any other thing in the world that can do that. Only the living
Word, which continues to be God-breathed.

*Dear God, all things pass into history except for You and Your
Word. How wonderful it is that Your Word transcends time,
is relevant in the present, and will live forever! Amen.*

evening
JOYFUL SERVICE

*Wherefore I put thee in remembrance that thou stir
up the gift of God, which is in thee.*

2 TIMOTHY 1:6 KJV

This passage is a reminder to every believer. It demonstrates that our God-given gifts
remain strong only through active use and fostering. Gifts left unattended or unused
become stagnant and, like an unattended fire, die. Just as wood or coal fuels a fire,
faith, prayer, and obedience are the fresh fuels of God's grace that keep our fires
burning. But this takes action on our part. Are you using the gifts God has given you?
Can He entrust you with more? Perhaps today is the day to gather the spiritual tinder
necessary to stoke the fire of God within.

*God, You have given me special talents and inspiring gifts. I
pray, open my eyes to sharing those gifts. Through faith and
obedience, I will joyfully use them to serve You. Amen.*

morning
HE HEARS ME

I love the LORD because he hears my voice and my prayer for mercy.
PSALM 116:1 NLT

Isn't that mind blowing? The almighty God of the universe who created and assembled every particle in existence hears us when we come before Him. Maybe we go to the Lord in song, praising. Maybe we spend some time reading and thinking about God's Word. Maybe we are praying to Him as we reach out for His comfort. Whatever we do, God hears us and is interested in what we have to say. Isn't that a great reason to love the Lord? May we never forget to give thanks to God daily for the opportunity that He provides us simply to be heard.

I have so many reasons to love You, Lord, so many reasons to worship and praise You. How grateful I am that You hear my voice! I love You, Lord. Amen.

evening
THREE IN ONE

I am Alpha and Omega, the beginning and the end, the first and the last.
REVELATION 22:13 KJV

What makes our God unique among the religions of the world? No other religion has a God whose Son is equal to the Father. The Jews and Muslims reject the idea of God having a Son. Only Christianity has a triune God—three persons in one God. The Bible is unique, because in it God fully reveals who He is. Since Jesus is fully God, let it renew our hope and faith in our Savior. He who created all things out of nothing will re-create this world into a paradise without sin.

Jesus, I learn how to live by Your human example, and I trust in You as my God—Father, Son, and Holy Spirit— three persons, one God, one perfect You! Amen.

ENDLESS SUPPLY OF LOVE
morning

We love because he first loved us.

1 John 4:19 niv

The power of God's love within us fuels our love when human love is running on empty. He plants His love within our hearts so we can share Him with others. We draw from His endless supply. Love starts with God. God continues to provide His love to nourish us. God surrounds us with His love. We live in hope and draw from His strength, all because He first loved us.

O God, the human love I know on earth cannot compare with Your love. When I feel empty, Your love fills me up. Your love is perfect. It never fails. Amen.

NEVER SETTLE
evening

For in him dwelleth all the fulness of the Godhead bodily. And ye are complete in him.

Colossians 2:9–10 kjv

Paul stated clearly that the fullness of deity lives in bodily form in Christ. He is God the Son, and when you have God in your heart, you are complete. You don't need anything added—whether ceremonies or so-called secret knowledge—to make you *more* complete. If the Spirit of Jesus Christ dwells in your heart and you are connected to God, you've got it all! Don't let anyone persuade you otherwise (Colossians 2:8). Don't settle for substitutes.

Jesus, You complete me. Since You dwell in my heart, I am forever connected with God and heaven. I have all that I need—salvation and Your perfect, eternal love. Amen.

morning
EXTEND HOSPITALITY

*Do not forget to show hospitality to strangers, for by so doing some
people have shown hospitality to angels without knowing it.*
HEBREWS 13:2 NIV

The author of Hebrews 13:2, most likely Paul, reminded Christians to extend hospitality to strangers. He suggested that some strangers might even be angels sent from God. Today, most strangers to whom we extend generosity and hospitality are probably not angels, but we can't know if someday God will allow us to entertain an angel without us knowing it. When you practice hospitality, God might be using you to minister to others. What are some ways that you can extend hospitality to strangers?

*Lord, teach me to be wise when extending hospitality to
strangers. Enlighten me. Teach me new ways to minister to
others and show them Your amazing love. Amen.*

evening
NEVER FORGOTTEN

"See, I have engraved you on the palms of my hands."
ISAIAH 49:16 NIV

In the middle of tumultuous times, it's tempting to proclaim that God has forgotten us. Both Israel and Judah struggled with the idea that God had abandoned them. But God took steps to contradict this notion. In an image that prefigures Jesus' crucifixion, God boldly proclaimed that His children were engraved on the palms of His hands. The nail-scarred hands that His Son would endure bear the engraved names of all of us who call upon Him as Savior and Lord. God does not forget us in the midst of our troubles! It is His nail-scarred hand that reaches down and holds our own.

*Jesus, the scars on Your hands are because of me—a testament
to my salvation. My name is engraved on Your hand as a
child of God. Oh, thank You, dear Jesus! Amen.*

morning
GOD KNOWS

*Your eyes saw my unformed body; all the days ordained for
me were written in your book before one of them came to be.*
PSALM 139:16 NIV

God knows the days of all people. Job said, "A person's days are determined; you have decreed the number of his months" (Job 14:5 NIV). The same knowledge applies to our new birth. He created us anew in Christ Jesus for good works "which God prepared in advance for us to do" (Ephesians 2:10 NIV). The God who knows everything about us still loves us. With the psalmist, let us declare, "Such knowledge is too wonderful for me, too lofty for me to attain" (139:6 NIV).

*God, how can You know all about everyone who has ever lived
or ever will live? Your ways are so far beyond my understanding,
and yet You love me. You are so wonderful! Amen.*

evening
EVERY MOMENT. . .

He will not let your foot slip—he who watches over you will not slumber.
PSALM 121:3 NIV

The psalms tell us that God does *not* sleep. He watches over us, never once averting His eyes even for a few quick moments of rest. God guards our every moment. The Lord stays up all night, looking after us as we sleep. He patiently keeps His eyes on us even when we roam. He constantly comforts when fear or illness make us toss and turn. Like a caring parent who tiptoes into a sleeping child's room, God surrounds us even when we don't realize it. We can sleep because God never slumbers.

*O God, how grateful I am that You never sleep. When
weariness overtakes me, You guard me like a mother who
watches over her child. I love You, Father! Amen.*

morning
CHILDLIKE FAITH

*Don't let anyone look down on you because you are young, but set an example
for the believers in speech, in conduct, in love, in faith and in purity.*
1 TIMOTHY 4:12 NIV

Much of the wisdom we gain comes through experiences we try to shed in an effort
to get back to a purer, more innocent state. Young believers can be a reminder to the
older generation of the joy and enthusiasm a pure faith can generate. And they have
another important task; after all, "peer pressure" doesn't always have to be negative.
The young are best positioned to bring other young people to God, and that is work
fully deserving of respect.

*Dear God, help me to rediscover childlike innocence, the simplicity of faith
without doubt. It is in that purest form of belief that I am nearest to You. Amen.*

evening
JOYOUS FEASTS

*The LORD said to Moses, "Speak to the Israelites and say to them:
'These are my appointed festivals, the appointed festivals of the
LORD, which you are to proclaim as sacred assemblies.' "*
LEVITICUS 23:1–2 NIV

During the feast of booths, the Israelites camped out in fragile shelters for seven days
as a remembrance of God's care and protection following their escape from Egypt.
This joyous feast took place at the end of the harvest season and included a time of
thanksgiving to God for the year's crops. Like the Israelites, let's use all our holidays
to celebrate God's goodness, reflecting on the blessings He has given us personally
and as a nation.

*Father, the secular world has excluded You from holidays,
especially those set to honor You. As for me, Lord, I will
worship You on holidays and every day. Amen.*

HIS LOVE ENDURES *morning* FOREVER

God, God, save me! I'm in over my head, quicksand under me, swamp
water over me; I'm going down for the third time. I'm hoarse from
calling for help, bleary-eyed from searching the sky for God.
PSALM 69:1–3 MSG

The psalm writers had a very real, genuine relationship with God. They sang praises to God; they got angry with God; they felt abandoned by God; they didn't understand God's slow response. . .and yet they continued to live by faith, deeply convinced that God would overcome. These ancient prayers remind us that nothing can shock God's ears. We can tell Him anything and everything. He won't forsake us—His love endures forever.

O Lord, You know the secrets of my heart. Teach me to talk to You through
every emotion and every circumstance. My focus belongs on You. Amen.

A STRONG *evening* SPRING

My voice shalt thou hear in the morning, O LORD; in the morning
will I direct my prayer unto thee, and will look up.
PSALM 5:3 KJV

We need to begin our busy days on a strong spring too. Not with just a good cup of coffee, but some time spent with our source of strength. Taking five minutes or an hour—or more if we're really disciplined—in prayer and Bible reading can make the difference in our day. No matter if we're facing wresting kids out of bed or fighting traffic all the way to work, that special time can give us a "spring in our step" today.

Thank You, Lord, for another day. Be my source of
strength today. In Jesus' blessed name, amen.

morning
RENEWAL OF ALL THINGS

*Peter answered him, "We have left everything to follow you! What then will
there be for us?" Jesus said to them, "Truly I tell you, at the renewal of all
things, when the Son of Man sits on his glorious throne, you who have followed
me will also sit on twelve thrones, judging the twelve tribes of Israel."*
MATTHEW 19:27–28 NIV

None of us will just occupy space in heaven. Our God is always productive. And this
job to which Jesus refers, that of judging the twelve tribes of Israel, will be given to
the disciples. Have you ever speculated as to what you might do in heaven? Well, don't
worry; it's not going to be anything like what you've done on earth. Your "boss," after
all, will be perfect. And the tasks you perform will be custom-tailored to you. "Job
satisfaction" will finally fit into our vernacular.

*Lord, I can't even imagine what You have in store for me in heaven. Please
keep me faithful to complete the duties You've called me to on earth. Amen.*

evening
HOLD ON TO HOPE

The prospect of the righteous is joy, but the hopes of the wicked come to nothing.
PROVERBS 10:28 NIV

Trusting in Jesus gave you new life and hope for eternity. So how do you respond when
life becomes dark and dull? Does hope slip away? When no obviously great spiritual
works are going on, do not assume God has deserted you. Hold on to Him even more
firmly and trust. He will keep His promises. Truly, what other option do you have?
Without Him, hope disappears.

*Dear heavenly Father, the day I met You was the day I
received life anew. My soul now overflows with hope,
love, peace, and joy. Thank You for saving me! Amen.*

morning
EVERYDAY BLESSINGS

But the eyes of the LORD are on those who fear him,
on those whose hope is in his unfailing love.
PSALM 33:18 NIV

The Lord of all creation is watching our every moment and wants to fill us with His joy. He often interrupts our lives with His blessings: butterflies dancing in sunbeams, dew-touched spiderwebs, cotton candy clouds, and glorious crimson sunsets. The beauty of His creation reassures us of His unfailing love and fills us with hope. But it is up to us to take the time to notice.

May I always be aware of Your lovely creation, Father
God. Your artistry never fails to amaze me! Amen.

evening
AN END TO MOURNING

"Blessed are those who mourn, for they will be comforted."
MATTHEW 5:4 NIV

How often do we think of mourning as a good thing? But when it comes to sin, it is. Those who sorrow over their own sinfulness will turn to God for forgiveness. When He willingly responds to their repentance, mourning ends. Comforted by God's pardon, transformed sinners celebrate—and joyous love for Jesus replaces sorrow.

Heavenly Father, thank You for replacing my sorrow with joy!
Your unconditional love floods my soul. You are good! Amen.

LOVING JESUS

Looking unto Jesus the author and finisher of our faith. . .

HEBREWS 12:2 KJV

God is writing a story of faith through your life. What will it describe? Will it be a chronicle of challenges overcome, like the Old Testament story of Joseph? Or a near tragedy turned into joy, like that of the prodigal son? Whatever your account says, if you love Jesus, the end is never in question. Those who love Him finish in heaven, despite their trials on earth. The long, weary path ends in His arms. Today, write a chapter in your faithful narrative of God's love.

God, thank You for helping me write my story. May my story touch the lives of others and be a light pointing them to You! Amen.

FIRST LOVE

But you must stay deeply rooted and firm in your faith. You must not give up the hope you received when you heard the good news.

COLOSSIANS 1:23 CEV

Do you remember the day you turned your life over to Christ? Can you recall the flood of joy and hope that coursed through your veins? Ah, the wonder of first love. Like romantic love that deepens and broadens with passing years, our relationship with Jesus evolves into a river of faith that endures the test of time.

Father, I am so thankful that You are faithful. Though human relationships may fail, You are a constant companion in my life. Thank You! Amen.

JOY: JESUS OCCUPYING YOU
morning

May all who fear you find in me a cause for joy,
for I have put my hope in your word.
PSALM 119:74 NLT

Have you ever met someone you immediately knew was filled with joy? The kind of effervescent joy that bubbles up and overflows, covering everyone around her with warmth and love and acceptance. We love to be near people filled with Jesus-joy. And even more, as Christians we want to be like them!

Lord, show me how to radiate Your joy in the presence
of others. I want to be a light for You. Amen.

FOREVER JOY
evening

We don't look at the troubles we can see now. . . . For the things we see
now will soon be gone, but the things we cannot see will last forever.
2 CORINTHIANS 4:18 NLT

A painter's first brushstrokes look like random blobs—no discernible shape, substance, or clue as to what the completed painting will be. But in time, the skilled artist brings order to perceived chaos. Initial confusion is forgotten in joyful admiration of the finished masterpiece. We often can't see past the blobs of trouble on our life canvases. We must trust that the Artist has a masterpiece under way. And there will be great joy in its completion.

God, You are the Master Artist. I trust You to create
a masterpiece with my life canvas. Amen.

morning
A NEW DAY

*GOD, treat us kindly. You're our only hope. First thing in the
morning, be there for us! When things go bad, help us out!*
ISAIAH 33:2 MSG

Every day is a new day, a new beginning, a new chance to enjoy our lives—because
each day is a new day with God. We can focus on the things that matter most: worshipping Him, listening to Him, and being in His presence. No matter what happened
the day before, we have a fresh start to enjoy a deeper relationship with Him. A fresh
canvas, every twenty-four hours.

*Before I get out of bed in the morning, let me say these words
and mean them: "This is the day that the LORD has made; let
us rejoice and be glad in it" (Psalm 118:24 ESV). Amen.*

evening
A LIMITLESS GOD

*Show me your ways, LORD, teach me your paths. Guide me in your truth and
teach me, for you are God my Savior, and my hope is in you all day long.*
PSALM 25:4–5 NIV

God has plans for our lives. But oftentimes we find ourselves standing in His way.
The solution is to not be so determined with our own plans and schemes that we
leave God out of the equation. Instead, look for His teaching. Make Him your number
one adviser. Search out His word for your direction and path. Know that all is well.
He is holding your hand as you walk, step by step.

*My hope is in You, dear Lord, for I know You have the best plan for my life.
Show me the way You want me to go. Lead me with Your wisdom. Amen.*

morning
CHANGE OF MIND

*Don't copy the behavior and customs of this world, but let God transform
you into a new person by changing the way you think. Then you will learn
to know God's will for you, which is good and pleasing and perfect.*
ROMANS 12:2 NLT

God wants us to renew our minds each and every day. He wants us to have attitudes
and ideals that reflect His goodness. He wants us to change ourselves and the world
from the inside out. For when we have our heads on straight, God will work to bring
the best out in ourselves to the good of all. So fix your face on God's—focus on His
light and way—and see how brightly you begin to shine.

*Lord, give me a God-attitude so that I can grow into the
woman You created me to be. In Jesus' name, amen.*

evening
A LONELY NUMBER

*"This is my command—be strong and courageous! Do not be afraid or
discouraged. For the LORD your God is with you wherever you go."*
JOSHUA 1:9 NLT

If you believe you are all alone in this world, you are believing in a lie. Because with
God, you are never alone. He is with you no matter where you go. Although you may
not be able to touch Him physically, you know deep down that He exists. You know
that He is real—and that when you reach out for Him with your entire heart, mind,
soul, and strength, your spirit will meld with His and you will experience an amazing
joy, one that cannot be expressed with words. So take heart. Be strong and courageous.
Leave fear and discouragement behind. God's with you. And He'll never let you go!

Lord, with You in my life, I need never be alone. Amen.

morning
QUEEN OF THE HILL

*Though the sheep pens are sheepless and the cattle barns empty,
I'm singing joyful praise to GOD. I'm turning cartwheels of joy to my
Savior God. Counting on GOD's Rule to prevail, I take heart and gain
strength. I run like a deer. I feel like I'm king of the mountain!*
HABAKKUK 3:17–19 MSG

Sing a song of joyful praise to God this morning. Before you know it, His strength will begin welling up within you. He'll make your heart truly sing. Instead of your being buried by your misfortunes, you'll be standing on top of them. Because of God and His amazing power, you are now Queen of the Hill. Your footing is sure. You have conquered your calamities! You are no longer a victim but a victor! Praise your Lord!

Lord, I praise Your name. I leap for joy at Your love for me. Amen.

evening
BECOME THE VISION

*Now may the God of peace. . .equip you with all you need for
doing his will. May he produce in you, through the power of
Jesus Christ, every good thing that is pleasing to him.*
HEBREWS 13:20–21 NLT

Take some time to look at yourself through God's eyes. Forget about your doubts, misgivings, and feelings of weakness. God has called you to a specific task and is just waiting for you to take on the mantle He has already fashioned—just for you! It's a perfect fit. All you need to do is believe and take that first step to become the vision God has of you.

*Dear Lord, show me who I am in Your eyes. Then help me become
whom You have already made me to be. In Jesus' name, amen.*

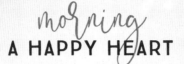

A HAPPY HEART

For the happy heart, life is a continual feast.
PROVERBS 15:15 NLT

Find some moments of pleasure in the smallest of things. Instead of focusing on the troubles that lie before you, make sure you take time out for all the good things that are happening. And if good things seem far and few between, *make* them happen. Do something that makes you laugh out loud or smile in utter contentment. Look to have a continual feast in the blessings of God as you serve Him and others with all the gladness in your heart.

Help me to find humor, joy, and contentment in the simple things in life, Lord. Give me a happy heart that continues to feast on Your goodness! Amen.

A WOMAN REBORN

"No one can enter the kingdom of God unless they are born of water and the Spirit. Flesh gives birth to flesh, but the Spirit gives birth to spirit. You should not be surprised at my saying, 'You must be born again.'"
JOHN 3:5–7 NIV

When you accepted Jesus, He gave you a new life. God once breathed life into you when you were born physically, but now you have been reborn spiritually. So erase the thought, *I was born that way,* that keeps playing in your mind. And replace it with God's truth: *I am a new creation in Christ, a daughter of God. With my Father, anything is possible because I can do all things through my Brother who strengthens me.* It's the new improved you, a woman reborn, now a sister of all, courtesy of heaven above.

God, thank You for this new life in Christ! Help me to let go of the old thoughts and embrace the truth. I'm a new creation! In Jesus' name, amen!

morning
GUILTY!

*If we confess our sins, he is faithful and just and will forgive
us our sins and purify us from all unrighteousness.*
1 JOHN 1:9 NIV

Sin leaves a spot—an indelible mark—on us. We can't hide it. We can't scrub it away. It marks us for life. Until *Jesus.* When we encounter Jesus, when we take Him at His Word and ask for His forgiveness, He performs in an instant what we could not perform in years of trying. The sin—all that ugliness of the past—is gone. *Poof.* No guilt. No condemnation. No doubt. When we make Him Lord of our lives, we get the best "laundering" job of our lives. What a joy, to be spot free!

*Father, thank You for removing not only my sin but the
lingering guilt as well. I'm so grateful, Lord. Amen.*

evening
REJOICING!

Always be full of joy in the Lord. I say it again—rejoice!
PHILIPPIANS 4:4 NLT

Have you ever heard a toddler laugh? Those adorable giggles are contagious. Before long you can't help but join in, your laughter filling the room. After all, nothing compares to the sheer joy of an innocent child. It bubbles up from the deepest, God-given place, completely unhindered by concerns, worries, or distractions. How many times do we become so burdened by life's complexities that we forget to rejoice? What would it feel like to let those giggles rise to the surface, even on the worst days? All we have to do is turn our focus from the pain to the glimpses of heaven right in front of us. Today, may your eyes be opened to many joy-filled moments.

*I'm grateful for the reminder, Father, that I can be filled with joy,
no matter the circumstances. Thank You, Lord. Amen.*

morning
USING YOUR GIFTS

We have different gifts, according to the grace given to each of us.
If your gift is prophesying, then prophesy in accordance with your faith;
if it is serving, then serve; if it is teaching, then teach; if it is to encourage,
then give encouragement; if it is giving, then give generously; if it is
to lead, do it diligently; if it is to show mercy, do it cheerfully.
ROMANS 12:6–8 NIV

What's your gift? What's your overarching talent or ability? Are you using it to the fullest? When you're flowing in the stream of God's best (i.e., His perfect will), you'll find plenty of opportunities to use those gifts. In fact, He just might open doors in ways that surprise and terrify and delight you! God is pretty amazing like that! He's got big plans for you!

Thank You for opening doors, Lord, so that I can use my gifts for You. Amen.

evening
LIVING IN HARMONY

Live in harmony with each other. . . .
Do all that you can to live in peace with everyone.
ROMANS 12:16, 18 NLT

Picture yourself at the symphony. The musicians file in, one by one, as the audience members take their seats. Before long, a violinist begins to warm up. Then a clarinet player. Then another musician. . . After a minute or so, you want to stick your fingers in your ears. It's a cacophony, dissonant and painful to the ears. This is what life is like when you're out of harmony with those around you. Maybe it's time to step back, wait for the conductor's cue, then link arms with your family, friends, and coworkers to play the most beautiful tune of your life.

Lord, sometimes I get caught up in the bickering and complaining
and don't see a way out. Thank You for teaching me the way
out, Father. I want to live in harmony with others. Amen.

morning
DREAMER

*"In the last days, God says, I will pour out my Spirit on all
people. Your sons and daughters will prophesy, your young
men will see visions, your old men will dream dreams."*
ACTS 2:17 NIV

Ah, the dreamer! She sees all of life's possibilities and believes every dream can come true. And she has no shortage of dreams either. Her creativity knows no bounds. She's got an idea a minute. How excited the Lord must be when He peers inside the hearts of his dreamer-daughters. He placed that creative bent inside of them, after all. Today, spend some time glancing back at some of the dreams God placed in your heart. Have all of them come true?

*Lord, I have plans. Ideas. Creative streaks. I know You placed
these dreams inside of me, and I can't wait to see which ones will
come to fruition. Thanks for entrusting them to me! Amen.*

evening
THINK ON THESE THINGS

*Finally, brothers and sisters, whatever is true, whatever is noble, whatever
is right, whatever is pure, whatever is lovely, whatever is admirable—
if anything is excellent or praiseworthy—think about such things.*
PHILIPPIANS 4:8 NIV

Single-minded. Such an interesting word! When you're single-minded, you are hyper-focused on the goal in front of you. Your gaze doesn't shift to the right or left. One of God's greatest desires is for His daughters to hyperfocus on good things: things that are noble, right, pure, lovely, and admirable. No more doubts, fears, or insecurities. From now on, single-minded aiming at a lovely target. Think on such things.

*Father, thank You for showing me how to think
on You so that my focus is sure. Amen.*

morning
HOPE TO THE FULL

*Now may the God of hope fill you with all joy and peace in believing,
that you may abound in hope by the power of the Holy Spirit.*
ROMANS 15:13 NKJV

The most beautiful thing about this prayer of Paul's is that he did not ask his readers to try to foster and maintain hope on their own, but rather that they would look to God, the source of hope. In sticking to and living out our faith, God fills us with hope. (He helps us with the sticking-to and living-out part also.) Joy and peace in what we believe allow us, with the help of the Spirit, to live hope-filled no matter the circumstance. And we abound, living fully, in the faith that things will turn out all right in the end.

God of hope, fill me with joy and peace to flourish in expectant faith. Amen.

evening
IMMORTAL DIAMOND

*Therefore we also, since we are surrounded by so great a cloud of witnesses, let
us lay aside every weight, and the sin which so easily ensnares us, and let us run
with endurance the race that is set before us, looking unto Jesus, the author and
finisher of our faith, who for the joy that was set before Him endured the cross.*
HEBREWS 12:1–3 NKJV

Faithful daughters of God cannot help becoming tired in the battle of the race. Yet they endure, not due to strength of their own but because they trust Jesus as Author and Finisher of their story of faith. Jesus saw the joy at the end. He endured the pain and the shame so that we could become His and inherit His beauty.

*Great Author, make me more like You,
to endure for a hidden but lasting joy. Amen.*

morning
AWAKEN THE DAWN

*Awake, lute and harp! I will awaken the dawn. I will praise You, O Lord,
among the peoples, and I will sing praises to You among the nations. For Your
mercy is great above the heavens, and Your truth reaches to the clouds.*
PSALM 108:2–4 NKJV

David's poetic lines reveal intentionality in starting the day with an attitude of praise. He writes of waking up early to thank God for His mercy and of wanting to make everything around him sing because of God's goodness. Sometimes the heart may be too hurt for such feelings. The only balm is spending time with Him and remembering He is at work before the rising of each new day. Like the lute and harp that David summons, we are all part of God's orchestra—each with their unique sound, all created to be in a harmony of praise.

*Awake my soul, O God, to the song of creation,
which was made to dance in tune with You. Amen.*

evening
RETURN

*"So you, by the help of your God, return; observe mercy
and justice, and wait on your God continually."*
HOSEA 12:6 NKJV

God has given us many analogies about our relationship with Him: Father and child, Shepherd and sheep, Master and servant. Children rebel, sheep wander, and servants run away. When we don't feel close to God, it's easy to think He has exited stage left, but this is a lie. We are the ones who move, leave, and stray from our relationship with Him. We have a Savior who freed us from the chains and bondage of sin. Search your heart for areas that you have strayed, then repent and return to your God.

*Father, forgive me for straying. Place a thirst
in my soul to never stray again. Amen.*

morning HOLY BOWL

In that day "HOLINESS TO THE LORD" shall be engraved on the bells of the horses. The pots in the LORD's house shall be like the bowls before the altar. Yes, every pot in Jerusalem and Judah shall be holiness to the LORD of hosts. Everyone who sacrifices shall come and take them and cook in them. In that day there shall no longer be a Canaanite in the house of the LORD of hosts.

ZECHARIAH 14:20–21 NKJV

What is holy? The prophet Zechariah sheds some light on what is holy. Holy is anything consecrated or dedicated to the Lord and for His glory. Use everything you have for God's glory. It doesn't matter if you are a janitor, lawyer, mother, teacher, or brain surgeon. Your skills and gifts are from the Lord and for the Lord.

Lord, help me to live a life that is set apart for You. Amen.

evening WILDERNESS BLOOM

The wilderness and the wasteland shall be glad for them, and the desert shall rejoice and blossom as the rose; it shall blossom abundantly and rejoice, even with joy and singing. The glory of Lebanon shall be given to it, the excellence of Carmel and Sharon. They shall see the glory of the LORD, the excellency of our God.

ISAIAH 35:1–2 NKJV

After the bleakness of winter, a small crocus blossoms and gives hope. We revel in its color and fragrance. There are times when our spiritual walk feels like a desert. There are few signs of life or progress, things are dry and brown, and it's hard to stay hopeful. But as Isaiah points out, God is our restorer and rainfall in a dry land. His glory makes our desert souls rejoice and blossom like the crocus. The excitement you feel for the coming spring. . .have you ever felt that excited about your time with the Lord?

Father, may I be as soil in the gardener's hands as I walk with You. Amen.

morning
LIGHT OF THE MORNING

"The God of Israel said, the Rock of Israel spoke to me: 'He who rules over men must be just, ruling in the fear of God. And he shall be like the light of the morning when the sun rises, a morning without clouds, like the tender grass springing out of the earth, by clear shining after rain.'"
2 SAMUEL 23:3–4 NKJV

Our God is just. We as followers of Christ and children of God must know and pursue God as He is revealed in the scriptures. His justice is like the light of the morning. The rising sun is constant; our Savior is constant. The same justice He gave to the Israelites is the same justice He gives to us. Know that there will be darkness, there will be night, but morning comes.

*Lord, help me to live a daily life aware of
You and dedicated to Your will. Amen.*

evening
LOVE GOD FIRST

Take good heed therefore unto yourselves, that ye love the LORD your God.
JOSHUA 23:11 KJV

There's nothing wrong with having nice things, but if we're not careful, our focus will center on things and not on God.

One reason we love possessions is because they feed a need in our lives—to have what others have, to feel important, to experience pleasure. Unfortunately, the need is bottomless. If we're not careful, we want more and more material possessions which only satisfy on a temporary basis.

The scripture today cautions us to take heed that we love the Lord our God. Don't allow temporary pleasures to take the place of God in your life. He's the only One who can fill that bottomless hole and make you feel complete.

Father, give me a craving for more of You. Amen.

morning
BE FILLED WITH JOY

*Now the God of hope fill you with all joy and peace in believing,
that ye may abound in hope, through the power of the Holy Ghost.*

ROMANS 15:13 KJV

Paul, the writer of today's verse, knew about battles, persecution, and rejection. He spent a lot of time writing his messages of hope while in jail. You may not be in a physical jail, but Satan may have you bound in a spiritual prison. It's time to break out of jail and be the victorious Christian you want to be.

1. Trust God to supply you with hope to make it during dark days.
2. Rely on God to fill you with joy and give you peace in the time of trouble.
3. Believe that God is who He says He is, that He has made a way for you through His Son, Jesus.
4. Allow the Holy Ghost to empower you to abound in hope.

*Father, empower me by Your Spirit to abound in hope as You fill
me with Your joy and peace through the Holy Ghost. Amen.*

evening
FREE THROUGH CHRIST

*Stand fast therefore in the liberty wherewith Christ hath made us
free, and be not entangled again with the yoke of bondage.*

GALATIANS 5:1 KJV

No matter what our past or present, Christ can set us free. There is no bondage that He cannot break, no power that can defeat Him. We become new creations in Christ when we surrender our lives to Him. The danger lies in our taking control and becoming entangled in the bondage of sin once again. We must allow Christ to be in complete control and then stand fast in the liberty through which He has set us free.

*Jesus, I surrender my life to You. Take control of my heart, and
help me to stand fast in the liberty that has set me free. Amen.*

SING A LITTLE *morning* SONG

Is anyone among you in trouble? Let them pray.
Is anyone happy? Let them sing songs of praise.
JAMES 5:13 NIV

James teaches us how to respond to life's experiences. He says if you're in trouble, pray about it. We're much better off when we pray about what's bothering us—no matter what the problem—than to let it show for the world to see. Likewise, if we're happy, we can let those around us know it by singing. When we pray about our troubles, we feel better and can then sing that song we feel in our hearts. Are you facing a problem today? Take it to God in prayer and let Him take care of it for you. If you're happy, then sing that little song you feel coming on.

Lord, help me to rely on You in times of trouble
and sing Your praises when I'm happy. Amen.

SERVE THE LORD *evening* WITH GLADNESS

Make a joyful noise unto the LORD, all ye lands. Serve the LORD with gladness:
come before his presence with singing. . . . Enter into his gates with thanksgiving,
and into his courts with praise: be thankful unto him, and bless his name.
PSALM 100:1–2, 4 KJV

Worship is a time of acknowledging God in our lives and showing Him we're grateful for all His blessings, a time to make a joyful noise and sing praises to Him. It's a matter of getting our priorities straight, deciding to give back to God a little of the time He's given us. Keeping God first in our lives means setting aside time to worship Him.

Father, help me to serve You by spending time in worship. Amen.

THE LORD WILL FIGHT FOR YOU
morning

*The LORD said to Joshua, "Do not be afraid of them; I have given
them into your hand. Not one of them will be able to withstand you."*
JOSHUA 10:8 NIV

When God fights for us, we have reassurance we are going to win. Often you can't tell your work from God's work, because He is working through you. And yet there are things only God can do. He wants us to boldly ask for what we need. He wants us to be in His work with Him.

*Heavenly Father, thank You for allowing us to partner with You in Your
work. Thank You that we can boldly go to the Creator of the universe and
ask for what we need, knowing You care deeply for each of us. Amen.*

A GLIMPSE OF HEAVEN
evening

*" 'He will wipe every tear from their eyes. There will be no more death' or
mourning or crying or pain, for the old order of things has passed away."*
REVELATION 21:4 NIV

Heaven will be a place of beauty. There will be no death, pain, fear, or impurity. God's creation will exist in the full glory He originally intended, not the wrecked-by-sin version we live in now. No sinfulness will mar it.

God gives us glimpses of heaven now to encourage us on our journey. He knows we can't see the whole picture, and He condescends to our frail humanity to give us what we need for the journey.

*Heavenly Father, thank You for Your loving care of us.
Show us glimpses of heaven when the journey gets rough,
and encourage us with what awaits us. Amen.*

THE DEFINITION OF FAITH
morning

*Now faith is confidence in what we hope for
and assurance about what we do not see.*

HEBREWS 11:1 NIV

In whom or what do you place your faith? God's character and His promises are faithful. Faith is the pathway to our relationship with God. We have faith to please God, to earnestly seek Him and believe in His reward, even when we can't see it with earthly eyes. We need to cultivate our eyes of faith, knowing that most of our reward for a faithful life will not be found in this life but in the next.

How do you grow your faith? Start with obedience. Worship, walk by faith, and share your journey with others. Faith will follow your obedience.

*Heavenly Father, thank You for making a relationship with
You possible. Help us to see You working in our lives. Amen.*

A WOMAN'S FAITH
evening

*Then Jesus said to her, "Woman, you have great faith! Your request
is granted." And her daughter was healed at that moment.*

MATTHEW 15:28 NIV

Jesus is delighted to grant this woman's request. He commends her faith, and He uses the same term of endearment, *woman*, that He used with His mother at the wedding where He turned water into wine. Jesus is proving to her that heritage doesn't determine her relationship with God; her faith does.

God invites you as His daughter to come to Him and relate to Him in a personal and loving way. Let Him show you how much He loves and values you.

*Lord Jesus, thank You for providing the way for us to have a
relationship with You. Thank You for loving us, for lifting us up
beyond our earthly heritage and giving us immeasurable value
in Your eyes. Remind us of how loved we are. Amen.*

morning
GOD'S GOT A PLAN

*"Here is a boy with five small barley loaves and two small
fish, but how far will they go among so many?"*
JOHN 6:9 NIV

Jesus simply needs us to trust Him with a little and then let Him work. He doesn't need us to do His work, but He allows us to be part of His process. In this Bible story, not only was there plenty to eat, but there were leftovers besides. These people had a physical need for food, and Jesus gave them spiritual food as well.

Spiritually, Jesus gives us everything we need to be satisfied and then even more, so it spills over onto others. When we seek God and put His kingdom first, He provides for our physical and spiritual needs. He is our satisfaction. He is the ultimate answer.

*Dear Jesus, thank You that You are not limited by what we can see or do.
Help us to see beyond this world and to trust You with the outcomes. Amen.*

evening
FINDING JOY IN WHAT YOU DO

So whether you eat or drink or whatever you do, do it all for the glory of God.
1 CORINTHIANS 10:31 NIV

Some people believe they will be fulfilled if only they could discover some solitary purpose, but lasting and deep fulfillment doesn't come from just fulfilling a purpose or even using one's greatest gifts and talents. It comes from using your gifts and talents *and* knowing whom you are using them for. It comes from serving God through what you do.

The artist who paints a picture simply to paint or just to make money will never experience the same joy as the artist who paints to glorify her Creator. Glorifying and loving God gives meaning and deeper joy to everything we do.

*Lord, please help me to love You so much that
everything I do flows from that love. Amen.*

morning
FREEDOM ISN'T FREE

*Not only so, but we also glory in our sufferings, because we know that suffering
produces perseverance; perseverance, character; and character, hope.*
ROMANS 5:3–4 NIV

Out of suffering comes. . .hope? It's true. Trouble ultimately produces hope. Suffering leads to greater character. Disaster leads to maturity. Attacks from Satan lead to strength. Why? Because freedom isn't free. It's typically paid for and bought with pain, problems, and crises that make us want to throw up our hands and scream.

So what should our response be? We rejoice. We must have the confident hope that something good is coming from our turmoil. We must choose to believe that a greater freedom is on its way.

*Lord, help me to remember that the trials I face are providing
for me a greater freedom when I submit to You. Amen.*

evening
LIVING BETWEEN THE PAIN OF EARTH
AND THE HOPE OF HEAVEN

*For just as we share abundantly in the sufferings of Christ,
so also our comfort abounds through Christ.*
2 CORINTHIANS 1:5 NIV

We must remember that in spite of what happens to us, God is good and He loves us, and He will ultimately make things right. Until then, we share in the sufferings of Christ and we wait. And with the power that comes from the Holy Spirit, we choose gratitude over self-pity and complaining. We cast our broken hearts, broken lives, and cares at His feet because He cares for us (1 Peter 5:7). We give Him our burdens, and in exchange, we receive rest (Matthew 11:28).

Living the abundant Christian life isn't about what happens to us. It's about how we respond to what happens to us.

*Lord, thank You that even though life is sometimes difficult, You have
given me all I need to be an overcomer through faith in You. Amen.*

WHEN YOU FEEL LIKE YOU ARE BLOWING IT

morning

Nothing in all creation is hidden from God's sight. Everything is uncovered and laid bare before the eyes of him to whom we must give account.

HEBREWS 4:13 NIV

Have you ever had a sense when you read the Bible that you just weren't measuring up? That you were totally blowing it? Hebrews 4:12–13 says that God's Word judges the thoughts and intentions of the heart. The conviction we feel is God's love in action, transforming us through His Word.

It's never His desire to burden us with guilt that leads to death, but to reveal our sin so we can experience life! Ah! Joyous liberty!

Lord, You know everything about me. You see the thoughts and intentions of my heart, and You purify me as Your Word judges both. This is the purification of my heart through Your Word as it corrects me and shows me where I am blind. Amen.

FEELING DISAPPOINTED?

evening

Though the fig tree does not bud and there are no grapes on the vines, though the olive crop fails and the fields produce no food, though there are no sheep in the pen and no cattle in the stalls, yet I will rejoice in the LORD, I will be joyful in God my Savior.

HABAKKUK 3:17–18 NIV

Praise God that He is at work. Praise Him that He hasn't left you. Praise Him for what He has done. Praise Him for what He is going to do. Praise Him in song. Praise Him with a shout. Like the psalmists did, don't ignore your disappointment, but don't wallow in it in unbelief either. Lift your burden to God and throw in a healthy dose of thanksgiving.

Lord, although life is sometimes difficult, and sometimes I am disappointed, I praise You for all the amazing things You have done in my life. How good You are! Amen.

morning
GOD IS BIGGER THAN THE WRONG DONE TO YOU

*"But if you do not forgive others their sins,
your Father will not forgive your sins."*
MATTHEW 6:15 NIV

Think about something someone has done to you that has demanded forgiveness. Do you believe God is bigger than the wrong? Are you convinced His love and His rule are redemptive? If so, let the person who has wronged you off the hook. Stop thinking that he or she has ruined your life and that you will never recover—because God is a redeemer.

*Lord, when someone wrongs me, I may want to lash out or hold
a grudge. Help me to remember that there is nothing that will
happen to me that You cannot redeem for my good and Your
glory. Help me to live in the freedom of this truth. Amen.*

evening
ONLY GOD GETS TO BE THE CAKE

"You shall have no other gods before me."
EXODUS 20:3 NIV

When we admit that a new home, the best furnishings, a six-figure job, a loving spouse, or even another child cannot fill us, we are in a very good place. At first, it may make us feel desperate because we come face-to-face with our emptiness. But it's a good kind of desperate, because it can lead to peace and rest.

Until then, we are like little children who scream in a panic while grasping at the sky, "I want!" But after we admit nothing in this world can satisfy like Christ, we can lie down in the gentle grass of "God's enough." And then comes rest from striving.

*Thank You, Lord, that You are enough. Help me to remember
that You are the only place I can find true satisfaction. Amen.*

HOW YOU CAN KEEP *morning* BELIEVING

For we live by faith, not by sight.

2 CORINTHIANS 5:7 NIV

Faith believes. In spite of what we can't see. In spite of what we don't understand. Faith always bends its knee to the God who made everything and knows everything. And faith remembers that this is not heaven, that this current life is a dot on the timeline of eternity. And faith is confident that, in time, God will make all things right. Maybe not this moment, maybe not next week, and maybe not next year. But when Christ returns, justice will be served, every wrong will receive its recompense, everything will be made beautiful, and everything will be made new. That's how we can keep believing.

Will you choose to believe God today?

Lord, give me the faith to follow You, no matter what happens in my life. Amen.

THE RIGHT *evening* ASSURANCE

And we know that all things work together for good to them that love God, to them who are the called according to his purpose.

ROMANS 8:28 KJV

This biblical promise doesn't apply to everyone. Only the ones who are following Christ can lay claim to the promise that God will work all things together for good. Those who trust and obey can rest in the assurance that everything (the good and the bad) fits together in the pattern He has laid out for them.

Lord, thank You for helping me bear my burdens and for keeping track of the things in my life. I know You are working all things for my good. In Jesus' name, amen.

morning
MORE THAN A PIECE OF FRUIT

*Thank you for making me so wonderfully complex!
Your workmanship is marvelous—how well I know it.*
PSALM 139:14 NLT

Women were designed by God to be beautiful. And He likes variety. If we're speaking about the plant world, think about the many species of flowers around the globe. They come in every imaginable shape and color and petal dimension. And each of them has its own unique glory. Maybe we should be more like the flowers—stay connected to the Source of our being, accept the sunshine and rain, and reflect His glory in how we grow.

*Lord, give me the right perspective of my body and
beauty. May I honor You with my being. Amen.*

evening
STAY CONNECTED

Give all your worries and cares to God, for he cares about you.
1 PETER 5:7 NLT

Prayer is your lifeline. It is the vital connection that keeps you in touch with the Father. And when we don't talk to Him, we shut Him out of the details of our lives. Of course, being omniscient, He is aware of what is going on anyway, but He wants us to invite Him in, to want to share our days with Him.

Have you prayed today? Don't see it as an obligation or a guilt inducer but as a chance to communicate with the One who loves you more than anyone else and who can do more about your situation than anyone else.

*Lord, thank You for being interested in
everything that concerns me today. Amen.*

morning SMILE AWAY!

Be glad in the LORD and rejoice, you righteous;
and shout for joy, all you upright in heart!
PSALM 32:11 NKJV

I think Jesus smiled a lot. We don't know what kind of temperament He had in His earthly form, but I believe He had the best traits of all the types—sanguine, choleric, melancholy, and phlegmatic. Certainly, His personality wasn't warped by the selfishness of sin and He always had time for others.

We are reminded often to be Christlike in our attitudes, words, and conduct. But what if we were to add to that list a challenge to be like Him in smiling at others? Of course, we don't know for sure, but there would certainly be nothing wrong with giving encouragement to others we meet throughout the day by letting our faces reflect the joy of the Lord in our hearts.

Lord, I want to be like You. Help me give others the gift
of my smile so that they can see You in me. Amen.

evening AN EXCLUSIVE PLACE

But now they desire a better, that is, a heavenly country. Therefore God is
not ashamed to be called their God, for He has prepared a city for them.
HEBREWS 11:16 NKJV

Think about the joy of arriving home for Christmas or coming to a family reunion, that moment when you walk in the front door to warm hugs and happy cries of welcome—that's the delight of every moment of eternity. Isn't it a comfort to know that we have this place waiting for us when this life is over?

Heaven is prepared for those who are in relationship with God. The only way to get there is by accepting the sacrifice of Jesus Christ's work on the cross. Salvation is an inclusive invitation to an exclusive place. Have you made plans to go?

Heavenly Father, thank You for preparing a heavenly
city where I can live for eternity. By Your grace, I will be
there with You when I die. In Jesus' name, amen.

morning
GOD IS GOOD

Praise the LORD, for the LORD is good; sing praises to His name, for it is pleasant.
PSALM 135:3 NKJV

Warm sunshine, brilliant flowers, rainbows after storms, newborn babies, friendships, families, food, air to breathe, pets, church dinners, sunrises, sunsets, beaches, forests, prairies, mountains, the moon and stars at night, and puffy clouds in the day. All around us are hints that God is good and that His works are beautiful and life-giving.

When disease or tragedy or hardship enters our lives, we can rest assured that God is not the author of these destructive things and that someday He will cleanse this globe of its misery and set everything right. Until then, He has given us His strength, His hope, and His promise. That is enough to keep us going.

Father God, I praise You. You are good. Your works are wonderful. I know You love me. Help me to trust Your plan and purpose for me. In Jesus' name, amen.

evening
FREE!

The Spirit who lives in you is greater than the spirit who lives in the world.
1 JOHN 4:4 NLT

Through the Holy Spirit, we have the power to overcome and carry on. Romans 8:37 (NIV) says, "We are more than conquerors through him who loved us." The Holy Spirit is always full of grace for the believer. Every conviction is for growth, sharpening, and disciplining, never guilt and shame.

Satan is right about one thing—we're not good enough; we fail over and over. But here is the difference: Our confidence is in Christ, not ourselves. And He has set us free!

Lord, thank You for setting me free. Speak into my heart, and continually remind me that I am clean in Your sight because of Your work, not mine. Amen.

THE WANT FOR *morning* WONDER

Praise the LORD God, the God of Israel, who alone does such wonderful things.
PSALM 72:18 NLT

We can regain our wonderment through reading God's Word. The more we learn about Him and our own condition, the more we can appreciate His love. Proverbs 25:2 (KJV) says, "It is the glory of God to conceal a thing: but the honour of kings is to search out a matter."

Is it time for you to examine the character of God in a fresh way? Pray today that He would open your eyes to His wonderful mysteries.

Father, restore in me the wonder of who You are. It has been too long since I have found myself amazed by Your love. Amen.

DON'T STOP *evening* PRAYING

The effective, fervent prayer of a righteous man avails much.
JAMES 5:16 NKJV

Jesus tells us to pray relentlessly, like a man who knocks on his neighbor's door in the middle of the night for bread. He said, "Ask and it will be given to you; seek and you will find; knock and the door will be opened to you. For everyone who asks receives; the one who seeks finds; and to the one who knocks, the door will be opened" (Luke 11:9–10 NIV).

Don't give up on your prayers. The answer is closer than you know.

Lord, there are many burdens that have gone unanswered, but I know nothing is impossible with You. Give me the strength to come to You daily. Amen.

morning
WITH ALL YOUR STRENGTH

Whatever your hand finds to do, do it with all your might.
ECCLESIASTES 9:10 NIV

Every single moment of life is a gift. *Every* moment has a purpose for God's kingdom. It's time to be zealous for righteousness in the course of everyday life, and God has promised a treasure trove awaiting us in heaven. The irony is that earthly life will also be filled with treasures—happy marriages, strong children, peace of mind, and joy unspeakable and full of glory.

> *God, I pray that my passion for You shows through my daily life. Put a fire in my soul that burns bright so others can see it. Amen.*

evening
ARE YOUR HANDS TOO FULL?

Trust in the LORD with all your heart.
PROVERBS 3:5 NKJV

Submission requires trust, and that can be difficult, especially if you've been disappointed before. But God has proven His faithfulness. Jesus said, "You believe because you have seen me. Blessed are those who believe without seeing me" (John 20:29 NLT).

Will you empty your hands? Let go of control and receive peace, joy, contentment, satisfaction, and confidence in its stead.

> *Jesus, give me the courage to give You control of my life. You already have it. Now teach me to rest in that. Amen.*

morning
SUFFERING CHANGES YOU. . .
FOR THE BETTER

After you have suffered a little while, [God] will himself restore you.
1 PETER 5:10 NIV

Don't despair in the dark places of suffering, but rather consider the ways God has used it to enrich your character. As the apostle Paul explained, "We also glory in tribulations, knowing that tribulation produces perseverance; and perseverance, character; and character, hope. Now hope does not disappoint" (Romans 5:3–5 NKJV).

In times of travail, watch as the Lord conforms you to His image, and consider yourself blessed.

Jesus, show me the value of my suffering,
and make me more like You through it all. Amen.

evening
GOD'S SYSTEM OF JUSTICE

Yet the LORD longs to be gracious to you; therefore he will rise up to show you compassion. For the LORD is a God of justice. Blessed are all who wait for him!
ISAIAH 30:18 NIV

The world's justice tells us we don't deserve God's graciousness—we've made too many mistakes—but God's justice is wrapped in love and mercy. Instead of pointing to our failures and telling us we're worthless, He forgives our sins and totally forgets them.

When we run into His arms of love and let His grace overwhelm us, we will long for more of Him. He's too magnificent to ignore. It's impossible to turn our backs on all He does for us. The natural response is to accept His compassion. He longs to give it and waits patiently until we're ready to receive.

Dear Lord, I long to receive Your gracious compassion. I yearn
for more of You! Help me set aside my own desires and fall down
before You, amazed by Your astonishing justice. Amen.

MY GOOD *morning* SHEPHERD

*"You are my flock, the sheep of my pasture. You are my people,
and I am your God. I, the Sovereign LORD, have spoken!"*
EZEKIEL 34:31 NLT

Jesus told a parable about the lost sheep. Though ninety-nine were safe, the shepherd searched until he found the one that was missing. Our Good Shepherd rejoices when He finds one sheep that strayed from the flock. He reminds us of the joy in heaven each time a sinner repents—when the Shepherd brings him safely from the wilderness to the sheepfold.

How desperately we need a Shepherd to care for us. Even though sometimes we act like willful sheep, God cherishes and protects us with every step we take.

*Heavenly Shepherd, no matter how far I stray, I know You
will find me and carry me home. Thank You for never giving
up on me, no matter how obnoxious I behave. Amen.*

FOREVER THE *evening* SAME

*"I am the LORD, and I do not change. That is why you
descendants of Jacob are not already destroyed."*
MALACHI 3:6 NLT

So many things in life change, but God doesn't. He won't throw us away because of the dumb things humans do. He hasn't resorted to stripping us of our free will, even though that would make things easier for Him. He didn't decide we aren't worth saving. He still invites us to work with Him.

And because He doesn't change, He will never destroy His people.

Jesus promised, "I am with you always, even to the end of the age" (Matthew 28:20 NKJV). And the writer of Hebrews said, "Jesus Christ is the same yesterday, today, and forever" (13:8 NKJV).

Because He doesn't change, we can look forward to eternity with Him. Just because of who He is.

*Dear Lord, I praise You for being changeless. As things around me change,
I can enjoy constant assurance, knowing You are forever the same. Amen.*

morning
HE WILL LIFT US UP

The LORD upholds all who fall, and raises up all who are bowed down.
PSALM 145:14 NKJV

In our daily lives, the Lord is the one who picks us up when we fall. Our falls may not be the kind that lead to broken bones, but we plunge into sin or slip on some stupid temptation or collapse into a pit of depression. Through everything that comes our way, He teaches us to depend on Him to lift us up and encourage us to go on. Always.

Precious Lord, I cannot fall so low that You won't rescue me. I rejoice in Your faithfulness, my Redeemer. You rescue me. Amen.

evening
GOD'S COMMAND

You made me; you created me. Now give me the sense to follow your commands.
PSALM 119:73 NLT

All God expects is obedience, and His rules are simple. He knows we will break His commandments, so He only asks that we love and trust Jesus. We can't just go through the motions or follow rituals, trying to get what we want. Our deep, genuine love and an intimate relationship are what He yearns for. The more we know Him, the easier it is to worship Him, to adore Him—to give back to Him the love He freely gives to us.

*Heavenly Father, following Your commands is so simple.
You loved me first. And I love You in return. Amen.*

morning
LIVE IN HOLY LIGHT

*"If you are generous with the hungry and start giving yourselves
to the down-and-out, your lives will begin to glow in the darkness,
your shadowed lives will be bathed in sunlight."*
ISAIAH 58:9–12 MSG

Jesus wants us to live an abundant life, and when we do—when we are full of His Spirit—we have plenty to share with the people He puts in our lives. That abundant overflow comes from spending time with God. When we pray, listen, read the Bible, meditate on His magnificence, and enjoy fellowship with other believers, we get filled to the brim. Whether we have material wealth or not, we will have spiritual riches to share with others.

We will "glow in the darkness" of the world. People will be drawn to the light they see in us. Our lives will be bathed in the Son's light, like noon on a clear, bright day.

Father, I long to shine Your light and joy in dark places. Amen.

evening
NO CONDEMNATION

*Who is he who condemns? It is Christ who died, and furthermore is also risen,
who is even at the right hand of God, who also makes intercession for us.*
ROMANS 8:34 NKJV

God the Father sees us through His Son. Jesus is eager to forgive the worst sinner. When we turn to Him, all our sins are washed away in His blood; we're spotless. And there's a glorious celebration in heaven whenever a sinner turns to Jesus.

No matter how filthy we feel, we're never more than a prayer away from being clean, as pure as if we never sinned.

*Thank You, Lord, for setting me free from the sin and guilt
that try to trap me. I praise You, because even though I don't
deserve it, You intercede for me continually. Amen.*

morning LEAD MY HEART

*May the Lord lead your hearts into a full understanding and expression
of the love of God and the patient endurance that comes from Christ.*

2 THESSALONIANS 3:5 NLT

If we try to control our own destiny, we flounder and our lives are full of confusion. We search for love in the things of this world and find broken hearts. We seek joy, only to face emptiness. We convince ourselves there is no truth, because we ignore reality. We waste time searching for things that bring no satisfaction.

When we bow our hearts and minds to the Creator and follow Him, we can bask in the calm of His unwavering peace. He leads us into a full understanding of true love and abundant life.

*Dear Father, I ask You to continually fill me with Your love.
Please lead me into a full understanding of Your love,
and keep me from choosing the wrong path. Amen.*

evening COMMON DAYS

*And so, dear brothers and sisters, I plead with you to give your bodies to God
because of all he has done for you. Let them be a living and holy sacrifice—
the kind he will find acceptable. This is truly the way to worship him.*

ROMANS 12:1 NLT

God tells us that He wants us to live a life of everyday worship. He wants to transform us from the inside out. This isn't about trying harder to please God or going to church more and giving more money. . .it's about letting the Spirit of God lead you in every moment and thanking Him along the way. It's about listening for His still, small voice and following Him—no matter what everyone else is doing.

*God, I want to worship You in all that I do. Show me
how to live a life of everyday worship. Amen.*

morning
THANK GOD

Hallelujah! Thank God! And why? Because he's good, because his love lasts. But who on earth can do it—declaim God's mighty acts, broadcast all his praises? You're one happy man when you do what's right, one happy woman when you form the habit of justice.

PSALM 106:1–3 MSG

You are the only one in charge of your attitude. Many things will happen today. Some good, some maybe not so good, but all are outside of your control. You can control how you respond to everything that happens this day. Why not thank God no matter what? Think that might change how well your day goes? Why not give it a try and see what happens!

God, please remind me in this moment of Your goodness and Your great love for me! Please help me to choose You in each moment. Help me thank You in every circumstance. Amen.

evening
A LIFE OF THANKS

My counsel for you is simple and straightforward: Just go ahead with what you've been given. You received Christ Jesus, the Master; now live him. You're deeply rooted in him. You're well constructed upon him. You know your way around the faith. Now do what you've been taught. School's out; quit studying the subject and start living it! And let your living spill over into thanksgiving.

COLOSSIANS 2:6–7 MSG

Jesus tells us that the greatest commands are to love God and love others (Matthew 22:36–40). Period. Nothing else matters if we aren't doing those two things! God's Word tells us that we are nothing without love. Ask God to transfer your head knowledge into heart knowledge so that you can start living in a moment-by-moment relationship with Christ.

When we live a life of love, it spills over into a life of thanksgiving.

God, please fill my heart with Your truths so that I can live a life of love. Move in me so that I can start living out what I believe with thanksgiving. Amen.

A SACRIFICE OF *morning* PRAISE

"Spread for me a banquet of praise, serve High God a feast of kept promises, and call for help when you're in trouble—I'll help you, and you'll honor me."
PSALM 50:7–15 MSG

In Hebrews 13:15 (NIV), God's Word tells us, "Through Jesus, therefore, let us continually offer to God a sacrifice of praise—the fruit of lips that openly profess his name." To sacrifice in worship means to have faith in God even when you don't feel like it. Even when you can't see Him anymore. The only way we can do that is through the power of Christ working in our lives in each moment. Because of the cross, we can rise above our circumstances and trust that the God of heaven has purpose for everything that comes our way. We are able to look at situations from God's perspective and trust Him no matter what.

*God, please increase my faith so that I can trust You
and worship You despite my circumstances. Amen.*

SAFE AND *evening* SAVED

I sing to GOD, the Praise-Lofty, and find myself safe and saved.
PSALM 18:3 MSG

God gives us His Word so that we won't be afraid. He is closer to us than we think. Whenever you feel afraid or lonely, call on His name. Ask Him to make Himself known to you. Copy Psalm 18:3 on a note card and read it again and again. God's Word is living and active, and the Spirit of God will remind you of these truths when you need them most. Don't be ashamed when you feel afraid. . .just take your fears straight to the only One who can free you from them. He will comfort you and cover you with His loving-kindness.

*God, please hide me in Your shelter and cover me with Your truth
and love. When I'm afraid, help me put my trust in You. Amen.*

morning
OVERFLOWING GRACE

They will pray for you with deep affection because of the overflowing grace
God has given to you. Thank God for this gift too wonderful for words!
2 CORINTHIANS 9:14–15 NLT

Because of Christ's work on the cross, God is overflowing with grace toward us. When He looks at us, He sees Jesus! Now we can go "boldly to the throne of our gracious God. There we will receive his mercy, and we will find grace to help us when we need it most" (Hebrews 4:16 NLT).

God, we come before You in thanksgiving today. Thank You for Your great
love and mercy toward us. Your gift is too wonderful for words! Amen.

evening
FILL YOUR MIND WITH GOOD

I'd say you'll do best by filling your minds and meditating on things true,
noble, reputable, authentic, compelling, gracious—the best, not the worst;
the beautiful, not the ugly; things to praise, not things to curse.
PHILIPPIANS 4:8–9 MSG

If you are typically a Debbie Downer, don't lose hope! Even if your mind goes directly to the negative, God can change you. He does this by transforming you and renewing your mind. Ask Him to daily fill your mind with good things—thinking the best about people and circumstances, not the worst. Seek the power of God to take every thought captive, and you'll begin to see a change in you!

God, please fill my mind with good things. Renew my
thoughts and make them obedient to Your will. Amen.

morning
GREAT EXPECTATION

All praise to God, the Father of our Lord Jesus Christ. It is by his great mercy that we have been born again, because God raised Jesus Christ from the dead. Now we live with great expectation, and we have a priceless inheritance—an inheritance that is kept in heaven for you, pure and undefiled, beyond the reach of change and decay.

1 Peter 1:3–4 nlt

If heartache and trials have marked your life, it's time for a new beginning. Take heart from Isaiah 43:19 (nlt): "For I am about to do something new. See, I have already begun! Do you not see it? I will make a pathway through the wilderness. I will create rivers in the dry wasteland."

If you are weary and burdened, take those burdens straight to the cross of Christ and allow Him to give you new life. Then be on the lookout—with great expectation—for the amazing ways that God shows up in your everyday life.

*God, today I will watch with great expectation
as You make Yourself known in my life. Amen.*

evening
SPIRITUAL MEDICINE

"The virgin will conceive and give birth to a son, and they will call him Immanuel" (which means "God with us").

Matthew 1:23 niv

Neediness has a solution. The One who will never leave us nor forsake us gives mercy and grace when we enter His throne room. He can redeem our losses, compensate our loneli-ness, understand our emotions, and satisfy our longings. How? By filling us with Himself. We have the fruit of the Holy Spirit when we focus on God. Colossians 3 gives practical steps for focusing our minds: put on love, let peace rule our hearts, fill our lives with the Word of Christ, sing to the Lord, and give thanks in all things. That is God's Rx for what ails us.

*God of mercy and grace, give me sensitivity to others
who are hurting, so I can point them to You. Amen.*

morning
THE PERFECT GIFT

*Every good gift and every perfect gift is from above,
and comes down from the Father of lights.*
JAMES 1:17 NKJV

We often seek material advantages, but God gives spiritual advances, often through adversity. Therefore, we must learn to receive all circumstances as wise gifts from God's loving hand. Viewing our troubles as tools to enhance our relationship with the Giver results in the joy He knew would be the "perfect gift" for our needs.

*Father, You have blessed me with many good and perfect
gifts, including adversity. May I be thankful for all
You give me, because it glorifies You. Amen.*

evening
A JOY FOCUS

*For the joy set before him he endured the cross. . . . Consider him who endured
such opposition from sinners, so that you will not grow weary and lose heart.*
HEBREWS 12:2-3 NIV

One way to keep a joyful focus is found in Psalm 68:19–20 (NIV): "Praise be to the Lord, to God our Savior, who daily bears our burdens. Our God is a God who saves; from the Sovereign LORD comes escape from death."

What if God does not deliver *from* a trial? Then He will sustain us *through* the trial by bearing our burdens with us every day.

When we "grow weary" and find ourselves "losing heart", let's focus on God our Savior, our sovereign Lord, our Burden-bearer. If the joy of the Lord is our focus, it will also be our strength (Nehemiah 8:10).

*God of my salvation, thank You for bearing my burdens and giving me
escapes from death. Help me stay joyful, because I'm focused on You. Amen.*

morning
A DAILY WALK WITH GOD

*And they heard the sound of the Lord God walking in the garden
in the cool of the day, and Adam and his wife hid themselves from
the presence of the Lord God among the trees of the garden. But the
Lord God called to Adam and said to him, Where are you?*

GENESIS 3:8–9 AMPC

How did Adam and Eve feel knowing God would come down from heaven just to spend time with them? Were they excited to see Him, or did they take His presence for granted?

You can experience God each day. He desires to spend time with you. He wants you, His child, to share your heart with Him. Are you there, waiting to hear His voice? Abide in Him and talk with Him today.

*God, forgive me for allowing the busyness of life to consume me.
Remind me that nothing is more important than abiding in You. Amen.*

evening
LOVINGLY CONNECTED

*I look up at your macro-skies, dark and enormous, your handmade sky-
jewelry, moon and stars mounted in their settings. Then I look at my
micro-self and wonder, Why do you bother with us? Why take a second
look our way? Yet we've so narrowly missed being gods, bright with
Eden's dawn light. You put us in charge of your handcrafted world.*

PSALM 8:3–6 MSG

God holds you close. You are precious and valuable to Him. His relationship with you runs deeper than even the tie you share with friends and family. You are lovingly connected to the Lord of the world without end.

*God, I am Yours, and You are mine. Thank You for loving me unconditionally
and desiring to have a relationship with me. You astound me. Amen.*

morning
FAITHFUL FRIEND

*The LORD kept his word and did for Sarah exactly what he had promised.
She became pregnant, and she gave birth to a son for Abraham in his
old age. This happened at just the time God had said it would.*
GENESIS 21:1–2 NLT

Regardless of what you are going through today, God is your faithful friend. Remind yourself of His presence and His promise to walk with you and never to leave you nor forsake you. Hold fast to Him and His promises!

*Lord, You are my closest, most faithful friend. I trust You to keep every
promise You have made to me. Because I know I can count on You, I'm
holding tight to You as You walk with me through my life journey. Amen.*

evening
LIVING THE TRUTH

*But I have trusted, leaned on, and been confident in Your mercy and loving-
kindness; my heart shall rejoice and be in high spirits in Your salvation.*
PSALM 13:5 AMPC

When you abide in Christ, you are equipped to battle negative thoughts. His Word comes alive within you, reminding you of His faithful promises.

Like David, you can hope again. You may not have the answers you think you need, but God is there—as He has always been.

David ends his prayer: "But I trust in your unfailing love; my heart rejoices in your salvation. I will sing the LORD's praise, for he has been good to me" (Psalm 13:5–6 NIV).

*Lord, sometimes I struggle to see the truth. Hide me in You
as I remember Your promises. You love me; You will not
fail me. You are my hope and expectation. Amen.*

morning
WHISPERS OF LOVE

*I am praying to you because I know you will answer, O God. Bend down
and listen as I pray. Show me your unfailing love in wonderful ways.*
PSALM 17:6–7 NLT

When those self-assaulting thoughts come to the forefront of your mind, refuse the
lies and focus on the many times God has come through for you. He loves you with an
everlasting love. He is faithful. He will never leave you. He is with you always. He has
given you a future and a hope.

*Thank You, God, for Your whispers of love. When negative thoughts
challenge me to give in and doubt, I will remember Your mercy,
compassion, and faithfulness. Lord, hear my prayer. Amen.*

evening
SECRETS OF THE KINGDOM

*He replied, "You are permitted to understand the secrets of the Kingdom
of Heaven, but others are not. To those who listen to my teaching,
more understanding will be given, and they will have an abundance
of knowledge. But for those who are not listening, even what little
understanding they have will be taken away from them."*
MATTHEW 13:11–12 NLT

Jesus told stories to crowds, but His disciples, who were also listening, were given more
knowledge than those who saw Jesus only on the surface. When you live in Christ and
walk closely with Him, when you go deep with Him, you too will see and experience
more than those who know Him superficially.

*Lord, I want to know the secrets of the Kingdom. Give me ears to hear, eyes
to see, and a heart that understands You on a deeper level. Help me to live my
life in accordance with the purpose You destined me for each day. Amen.*

morning LET YOUR SOUL RETURN

The law of the Lord is perfect, converting the soul; the testimony of the Lord is sure, making wise the simple; the statutes of the Lord are right, rejoicing the heart; the commandment of the Lord is pure, enlightening the eyes.

PSALM 19:7–8 NKJV

You grow in relationship with your heavenly Father as you come to understand Him and His ways through the Bible. Just as the sun restores a darkened earth's light, the Word of God restores your entire person, bringing your mind, will, and emotions back to that divine connection for which you were created—a relationship with Him.

Jesus, I desire Your truth found in the holy scriptures as much as I desire sunlight. Let Your Word renew my soul, and bring me into a closer relationship with You. Amen.

evening QUIET MOMENTS

The Lord is my shepherd; I shall not want. He makes me to lie down in green pastures; He leads me beside the still waters. He restores my soul. . . . Yea, though I walk through the valley of the shadow of death, I will fear no evil; for You are with me.

PSALM 23:1–4 NKJV

If you are not intentional about spending time with God, before you know it, you have become distant or have detoured away from Him. You find your soul is hungry for His presence and peace.

God is calling you to reconnect. No matter where you are, when you recognize your need for Him, stop whatever you are doing and step away from others. Once you are alone with Him, establish a reconnection. Allow His presence to wash over you and restore your soul.

Lord, when life begins to consume me, speak to my heart and draw me to You. Help me to disconnect from the busyness of this world and reconnect with Your. Amen.

IN THE MIDDLE *morning* OF IT ALL

*Six days later Jesus took Peter and the two brothers, James and John,
and led them up a high mountain to be alone. . . . Peter exclaimed,
"Lord, it's wonderful for us to be here!". . . But even as he spoke, a bright
cloud overshadowed them, and a voice from the cloud said, "This is
my dearly loved Son, who brings me great joy. Listen to him."*
MATTHEW 17:1, 4, 5 NLT

You may have experienced some rough patches in your life, a time when you were discouraged, praying and standing in faith day after day, yet getting no tangible results. And then, *wham!* God showed up in an amazingly big way.

Times like those should encourage you. For answered prayer will give you the courage to trust God more in the times when it seems like He's silent.

*God, You are in the middle of it all. Thank You for being so
faithful, always at work, providing Your very best for me! Thanks
for giving me the confidence to trust You more every day.*

SPRING EVENTUALLY *evening* COMES

*The LORD is my strength and my song; he has given me victory. This is
my God, and I will praise him—my father's God, and I will exalt him!*
EXODUS 15:2 NLT

Wouldn't it be nice if something or someone would predict your future? Will the figurative storms in your life continue to rage or cease? How long will a season of hardship and suffering continue? Regardless of today's shadow, spring will inevitability come in your own life. The cold, dark, bitter challenges you might be facing will eventually end. As you cling to the promises found in scripture, you will find hope. Blossoms will bloom!

*Father, whether I'm walking through heavy snowdrifts or
dancing in a field of lilies, I'll praise You because I believe
that spring is on its way or has already come!*

morning
TO SERVE OR NOT TO SERVE?

"You must serve only the Lord your God."
EXODUS 23:25 NLT

Jesus must have understood David's heart when he said, "Love the Lord, all you godly ones! For the Lord protects those who are loyal to him, but he harshly punishes the arrogant" (Psalm 31:23 NLT).

As you go about the day, be mindful of who you are serving—Jesus Christ—and how you can serve others out of the love you have for Him. Focus on serving God and leading by His example. Doing so will be more fruitful and satisfying than anything this world has to offer.

Jesus, I need to remain connected to You by serving and leading in the ways that glorify You. May my life be an instrument—a reflection—of You. Amen.

evening
FIRST THINGS FIRST

" 'Love the Lord your God with all your heart and with all your soul and with all your mind.' This is the first and greatest commandment. And the second is like it: 'Love your neighbor as yourself.' "
MATTHEW 22:37–40 NIV

Take a moment to love God with your whole being. Then do some self-reflecting. See if there's something for which you need to forgive yourself—and do so. Then extend that same love and forgiveness toward others. Ah, how freeing! Like David, you can now say to God, "You are my hiding place; you will protect me from trouble and surround me with songs of deliverance" (Psalm 32:7 NIV).

Jesus, You are the greatest thing in my life! I revel in the love You have for me, the love I have for others and myself, and the love I have for You. Thank You for helping me set my priorities straight. Amen.

morning
SING A NEW SONG

He has given me a new song to sing, a hymn of praise to our God.
Many will see what he has done and be amazed.
They will put their trust in the LORD.
PSALM 40:3 NLT

Sing a song of praise for what Jesus has done in your life, how He heals and restores you! David wrote, "O LORD my God, you have performed many wonders for us. Your plans for us are too numerous to list. You have no equal. If I tried to recite all your wonderful deeds, I would never come to the end of them" (Psalm 40:5 NLT).

How wonderful to sing a never-ending song about all the amazing things Jesus has done in your life, how He turns all your sorrow into joy!

Lord, help me to have an endless supply of praise for You. Your never-ending wonders give me hope. To You I sing a new song! Amen.

evening
CALMER OF SOULS AND STORMS

[Jesus' disciples in the boat] all saw Him and were agitated (troubled
and filled with fear and dread). But immediately He talked with them
and said, Take heart! I AM! Stop being alarmed and afraid.
MARK 6:50 AMPC

Remember who Jesus is and the amazing things He has done for you. Never think He's overlooking you. Take courage that you will recognize His voice, His presence, and His power when He is near. Be assured He's looking out for you. He will never pass you by. He has words to calm your spirit. He's ready to get into your boat and still your storms. Simply allow Him into your vessel.

Lord, come to me now. Speak to me. Calm my inner and outer storms. Amen.

morning
BE OPENED!

Looking up to heaven, He sighed as He said, Ephphatha, which means, Be opened! And his ears were opened, his tongue was loosed, and he began to speak distinctly and as he should.
MARK 7:34–35 AMPC

What proof that Jesus is the Messiah! That He is the One on whose arrival, "the eyes of the blind shall be opened, and the ears of the deaf shall be unstopped. Then shall the lame man leap like a hart, and the tongue of the dumb shall sing for joy. For waters shall break forth in the wilderness and streams in the desert" (Isaiah 35:5–6 AMPC)!

As you spend time in the restful, yet rejuvenating, presence of Jesus, be open! Allow His presence to sweep into your eyes, ears—and heart. Doing so will fill you with joy, prompting you to break out in prayer, praise, and song!

Jesus, I come to You in this private place, opening up my heart, soul, body, mind, and spirit to Your healing presence. Ah! What deep abiding joy!

evening
CONSTANT HELP

Lord, I believe! [Constantly] help my weakness of faith!
MARK 9:24 AMPC

Jesus has one request when you ask for help with your own issues: Take the *if* out of the equation when it comes to believing in His power. Have faith that *He can do* anything in your life, that for Him *nothing is impossible.*

But when (and *if*) you do fall short in faith, know that the Lord will constantly help you, pouring on you more than a sufficient amount of grace, enabling Him to work even through your weakness.

No matter what your level of faith, constantly call on Jesus. He will come, grip your hand, and lift you up into a life of seemingly impossible miracles.

Jesus, everything is possible with You in my heart. Help me to believe this more and more each day. Amen.

morning
IN GOD'S MIND

*I know and am acquainted with all the birds of the mountains,
and the wild animals of the field are Mine and are with Me, in My mind.*
PSALM 50:11 AMPC

No matter where you go or what you do, you are with Him—You are in God's mind. There is nothing you can hide from your Master, your Creator.

Allow His Word, His voice, to speak to you. Meld your mind with His. Seek the wisdom He is bursting to share. Know Him as He knows you. Love Him as He loves you.

For when you become one with the great I AM, nothing He has will ever be out of your reach.

*I want to know You, Lord, as You know me. I come to You now,
opening myself to You. Enter into my heart and mind. Amen.*

evening
FOCUSED ON JESUS

*And Moses made a serpent of bronze and put it on a pole, and if a
serpent had bitten any man, when he looked to the serpent of bronze
[attentively, expectantly, with a steady and absorbing gaze], he lived.*
NUMBERS 21:9 AMPC

"Just as Moses lifted up the serpent in the desert" (John 3:14 AMPC), so was Jesus lifted up to save you. So look away from all that distracts to Jesus, the Author and Finisher of your faith (Hebrews 12:2). And not just with a casual glance, a once-in-a-while glimpse, a just-in-case peek, but with an all-consuming, all-absorbing gaze.

Take some time to really "see" your Savior. Step away from the world and put your spiritual eyes on the prize of your life. Cling to Him. See Him. And He will save you.

*Lord, I'm here, seeking Your face, ready to melt in Your
presence, as I lift my eyes to Your saving grace! Amen.*

morning
PROMPTINGS OF THE SPIRIT

Now there was a man in Jerusalem whose name was Simeon. . . .
And prompted by the [Holy] Spirit, he came into the temple [enclosure].
LUKE 2:25, 27 AMPC

When you are close to God, you are in tune with the Holy Spirit. You can feel His nudges and promptings. You can hear His leadings.

Take some time today to draw close to God. "Seek the LORD while He may be found, call upon Him while He is near" (Isaiah 55:6–7 NKJV). Be open to His Spirit's leadings. Follow His promptings. If you don't, you will always be wondering what you might be missing.

Lord, keep me open to Your Spirit's nudges. I don't want to
miss anything You may have in store for me. I want to see Jesus
and His power in my life! In His name I pray, amen.

evening
HEART GUARD

His mother kept and closely and persistently guarded all these things in her heart.
LUKE 2:50–51 AMPC

When reading God's Word or examining His promises, you may not totally understand what He is trying to tell you. And He doesn't expect you to. After all, His thoughts are so much higher than any human's. But what you can do is follow Mary's example. Seek out God's wisdom, ask for clarity, relish His every word, and treasure it in your heart, knowing that someday you will understand it all.

Jesus, I treasure Your Word. Help me to hold it deep within
my heart, whether or not I understand it, for I know it will
determine the course of my life [Proverbs 4:23].

morning
GOD POWER

Jesus was baptized. As he was praying, the sky opened up and the Holy Spirit, like a dove descending, came down on him. And along with the Spirit, a voice: "You are my Son, chosen and marked by my love, pride of my life."
LUKE 3:21–22 MSG

What a great example of the power you have access to in your life! Just as Jesus' prayers could open up the sky, your prayers can move mountains. You also have a three-man team on your side. Like Jesus, you have a Father God who loved you—before you ever loved Him (Romans 5:8). Because of this great love, this Father God sent His Son not only to seek you—but to save you (Luke 19:10). And then He left behind the Spirit to draw you to Him (John 16:13–14).

What more could a woman want—or need?

In You alone do I have power, Lord. May I use it for Your good.

evening
YOUR MISSION

Let all that I am wait quietly before God, for my hope is in him. He alone is my rock and my salvation, my fortress where I will not be shaken.
PSALM 62:5–6 NLT

It takes commitment to make sitting silently before the Lord a priority. But only when you do so will you be able to, at all other times, step into the fortress where you cannot be shaken.

Make it your mission to seek the Lord in silence. Expect Him to be there and refill and refuel you. Make your motto the words "I wait quietly before God, for my victory comes from him" (Psalm 62:1 NLT).

Lord, all I need can be found in You. So here I am, Lord, seeking Your presence, hoping in You alone, my Rock and my Refuge. Amen.

morning
ON THE RUN-WITH GOD

*O God, You are my God, earnestly will I seek You; my inner self thirsts for You,
my flesh longs and is faint for You, in a dry and weary land where no water is.*
PSALM 63:1 AMPC

Even though David was on the run, even though he was out of his comfort zone, he
hadn't forgotten the most important thing: his love, worship, and pursuit of God.

When all seems lost in your life, when those who once loved you now curse you,
when you are relegated to a barren wasteland, remember Psalm 63. Know that the
most important thing you have—faith in God—is there for you to cling to and rejoice
in. He is all the comfort you need, no matter where you are.

You, Lord, are my all in all. You alone are my comfort zone. You are all I need.

evening
WHAT ARE YOU SAYING?

"And you—what are you saying about me? Who am I?"
LUKE 9:20 MSG

Knowing something and living it out are two different things. There's *knowing* the
truth, and then there's *living* the truth. Often, it's hard to do both at once. But the
difficult thing is that how you live speaks to others about what you know to be true.
And many times, how you live speaks much louder.

So take some time to reflect. What is *your* life saying about Jesus?

Lord, let my life speak the truth about You. Amen.

morning SHINE

May God be gracious to us and bless us and make his face shine on us—so that your ways may be known on earth, your salvation among all nations.
PSALM 67:1–2 NIV

Humans can't comprehend the brilliance of God. Thousands and thousands of years ago, people considered the sun a god. They could not imagine anything greater—a force more powerful than this ball of fire that gave life to the world. They could not imagine a power so boundless that it could simply speak the light into being.

But God does not so much want to light the world as He wants to light you. He wants your face to reflect His light, so that His ways may be known among all nations. The sun only reaches so far. The night still comes. But you, His daughter, can praise His name all the time.

Creator God, thank You for shining on me. Amen.

evening ENJOYING THE JOKE

Jesus was filled with the joy of the Holy Spirit.
LUKE 10:21 NLT

Many a woman thinks that if she works hard enough, if she studies enough, if she obeys enough, and if she's serious enough—then at the end of all of that, that is when Jesus will reward her with the power she wants in her life. That's when He will give her the reins.

But Jesus turns all that on its head. He loves you before you ever start the work, and He loves you when you have become exhausted. And though for certain there's a reward for those who remain steadfast and obey Him—the reward looks nothing like the prizes that come with gold statues and silver medals and piles of cash. Instead, it may be the weight of more responsibility, the sweat of more service, the sweet pain and blessing that comes with more love.

That Jesus—He has quite the sense of humor.

Lord, I'm glad You let me in on the joke. Amen.

morning
CHANGE FOR THE BETTER

*"The LORD your God will change your heart and the hearts
of all your descendants, so that you will love him with
all your heart and soul and so you may live!"*
DEUTERONOMY 30:6 NLT

For you to become new in Christ and take up the path of obedience, you cannot do it on your own with a sinful, selfish heart. God has to change you—and so He changes your heart to want Him more. You will still sin. You will still fall into the old habit of thinking of yourself too much. But you will want to be better, do better. And the longer you travel with Him and let Him work in your life, the more your heart can conform to the shape of His love.

God, change my heart so I can love You more. Amen.

evening
TRUE LIGHT

"See to it, then, that the light within you is not darkness."
LUKE 11:35 NIV

How many times have you felt a surge of happiness or a thrill of purpose, only to later realize that what you thought was a solid change in your heart was really created by a fleeting emotion or an artificial cause? The light of Jesus won't leave you wanting. It won't come in a moment and leave you in the next. It will stay and grow and give warmth and banish every bit of darkness.

Lord, help me be able to discern true light from darkness. Amen.

morning
THE CONFESSION

You, God, know my folly; my guilt is not hidden from you.
PSALM 69:5 NIV

There is beauty in knowing and living with God. When your eyes are on Him, you can see your own faults more clearly. But also you have hope that He will not leave you sinking down under the weight of those faults. He will reach down into your sorrow and your sorry-ness, and lift you up into His grace.

Dear Lord who sees me, help my eyes to stay trained on You. Amen.

evening
BIRD BUSINESS

"How much more valuable you are than birds!"
LUKE 12:24 NIV

It's not a bad thing to make plans—it's just a stifling thing to *live* for those plans. God wants you instead to keep going about the business He has created you to do—to love one another, to tell others about Jesus, and to love God with all your heart, soul, mind, and strength. To seek His kingdom first, and then all the rest will fall into place. That is His promise! And if this God of yours, who created such beautiful little feathered creatures, sees fit to take care of their needs, do you really believe He will neglect yours?

Father God, teach me not to fret about tomorrow. Amen.

morning
FROM BIRTH ON UP

*From birth I have relied on you; you brought me forth
from my mother's womb. I will ever praise you.*
PSALM 71:6 NIV

From the moment you were born (and even before that), whether you know it or not, you began relying on God every minute of your life. He gave you the parents you have. He knitted your body into the particular shape it would be, along with molding your particular set of abilities and challenges.

So praise Him today for being there for you from day one. Praise Him for providing capable hands to care for you. Praise Him for making you who you are today!

God, I praise You for making me, me. Amen.

evening
OUR PORTION

*My flesh and my heart fail; but God is the strength
of my heart and my portion forever.*
PSALM 73:26 NKJV

Just a piece of God fills a person up to overflowing. A portion of God is like the eternity set in the human heart that is mentioned in Ecclesiastes 3:11—no one can find out what that means or how God works, yet each person has this longing for something more and bigger and more beautiful and far beyond what she can know or see.

Who do you have in heaven but God? No one. He is all you have. Who on earth is like Him? No one. There is no one who comes remotely close. But with God as your portion, what else could you possibly need?

God, thank You for sharing You with me. Amen.

morning HOSANNA!

"Blessed is the king who comes in the name of the Lord!"
LUKE 19:38 NIV

As Jesus approached Jerusalem and saw the crowds, He actually wept over the city. But it seems He was not weeping because their acts of worship were so moving. He wept because it was all coming a bit too late. And the day was coming, He foretold, when their enemies would surround the city and crush them from every side. They had discovered too late what would bring peace to their city. They did not even now recognize God in their midst.

But you can. You know who Jesus is. And you can welcome Him into your heart, mind, family, household, and city today. You can sing songs of praise to Him and worship Him as your living, resurrected King, the Son of God, and the one Messiah. And you can go to Him to find peace.

Lord Jesus, show me the way to peace today. Amen.

evening GIVE FROM YOUR HEART

*"Truly I tell you," he said, "this poor widow has put in more than
all the others. All these people gave their gifts out of their wealth;
but she out of her poverty put in all she had to live on."*
LUKE 21:3–4 NIV

Your Lord loves a cheerful giver! He sees not just the gift but the heart of the giver. When the widow in this story from Luke 21 gave her last coin, Jesus declared her gift the most precious of all. It was of very little value in the marketplace, but in God's economy, it was greater than all the other offerings presented at the temple that day. It was all she had left to live on, and she chose to give it to God sacrificially and cheerfully.

Give from a thankful heart. Give generously and often. In doing so, you will please God.

*Dear God, help me to be a cheerful giver. I trust You to
provide for me all the days of my life. Amen.*

morning
EVERLASTING WATER

The woman left her water jar beside the well and ran back to the village, telling everyone, "Come and see a man who told me everything I ever did! Could he possibly be the Messiah?"

JOHN 4:28–29 NLT

When the woman at the well met Jesus, *truly* met Him, she tossed her water jar aside. She did not walk, but ran into the town to tell everyone about the Messiah.

Imagine her: skirt flying, arms flailing, a smile spread full across her sun-scorched face. The head that had once hung in shame now turned upward to heaven, a changed countenance mirroring a new heart.

Today what stands between you and reckless abandon for Christ?

Jesus, may I be like this woman who left the well, experiencing reckless abandon for You! Amen.

evening
GOOD SHEPHERD

Then we your people, the sheep of your pasture, will praise you forever; from generation to generation we will proclaim your praise.

PSALM 79:13 NIV

Listen for the still, small voice of your Good Shepherd. He may be calling you to pursue a dream you think is unattainable, a reminder that nothing is impossible with God. He may be asking you to reach out to another woman or a child who desperately needs a word of encouragement or a bit of help. This too is a reminder that He will not call you to that which you cannot accomplish in His name.

Praise your heavenly Father today. Thank Him for being such a loving Shepherd. He will never lose sight of His own. May your ears always be fine-tuned to His voice.

Good Shepherd, lead me today in Your everlasting ways. Amen.

REMAIN A FAITHFUL WITNESS
morning

*"Whoever belongs to God hears what God says. The reason
you do not hear is that you do not belong to God."*
JOHN 8:47 NIV

Be patient. Pray for those in your life who do not know Jesus, who scoff at your "religion" and smirk when you explain it as a relationship with the Savior. Know it is only through the work of the Holy Spirit that their ear plugs can be removed. In due time, and as a result of your prayers and witness, they may come to know Christ.

There is no celebration like that of a Christ rejecter–turned–Christ follower! Don't give up on the Sauls in your circle just because they have not heard God's voice. . .yet.

*Jesus, give me the endurance I need to bear the rejection of nonbelievers in
my life. I pray that one day they will come to know You as Lord. Amen.*

YOUR PILGRIMAGE
evening

Blessed are those whose strength is in you, whose hearts are set on pilgrimage.
PSALM 84:5 NIV

When someone cuts you off in traffic today, look to Jesus. When a situation at work frustrates you, stay the course. It is as if there are a million naysayers lining the sides of the track, but Jesus stands at the finish line cheering so loudly for you that His voice drowns out all the others.

You are a child of God, a daughter of the Most High, saved by grace and set on a path for success. Set your mind on the pilgrimage. God will honor your steadfastness of heart.

*God, help me to keep my eyes on You,
the Author and Perfecter of my faith. Amen.*

morning
LIFE VS. DEATH

"The thief does not come except to steal, and to kill, and to destroy. I have come that they may have life, and that they may have it more abundantly."
JOHN 10:10 NKJV

When you consider the difference between the father of lies and the Father of Lights, note this. Satan kills; Christ gives life. Satan destroys; Christ builds and rebuilds. Satan steals; Christ gives good gifts.

Live the abundant life that is offered to you as a believer. Reject the temptations of the devil. Run to Jesus. In Him, there is life abundant and free.

Jesus, You are the Giver of all good gifts. Bind Satan from my life that I might follow You always. Amen.

evening
CRY OUT TO GOD

GOD, you're my last chance of the day. I spend the night on my knees before you.
PSALM 88:1 MSG

The psalmist was in misery and cried out to God. He felt as though he were near death. Been there?

During such times, you must rely on God. You may not feel Him or sense His presence, but His Word declares that He will never leave you nor forsake you.

Talk to God first thing in the morning and just before your head hits the pillow at night. He is your refuge and your strong tower in times of trouble. A brighter day will come. Joy comes in the morning. Hold on tight to God. Find strength in knowing you are never, ever alone.

God, I find comfort in knowing You are always with me and will always see me through to the other side of sorrow. Amen.

morning
TRIED AND TRUE

As for God, his way is perfect; the word of the LORD is tried: he is a buckler to all them that trust in him.

2 SAMUEL 22:31 KJV

Today, no matter what you are up against, spend some time with David's song of praise, recounting the victories and grace the Lord has given you. Reminding yourself of His goodness and His help in the past will give you hope for the waiting—just as it did for one famous shepherd-king.

Lord, I praise You for being tried and true! Amen.

evening
HIS BEAUTY, YOUR FOUNDATION

Let Your work appear to Your servants, and Your glory to their children. And let the beauty of the LORD our God be upon us, and establish the work of our hands for us.

PSALM 90:16–17 NKJV

Solomon would have just been some other king if God hadn't given him the tools to be a great one. Perhaps you know believers whose flourishing work is built on their love for God, and you wonder how you could ever measure up to their "holiness." Leave the comparison game behind and turn to your Maker. Examine His glorious work in scripture, in your life. Ask Him to show you His beauty and establish the works of your hands wherever you labor—in your community, workplace, church, or home. He *will* answer.

Lord, may Your beauty establish the works of my hands!

morning
MADE TO BE MAKERS

King Solomon sent to Tyre and brought Huram. . . . Huram was filled with wisdom, with understanding and with knowledge to do all kinds of bronze work.
1 KINGS 7:13–14 NIV

Since you are made in His image, the Creator made you to be a maker! No matter the amount of your talent, He delights in your creativity.

Maybe creativity feels like a splurge to you, or someone told you it's not as important as other pursuits. But God intends for you to use and develop all His good gifts. Ask Him to give you courage to explore your creativity, to give you the wisdom and freedom to make as He does. Who knows what beautiful, truthful, excellent things He has in store for you to create?

Father, thank You for making me creative like You! Help me to use my gifts well.

evening
RIGHT ON TIME

He asked her, "Woman, why are you crying? Who is it you are looking for?" Thinking he was the gardener, she said, "Sir, if you have carried him away, tell me where you have put him, and I will get him." Jesus said to her, "Mary." She turned toward him and cried out in Aramaic, "Rabboni!" (which means "Teacher").
JOHN 20:15–16 NIV

On your heavy-heart days, you might not really expect Jesus to show up. But turn around, dear friend! Your Savior calls you by name, and His grace is always right on time. Think back on how Jesus has renewed your joy in the past: sending just the right scripture, a call from a friend, or a surprise refund when your paycheck was beyond stretched. With Mary, bear witness to His love and presence today!

*Thank You, Jesus, that You are always on time.
Your grace is enough. You are enough.*

DAY 148

morning
SHINING BRIGHTLY

Light is sown for the righteous, and gladness for the upright in heart.
PSALM 97:11 KJV

Until heaven comes and God's light fills the Holy City, making the sun and moon obsolete (Revelation 22:3, 5), be confident that Jesus, the Light of the World, is lighting your way. As you spend time in the Word and prayer, He will help you cultivate joy in the midst of uncertain bends in the path. As the season of summer blooms—months of bustle and fruitfulness, of gardens and relationships growing in the sunshine—may you reap a harvest of irrepressible joy as you grow closer with your faithful God who lights your pathway through any darkness, through any valley (Psalm 23:4).

Father, fill me with Jesus' joy so I may shine just as brightly! Amen.

evening
PRACTICING HIS COMPASSION

Know that the LORD is God. It is he who made us, and we are his; we are his people, the sheep of his pasture.
PSALM 100:3 NIV

Practicing being like God in His compassion helps you grow closer to His heart. You will learn to love as He loves, helping people who feel overlooked to know, through your care, that He is the God who sees, who provides. As you draw strength from your Good Shepherd's compassionate care toward you, how will you share His love with the vulnerable people around you?

Father, Your love is so beautiful. Lead me to the hurting people who need Your love today so I can share the hope and joy You have given me.

morning
BOUNDARY LINES

You have set a boundary that they may not pass over,
that they may not return to cover the earth.
PSALM 104:9 NKJV

After the flood, God put a rainbow in the sky as a promise. He made a covenant with humans that He would never again flood the earth. He told the waves they would never come forth with such a vengeance again.

God sets forth boundaries in your life as well. Those "boundary lines" fall for you in "pleasant places" (Psalm 16:6 NIV).

Even if you are facing your own "flood" in life—unemployment, loss, disappointment, or depression—God is your portion. Your joy is found in Him, not your circumstances. He is always with you and always has your best interest at heart.

God, thank You for being all I need. Amen.

evening
ATTITUDE MAKES THE DIFFERENCE

I will sing to the LORD all my life; I will sing praise to my God as long as I live.
PSALM 104:33 NIV

If you determine to sing to the Lord all the days of your life, as the psalmist did, you will have a hard time listing off all your troubles to everyone who will listen. It's pretty tough to sing praises to Jesus while whining about what aches.

Happiness is a choice. If you have the joy of the Lord planted deep within your soul, you will be able to shine for Him, regardless of your circumstances. Commit today to praise Him all the days of your life. It will make all the difference in the world!

Heavenly Father, You are so good. You are my provider and my companion. Whether I have plenty or am in need, whether I am among others or on my own, You are my God and I will praise You. Amen.

morning
GOD OF MIRACLES

*He listened to Paul as he was speaking. Paul looked directly at him,
saw that he had faith to be healed and called out, "Stand up on
your feet!" At that, the man jumped up and began to walk.*

ACTS 14:9–10 NIV

Do you believe as this man did? Do you wake up each day expecting the Lord to do great things? Or have you given up on a big dream in your life?

You serve a God who is powerful enough to make a lame man stand up and walk! Believe in Jesus. He's above and beyond all you can imagine. He can bring beauty from ashes in your life. He can make dry bones live again.

*God, give me hope where I am hopeless. You are a God
who still works miracles in Your children's lives. Help me to
believe. Help me to stand up on my feet again! Amen.*

evening
OUT OF NOWHERE

He opened the rock, and water gushed out; it flowed like a river in the desert.

PSALM 105:41 NIV

Abide in Christ. Read His Word. Stand on His promises. He has called you more than a conqueror (Romans 8:37); He has promised you hope and a future (Jeremiah 29:11); and He will never leave nor forsake you (Hebrews 13:5).

You may never see water flood out of a rock, but get ready. There are blessings ahead of you that will seem to come out of nowhere! God has a bright future in store for you and is able to do above and beyond what you can imagine in your wildest dreams.

*Father, help me to believe in miracles. I know
You have a good future for me. Amen.*

morning
REMEMBER GOD

They soon forgot His works; they did not wait for His counsel.
PSALM 106:13 NKJV

Take a moment today. Name the places and times God has blessed you beyond measure. He longs to do so again. In the moments when the grass appears greener elsewhere, rest in the unsettledness of today. It's okay if you cannot see the way. You know the Way Maker.

God is *for* you. Just as His heart was for the Israelite people, His heart beats for all who call Jesus Lord and Savior. Remember Him. Count your blessings. Trust God, who is the same yesterday, today, and tomorrow.

Father, help me to be faithful. To remember the "wheres" and "whens" of your hand of blessing on me and my life. Find me loyal and thankful this day. Amen.

evening
SHARE THE LOAD

He sent two of his helpers, Timothy and Erastus, to Macedonia, while he stayed in the province of Asia a little longer.
ACTS 19:22 NIV

Are you so busy trying to do everything yourself that you cannot do any one thing well? If so, ask God for wisdom in learning how to manage your time and energy. When you are with your family, be fully present. When you are working, focus on each task and complete it for the glory of God, whether you are sending emails or folding laundry.

Rest when needed. When you return to the tasks at hand, you will be refreshed and ready, at ease and focused, leading to a job for the Lord well done.

Father, I know I cannot be all things to all people at all times. Help me be wise with my time and energy. Amen.

GETTING OUT OF *morning* THE DESERT

*He turned the desert into pools of water and the
parched ground into flowing springs.*

PSALM 107:35 NIV

Do you find yourself in the desert? Is life dry and boring? Are you parched from the sameness of it all? Look up! God is more than able to bring you out of that place. He can turn your desert into pools of water and bring new life to the lifeless.

When you are busy about God's work, you won't have as much time to feel bored with life. You will find that He can bring joy to replace sorrow and a feeling of value that trumps that desert place every time!

*God, lead me today as I consider ways to use the gifts
and abilities You have bestowed on me. Amen.*

GOD-CENTERED *evening* REQUEST

*Solomon son of David established himself firmly over his kingdom,
for the LORD his God was with him and made him exceedingly great.*

2 CHRONICLES 1:1 NIV

David's son Solomon got a firm grip on the kingdom of Israel, not because he was self-centered but because He was God-centered. And because Solomon stuck so close to God, God stuck close to Solomon—"and made him exceedingly great."

Solomon was a person totally devoted to God, who sought God while He was near (Isaiah 55:6–7)—a great example for any human to follow!

What would you like to ask God for? If your request is heart-centered, God-serving, and selfless, God will surely grant it—and more besides!

*God, help me to search my heart, to find the request I want to make of
You that would further Your kingdom. May it please You. Amen.*

morning
YOU ARE LOVED

*For great is your love, higher than the heavens;
your faithfulness reaches to the skies.*
PSALM 108:4 NIV

God's love for you is higher than the heavens. His faithfulness reaches to the skies and beyond. Rest in that love today.

With God, there is no time or space. He is not limited by feelings or circumstances. He has no earthly constraints. He promises in His Word that He will never leave you. Bank on it. Today, start living like a daughter of the King. Hold your head high. You are dearly and infinitely loved.

Thank You, Father, for Your great love for me. Amen.

evening
JESUS STANDS NEAR

*The following night the Lord stood near Paul and said, "Take courage!
As you have testified about me in Jerusalem, so you must also testify in Rome."*
ACTS 23:11 NIV

Christ stands with you every single day of your life. Listen. Do you hear Him now? He whispers words of affirmation, which He spoke over your ancestors—words He will speak to your descendants. Be still now. Hear Him:

"You are Mine. You are a beloved sheep of My pasture, and I am your Good Shepherd. Be bold in My name, for I have declared you more than a conqueror. I've breathed new life into you. You are cherished. Be strong and courageous, because I go with you into battle. I'll help you share your story. Your testimony will draw others to My side so that I may stand near to them as well!"

Father, help me to remember that You are always standing near me. Amen.

morning
THE MAZE OF LIFE

The fear of the LORD is the beginning of wisdom;
all who follow his precepts have good understanding.
PSALM 111:10 NIV

Have you ever tackled the challenge of a corn maze? Just when you think you have discovered the way out, you run into another wall of stalks! With twists and turns galore, you find yourself backing up, plotting your path again and again. Eventually you find the way out, usually with the help of a friend calling to you from the exit!

Like a faithful friend at the end of the corn maze, God is constantly speaking to, encouraging, and calling out directions to you. It's your job to listen. Fear the Lord. Follow His instructions. These steps will give you a great jump start toward peace and joy as you navigate through an uncertain life.

Heavenly Father, develop in me a healthy fear of You.
Guide me as I follow Your ways. Amen.

evening
NO FEAR OF BAD NEWS

They will have no fear of bad news; their hearts are steadfast, trusting in the LORD.
PSALM 112:7 NIV

Scripture does not say you will not face trouble. It does not claim that bad—*really* bad—things cannot touch your life. What it does promise is that you, Christian sister, will never go it alone. God is at—and on—your side.

Stay true to Him. Put your faith in the One who will hold you tight and walk with you when bad news does come. Trust He knows what's best for you. He's got this.

Thank You, God, that I never have to fear bad news. Amen.

morning
ALL FALL, ALL FREE

All have sinned and fall short of the glory of God, and all are justified freely by his grace through the redemption that came by Christ Jesus.
ROMANS 3:23–24 NIV

Everyone has fallen, but everyone is made worthy by the gift of the grace of God. It's a mysterious gift—one that doesn't just add to who you are or what you have, like other possessions that bestow some added honor or wealth. It's a gift that changes where you stand. Without this grace, you sink to the bottom of the sea. With it, you can walk on water to meet your Savior.

God, thank You for my gift of grace! Amen.

evening
BE GLAD

The LORD has done it this very day; let us rejoice today and be glad.
PSALM 118:24 NIV

What has God done for you today? Open your eyes and see the works He has performed. Maybe He kept you safe on your commute to work. Maybe He sent rain to water dry fields. Maybe He cleared the clouds and gave you a bit of sunshine to start your morning. God shows His love and care for you every day, all day long, in both big and small ways. Don't forget to look around and see what God is doing for you and for others today. Then rejoice and be glad!

God, I'm so glad You love me! Thank You! Amen.

morning
ACCESS DOOR

*Therefore, since we have been justified through faith, we have peace
with God through our Lord Jesus Christ, through whom we have
gained access by faith into this grace in which we now stand.*
ROMANS 5:1–2 NIV

Accepting Jesus as your Lord and Savior gives you special access to the center stage of God's theater. You don't have to stay in the shadows watching a more joy-filled life go by. God invites you to step into His light and live boldly in the scenes He has written just for you. He is your director and guide, your manager and your adoring audience. And He is the author of your life, the gifter of grace.

Though you may sometimes get butterflies in your stomach, you don't have to be afraid to use your voice. You can find peace in the certainty that God will be with you every minute.

God, thank You for Your matchless grace. Amen.

evening
DEAD OR ALIVE?

Count yourselves dead to sin but alive to God in Christ Jesus.
ROMANS 6:11 NIV

Sin keeps you so wrapped up in yourself, you can't see any other way to live or any other person to live life with. The only way to escape that kind of existence is to kill it—to die to sin. To be baptized into the death of Christ and raised in new life with Him.

Does dying to sin mean you will never sin again? Never make a mistake? Never choose to do wrong? No. Accepting Christ does not make you perfect—at least not all at once. It does, however, give you purpose. And that purpose becomes the driving force behind your choices and actions. What is that purpose? To love the Lord your God with all your heart, mind, soul, and strength, and to love others as you love yourself. That's really living!

God, thank You for making me alive in You. Amen.

morning
IN ALL THINGS

*We know that in all things God works for the good of those who
love him, who have been called according to his purpose.*

ROMANS 8:28 NIV

God is always at work. He doesn't take vacation days. He doesn't ever stop knitting you together and unfolding His grand story. Even at the times when you feel your weakest, when you don't even know what to pray for and can't find the words to say, the Spirit helps you and speaks for you. No matter how you feel, where you are, what you are doing, or who you are with—God is working for your good.

*God, I want to join You in Your work.
Teach me to be a good servant for You. Amen.*

evening
AWAKE

He who watches over you will not slumber.

PSALM 121:3 NIV

If you have ever taken care of a small child who is sick in the night, you know what it's like not to slumber. Even when you get so tired that your eyelids won't stay open, you can't really get into a deep sleep. A small sound—a sniffle, a cough, raspy breathing—wakes you.

God watches over you like a parent watching over a sick child in the night. Except God's eyes never shut, and He never tires. He is always there to comfort you, guide you, and hold you in His strong arms.

God, thank You for watching over me even when I don't realize You are. Amen.

morning
THE SACRED MUNDANE

*Take your everyday, ordinary life—your sleeping, eating, going-to-work,
and walking-around life—and place it before God as an offering.*
ROMANS 12:1 MSG

Wake up. Turn off your alarm. Get up and get dressed and get moving. Pour the cereal and brew the coffee. Brush your teeth. Grab your keys and go.

God wants your mundane minutes and your sacred seconds and everything in between. Why? Because that is one of the best ways you can worship Him—by giving over body, mind, and soul as an act of living, breathing sacrifice.

If you actually actively gave over your schedule to God, praying through your day and committing to honor Him in your actions, how do you think that might change you? What might happen to your day if you offered every piece of it to God?

*Lord, take my body and my time—I offer them to You. Please
show me Your will, and I will serve You all my days. Amen.*

evening
WHAT GROWS FROM GRIEF

Those who plant in tears will harvest with shouts of joy.
PSALM 126:5 NLT

The people of Israel knew sorrow and disappointment. So many times, either through their own wrong actions or the actions of others, their lives were thrown into turmoil. And suddenly the Promised Land seemed too far to reach, or the temple crumbled, or the enemies appeared on every side—and there was no way out.

But God always came back for them, and as the psalmist records here, He brought them home to Jerusalem.

God will remember you too. So start again. Take up the faith of the farmer and plant your seeds, watering them with tears. Trust in the One who can make anything grow—even in the wilderness of grief.

*Lord, sometimes life seems so hard. Help me to remember that You
are always with me and that Your promises never fail. Amen.*

morning
DIFFERENT GIFTS

God gives the gift of the single life to some, the gift of the married life to others.
1 CORINTHIANS 7:7 MSG

Do you consider your life a gift? Or do you find yourself wondering if there's a better life out there somewhere?

Take a good look at your blessings. If you are married, think of all the ways you are grateful to have a partner with whom to go through life. If you are single, think of the scope for service that's available to you.

Be thankful for the gift of where you are right now, and show your gratitude in how you live and love and work for God.

*Lord of all, thank You for showing me all the
ways I am blessed right now. Amen.*

evening
LET YOUR LIFE BE A SONG FOR HIM

I will praise You with my whole heart; before the gods I will sing praises to You. I will worship toward Your holy temple, and praise Your name for Your lovingkindness and Your truth; for You have magnified Your word above all Your name.
PSALM 138:1–2 NKJV

You were born to worship—to live, to move in God. You were created to be an instrument of praise. Worship from your lips ushers you into His presence and brings Him pleasure.

One of the greatest gifts you can give God—aside from your heart through salvation—is worship. Take time to fully express your adoration of Him. Invite Him to show you who He has created you to be. As you become one with Him, your life becomes a song of praise for Him.

*Lord, I praise You. Thank You for Your loving-kindness
and truth. I want to be an instrument of praise to You.
May my life bring You pleasure in all I do. Amen.*

GOD IS ALWAYS *morning* THINKING ABOUT YOU

You saw me before I was born. Every day of my life was recorded in your book. Every moment was laid out before a single day had passed. How precious are your thoughts about me, O God. They cannot be numbered!

PSALM 139:16–17 NLT

Have you ever wondered what God thinks about you? Not a moment passes that you are not in His thoughts. From the very beginning of time, your Father's thoughts for you compelled Him to send His Son, Jesus, to the cross so you could have an eternal relationship with Him. Even amid the most trying personal crisis of Jesus' life—while hanging on the cross—*you* were on the heart of the Father.

What a powerful revelation to know you are on God's mind.

God, thank You for reminding me that because every day of my life is recorded in Your book, nothing about my life catches You off guard. Amen.

DRINK OF HIS *evening* GLORY

I saw the Lord sitting on a throne, high and lifted up, and the train of His robe filled the temple. Above it stood seraphim; each one had six wings: with two he covered his face, with two he covered his feet, and with two he flew. And one cried to another and said: "Holy, holy, holy is the LORD of hosts; the whole earth is full of His glory!"

ISAIAH 6:1–3 NKJV

The earth truly is full of God's glory. Each new day, God takes the time to paint the sunrise and fill the evening sky with a light show.

He wants you to step outside of the everyday chaos to experience His presence and His glory. He speaks to you in the little and big things found in His creation. Your heavenly Father pours out His artistic beauty simply for your joy and pleasure.

Heavenly Father, thank You for filling the earth with Your glory.

morning
PRECIOUS TIME WITH HIM

I say to the LORD, "You are my God." Hear, LORD, my cry for mercy.
Sovereign LORD, my strong deliverer, you shield my head in the day of battle.
PSALM 140:6–7 NIV

Regardless of today's workload or your planned to-dos, resist the pressing urge to jump into your busyness first thing. Instead, determine to spend some time with the Lord.

Pour a cup of tea and sit in your favorite chair. Look out your window to whatever nature might surround you. Better yet, take a nice leisurely walk around your neighborhood or in a park. Either way, begin to pray quietly. Stop for a moment to drink in your surroundings, the beauty that reflects your Creator.

How wonderful that in these quiet moments, God takes every opportunity to remind you that He cherishes the precious time you spend with Him.

Lord, forgive me for being distracted. I will make time for You—
especially today. Give me a visible glimpse of You.

evening
A QUIET CONFIDENCE

For thus said the Lord God, the Holy One of Israel: In returning
[to Me] and resting [in Me] you shall be saved; in quietness
and in [trusting] confidence shall be your strength.
ISAIAH 30:15 AMPC

Make it a point to return to God daily. Rest in Him. Stop your running around (mentally and physically) and be still and know that He is God (Psalm 46:10). In so doing, you will be refreshed. And as you quietly and confidently trust in Him, you will find unlimited strength and joy.

Lord, thank You for a quiet confidence in times of waiting.
Thank You for taking my hand and leading me through this
season. Help me to be obedient to all You have asked me to do.
Help me to hear You and respond with confidence. Amen.

morning
SHOW 'EM WHO LIVES IN YOU

*Examine yourselves as to whether you are in the faith. Test yourselves.
Do you not know yourselves, that Jesus Christ is in you?*
2 Corinthians 13:5 nkjv

Paul wrote, "I don't just do what is best for me; I do what is best for others so that many may be saved. And you should imitate me, just as I imitate Christ" (1 Corinthians 10:33–11:1 nlt). When you abide in Christ, His character—His nature and all of His attributes—shines out from within you. You are God's sanctuary; His Spirit lives in you. Christ in you is the hope of His glory demonstrated to those all around you (Colossians 1:27). Each day, choose to show 'em who lives in you!

*Christ Jesus, You live and dwell in me. Let my life shine for Your
glory. Let Your purpose and presence in my life point others to
relationship with You because of the choices I make today. Amen.*

evening
DELIGHTFULLY YOU

*You [Judah] shall no more be termed Forsaken, nor shall your land be
called Desolate any more. But you shall be called Hephzibah [My delight is
in her], and your land be called Beulah [married]; for the Lord delights in
you, and your land shall be married [owned and protected by the Lord].*
Isaiah 62:4 ampc

Your name at birth is the first gift from your parents *and* your first identity. But no matter how you have been labeled until now, God has given you a new name.

Let go of the other names you may have accumulated throughout life: Too Heavy, Too Tall, Not Smart Enough, Not Pretty Enough, Too Much Trouble. You *are* enough. . .and not too much. God is not seeking perfection, beauty, or grace. He is seeking *you*. Bloom in the love of a Father who has renamed you His Delight.

*Father God, thank You for delighting in me. Help me to fully accept my
new name and live as one accepted and adored by her Father. Amen.*

morning
FULLNESS

*I pray that you, being rooted and established in love, may have
power. . .to know this love that surpasses knowledge—that you
may be filled to the measure of all the fullness of God.*
EPHESIANS 3:17–19 NIV

The fullness of God is like the deep pool at the base of a mountain waterfall. Immerse yourself in the great incomprehensible mystery of who God is—an all-knowing and all-powerful being who *chooses* friendship with you. He is enduringly faithful but forgives all of your unfaithfulness. He is God, the mighty warrior of the Old Testament, and Christ, the gentle lamb of the New.

Though God is unfathomable, He delights in revealing Himself to you so that you may be filled to the brim with the fullness of God.

*Father God, help me absorb the deep and extravagant
love with which You fill me to the brim. Amen.*

evening
FORGET ME NOT

*Does a young woman forget her jewelry, a bride her wedding ornaments?
Yet my people have forgotten me, days without number.*
JEREMIAH 2:32 NIV

Each morning God is smiling when you open your eyes. He wants to talk with you. Time in His Word is like sitting down to coffee with the best of friends. He meets you there and prepares you for your day.

When it's time to get dressed, remember to slow down long enough to add your most valuable accessory: a spirit warmed and refreshed by the Spirit of God. Just as a woman remembers to put on earrings or a necklace, take a mental and spiritual moment to clothe yourself with the truth of God. And just as a bride places a veil on her head, pause and adjust your thoughts to remember God in His greatness and generous love.

God, I love that You want to spend time with me! Help me to forget You not. Amen.

morning
LIGHT

*For you were once darkness, but now you are light in the Lord. Live
as children of light (for the fruit of the light consists in all goodness,
righteousness, and truth) and find out what pleases the Lord.*
EPHESIANS 5:8–10 NIV

The transformation that changed you from darkness to light is no less dramatic than what your Creator God did in transforming this world. You are a new creature. Live like a new creature. Give up any ties with the dark, and please God instead. For He is your source of abundant life, joy, peace, and love.

Determine to live each day in the light. Seek God in scripture and in prayer. Thank Him for His gifts. Praise Him for being a great God who transforms. Enjoy life in the light.

*God, help me live as a child of light and be drawn to
the best of what is good, right, and true. Amen.*

evening
STANDING STRONG

*Finally, be strong in the Lord and in his mighty power. Put on the full armor
of God, so that you can take your stand against the devil's schemes.*
EPHESIANS 6:10–11 NIV

Satan loves to batter you with shame that you haven't done enough or the idea that God can't possibly forgive you *again*. The enemy takes pleasure in making you doubt your salvation or in making you think that God could never love someone like you. The enemy wants to trick you into losing the peace and joy of abundance in Christ.

No worries. Your God-given armor has you covered. It's your task to put each piece on with focus, understanding that the battle has already been won. Stand strong. God's power looks mighty good on you.

*God, I'm thankful for Your mighty power and protective armor. Now
help me stand firm, exchanging Your truth for the enemy's lies, confident
in the knowledge that You are the One who fights for me. Amen.*

morning
GOD'S TRADEMARKS

God's Message: "Don't let the wise brag of their wisdom. Don't let heroes brag of their exploits. Don't let the rich brag of their riches. If you brag, brag only of this and this only: That you understand and know me. I'm God, and I act in loyal love. I do what's right and set things right and fair, and delight in those who do the same things. These are my trademarks." God's Decree.

JEREMIAH 9:23–24 MSG

Busyness, volunteering, and achievements can be added to the list of things that are outer signs of worth. And you may tend to rely on those exterior things to demonstrate your worthiness. Yet your heart will be happiest when you find your worth in God.

As you understand and know Him, you will bask in His loyal love, and all those insecurities that cause you to find significance elsewhere will fade away.

Thank You, Lord, that Your heart desires the best of relationships with me. Help me know and understand You! Amen.

evening
GATHERED UP

So spacious is he, so expansive, that everything of God finds its proper place in him without crowding. Not only that, but all the broken and dislocated pieces of the universe—people and things, animals and atoms—get properly fixed and fit together in vibrant harmonies, all because of his death, his blood that poured down from the cross.

COLOSSIANS 1:19–20 MSG

No matter how broken up or beat down you may feel, you are—in reality—gathered up, contained in Jesus. You are restored, all in one piece, all in one place in the absolute fullness of God.

When you comprehend that the scattered pieces of yourself are gathered up and redeemed, the fissures that have left you painfully cracked can heal. You can look at yourself with the word *reconciled* scripted around you in flowing circles. You are complete.

God, help me walk today as one who is gathered up, redeemed, and healed. Amen.

morning
BELOVED SHEEP

*"I myself will gather the remnant of my flock out of all the countries where I
have driven them and will bring them back to their pasture, where they will be
fruitful and increase in number. I will place shepherds over them who will tend
them, and they will no longer be afraid or terrified, nor will any be missing."*
JEREMIAH 23:3–4 NIV

Being God's sheep means that you can reside in a peaceful pasture, green with peace
and gladness at any time or place. When you feel a little beat up by life outside the
pasture, you can remember that your Good Shepherd understands. He promises not
to lose even one of His fold. He keeps a careful head count and goes in search of those
who wander off.

*Thank You, Good Shepherd, for providing what I need
in a pasture. I trust You to care for us all. Amen.*

evening
ARMLOADS OF BLESSINGS

*Bring rains to our drought-stricken lives so those who planted their crops
in despair will shout "Yes!" at the harvest, so those who went off with
heavy hearts will come home laughing, with armloads of blessing.*
PSALM 126:6 MSG

There are so many moments that can't be explained in this life. And although you may
not be able to figure out why certain things happen in your life or the lives of those
you love, you can be sure God will use those trials for your ultimate good. To further
His will. To mold you into the daughter He created you to be.

God will eventually turn your despair into delight and your tears into laughter.
He's poised to fill your arms with blessings.

*Father, give me faith and endurance to keep
going even when the going gets hard. Amen.*

morning
WHOLEHEARTEDNESS

*"For I will set My eyes on them for good, and I will bring them back
to this land; I will build them and not pull them down, and I will plant
them and not pluck them up. Then I will give them a heart to know
Me, that I am the LORD; and they shall be My people, and I will be
their God, for they shall return to Me with their whole heart."*

JEREMIAH 24:6–7 NKJV

Life may have left your heart bruised and broken, but God can do what no one else
can. He can give you a new heart—one that comprehends His greatness.

Your heart is safe with your faithful God. It can expand and dream.

Return to Him now. Discover the freedom of hoping in a future that is good. Find
your ease in loving God with your whole heart. Grasp the deep and abiding love with
which He first loved you.

God, help me grasp Your wholehearted love for me. Amen.

evening
GREEN GARDEN

*A life devoted to things is a dead life, a stump;
a God-shaped life is a flourishing tree.*

PROVERBS 11:28 MSG

A God-shaped life glistens inside and out. But spending time on things that don't bring
enthusiasm to your spirit will leave you feeling dead inside. Excessive TV watching or
internet surfing can cause numbness. Watch out for and avoid things that dry up your
sap and stunt your growth! Instead, pursue flourishing life provided by the Father,
striving to spend less time in the world's shadows and more time in the Son's light.

*Father God, I want all You have to offer!
Help me embrace a God-shaped life. Amen.*

morning

BEAUTIFUL CHANGES

If you love learning, you love the discipline that goes with it—how shortsighted to refuse correction!
PROVERBS 12:1 MSG

Change occurs in you as you spend time with God, learning about Him from His Word. His truths go into the dark places of your heart and let in light. As you understand how completely you are loved and accepted, you will find the courage to let go of the ideal, of perfection. You will let go of fear and worry as you grow to trust God more and more.

When you believe deeply that God will never, ever abandon or reject you, you can let go of old habits and thought patterns that have kept you frozen in place. As you begin loving learning and thriving on correction, you will find more and more pleasure in your inner beauty.

God, thank You for working out Your beautiful salvation in me. Amen.

evening

HIDDEN THINGS

"This is GOD's Message, the God who made earth, made it livable and lasting, known everywhere as GOD: 'Call to me and I will answer you. I'll tell you marvelous and wondrous things that you could never figure out on your own.'"
JEREMIAH 33:2–3 MSG

God's answers are sometimes long in coming, and other times they're quick; but He always hears when you call Him and is not slow to speak. He unravels every single mystery as you patiently listen for, then follow His promptings. The beauty is in your relationship with Him. The almighty Father God whispers into the ear of His beloved daughter, telling you the wondrous things only He can impart. Listen and attend carefully. For at times, He speaks softly to your spirit. At other times, He will gently nudge your soul.

Need to know how to reach a troubled heart? Perplexed about relationships? Want to feel whole and safe amid transition? Call to God. He will answer, advise, and amaze you.

Father God, help me know when You are speaking.
Quiet my soul to listen. Amen.

morning
YOUR HEART'S DESIRE

Souls who follow their hearts thrive;
fools bent on evil despise matters of soul.
PROVERBS 13:19 MSG

Scripture promises that if you delight in the Lord, He will give you the desires of your heart (Psalm 37:4). Trusting God to do so might not seem reasonable or safe if you have had disappointments in the past. Yet God alone is worthy of your total confidence. Because He loves you like no other, you can trust Him. Have confidence in all He is doing in your life, as well as what He plans to do.

God, thank You for the delights You bring to my life.
I trust You to bring good things in my future.

evening
HEART WEIGHTS

The heart of the righteous weighs its answers, but the mouth of the
wicked gushes evil. The LORD is far from the wicked,
but he hears the prayer of the righteous.
PROVERBS 15:28–29 NIV

The righteous—you who are made right by being made new creations in Christ—attract God. He is close to you. When you pray, the Holy Spirit takes the whispers of your heartstrings and brings them to the Father. The Lord hears your prayers, the prayers of His child. The only thing that interrupts heavenly cell service is sin, and forgiveness is only a prayer away.

The Lord is far from the wicked but near the righteous. Learn it. Live it.

King of kings and Lord of lords, may I weigh my decisions.
May I recognize the candidates You seek and who seek You.
Thank You that You hear me, whatever my needs are.

morning WORKING OUT

It pays to take life seriously; things work out when you trust in GOD.
PROVERBS 16:20 MSG

Today's verse reads like a contradiction:

The first part says, take life seriously. Concentrate without frills or fun.

The second, it will all work out. Don't worry, be happy. What goes around comes around.

Although the two statements seem to collide, God's Word is true and does not lie. Things work out for those who take life seriously.

When you live as God directs, both vertically and horizontally, things will work out for you. You can count on it.

Eternal, wise God, I trust everything will work out when I live according to Your plan as revealed in Your Word. Amen.

evening HEAVEN'S ART GALLERY

A present is a precious stone in the eyes of its possessor; wherever he turns, he prospers.
PROVERBS 17:8 NKJV

When God gives you a gift, He expects you to use it. Like parents who treasure their children's schoolwork, He awaits your efforts. If human parents give each picture, essay, and test a place of honor on the refrigerator, what will God do with *your* work?

When you delight in the gifts God gives to you, returning them to His use, He treats them as precious. He showers more gifts on you. He wants to fill His art gallery with your works.

Loving Father, may I treasure Your gifts to me, polishing them, sharing them in praise to You. May any increase flow back to You and Your kingdom.

morning
LIFE, FULL AND TRUE

*"Imagine a person who lives well, treating others fairly, keeping
good relationships. . .lives by my statutes and faithfully honors
and obeys my laws. This person who lives upright and well shall
live a full and true life. Decree of GOD, the Master."*
EZEKIEL 18:5, 9 MSG

An upright existence, time lived the way God wants, will bring you the benefit of a full and true life—love, joy, peace, and all the fruit of the Spirit.

A true life frees you to be transparent, 100 percent single-minded in your loyalty to God, as you enjoy the continual presence of your all-knowing, all-powerful, loving Father.

Pretense ends. You are who you say you are. God fits you with a life custom-made for you.

*Living God of truth, fill me with the knowledge and love for
Your Word so that I will have that full and true life.*

evening
GOD THE DRAGON

*Do you see what we've got? An unshakable kingdom! And do you see how thankful
we must be? Not only thankful, but brimming with worship, deeply reverent
before God. For God is not an indifferent bystander. He's actively cleaning
house, torching all that needs to burn, and he won't quit until it's all cleansed.*
HEBREWS 12:28–29 MSG

God invests Himself completely in you, His child. He's not an indifferent bystander. Like a dragon, He purifies and protects His treasure with fire.

When God turns up the heat of trials in your life, rejoice that He is making you perfect, holy, His work complete.

*Lord, thank You for burning away what needs to be cleansed. I trust the
transformation process to You as I hide under the shelter of Your wings.*

morning
LESSON PLAN

*Then shall they know, understand, and realize positively that I am the
Lord their God, because I sent them into captivity and exile among the
nations and then gathered them to their own land. I will leave none of
them remaining among the nations any more [in the latter days].*

 EZEKIEL 39:28 AMPC

One thing rings crystal clear in the Bible: God wants you to know Him. It echoes from
the psalmist's prayer, "Let be and be still, and know (recognize and understand) that
I am God" (Psalm 46:10 AMPC), to Paul's prayer that the Ephesians would be given a
"spirit of wisdom and revelation [of insight into mysteries and secrets] in the [deep
and intimate] knowledge of Him" (Ephesians 1:17 AMPC).

Whatever it takes, God will make you see Him as He is. Look for Him in all circumstances of your life, good and bad, beginning today.

*Omniscient God, fill my heart with a hunger
to know You more and more. Amen.*

evening
BLINDFOLD FAITH

*Though you have not seen him, you love him; and even though you do not see
him now, you believe in him and are filled with an inexpressible and glorious
joy, for you are receiving the end result of your faith, the salvation of your souls.*

1 PETER 1:8–9 NIV

Today you live in between the seen and the unseen. A few hundred believers knew
Jesus in the flesh. The day is coming when you will see Jesus as He is (1 John 3:2). But
although today you can't see Jesus with your physical eyes, you offer the certainty of
your faith. You love Jesus because He first loved you and died for you.

You believe and accept the rich gifts He showers on you, including your salvation.
By faith you see the joy beyond.

You don't trust because you know. You know because you trust.

*Invisible God, thank You for opening my eyes of faith
and enfolding me in Your loving embrace. Amen.*

morning
OTHERWORLDLY

*See how very much our Father loves us, for he calls us his children,
and that is what we are! But the people who belong to this world don't
recognize that we are God's children because they don't know him.*

1 John 3:1 nlt

Since many people do not know or understand your heavenly Father, chances are you will be misunderstood. Your customs and behavior will seem strange and otherworldly. In one of his letters, Peter addresses Christians as sojourners and exiles. How true this is! He calls you this, because you are seeking a better country to call your own. You know that your stay here is fleeting.

When the pressures of this world are overwhelming, remember that your Father has lavished His love on you. He is your refuge. He is your home.

*Father, when I feel misplaced and alone, remind me that my hope
rests in the promise of abundant, eternal life in a better country.*

evening
FOREVER BRIDE

*"I will betroth you to me forever; I will betroth you in righteousness
and justice, in love and compassion. I will betroth you in
faithfulness, and you will acknowledge the Lord."*

Hosea 2:19–20 niv

These verses may seem distant and irrelevant in the modern world. But as a Christian, you have been adopted into God's nation. You are one of His people, a citizen in His kingdom. When you bow before idols—which can be anything from money to relationships—it grieves the Lord. He is a jealous God, desiring your undivided attention.

But the most astonishing thing is that you are also betrothed to Him to be His bride—beautiful, pure, honored, and cherished. God offers to purify those who enter into a covenant with Him. His wedding gift to you is righteousness, justice, love, compassion, and faithfulness. In all of these things, He never fails or falters.

Rejoice! For you are God's forever-bride.

Lord, You are the ultimate lover of my soul. Thank You for pursuing me.

morning
PERFECT LOVE

There is no fear in love. But perfect love drives out fear, because fear has to do with punishment. The one who fears is not made perfect in love.
1 JOHN 4:18 NIV

God designed you to experience perfect love. This kind of love fortifies and sustains. It places you on solid ground. It surrounds you and fills you up. And it sets you free from fear. Can you fathom a love so whole, so pure? It might be difficult for you to imagine such a perfect love, because no one has ever offered it to you—except for the One who laid down His life for yours, who shouldered God's wrath in order to spare you. His love is perfect and utterly selfless. In it there is no fear of condemnation. No fear of unfaithfulness. No fear of separation. Death's sting has been erased.

Jesus, how exquisite and deep Your love is for me.
Give me the eyes to see it. Turn my heart toward it daily.

evening
A CHOICE OF WISDOM

"Those whom I love I rebuke and discipline. So be earnest and repent."
REVELATION 3:19 NIV

God loves you even more than a mother loves her own child—imagine!—so you can be assured that if you need discipline of any kind, it will be essential. His Word says that when those times of rebuke come, you should be earnest and repent. The wailing, pouting, and stomping will only prolong your misery, keeping you in harm's way and from living your life with all the victory God intended for you.

The next time you receive discipline from God, embrace that unfathomable love by accepting—with an attitude of remorse and a heart for sincere change—the insight He brings. It will never be a decision full of regret, but a choice of wisdom and a source of future joy!

Spirit, when I've gone astray, give me a sincere
heart for repentance and change. Amen.

morning
A JOY IN FAITHFULNESS

A faithful person will be richly blessed.
PROVERBS 28:20 NIV

When loyal and dependable people show up on the scene, they are a breath of fresh air. There is a joy and peace to faithfulness—even a winsomeness. You listen to what those people have to say. When they give you their word, it means something. Those kinds of people are the faithful ones, the ones you want on your side.

God says those faithful people will be blessed. Of course, blessings from God may not mean wealth, but any gift from God is never a disappointment. It will be something you can look forward to with great anticipation.

How can you learn to be faithful in word and deed? Hold fast to the scriptures. Stay near the Lord. And ask for the supernatural ability to be that person of integrity.

Lord, let all the days of my life find me faithful in ways that please You! Amen.

evening
DEEP WATER

But Jonah ran away from the LORD and headed for Tarshish.
JONAH 1:3 NIV

When God told Jonah to preach to the people of Nineveh, he refused. Then Jonah decided that fleeing the scene would fix the problem. But it only got Jonah in deep water.

But there's good news. As He did for Jonah, God will take you back, restore you, place you just where you need to be. And that will bring you not to a place of fear but to a place of freedom and joy.

Lord, help me to know the best place to run is into Your loving arms. Amen.

JOY TO YOUR *morning* SOUL!

The LORD is good, a refuge in times of trouble.
He cares for those who trust in him.
NAHUM 1:7 NIV

How can you live to please the Almighty when all the fallen earth seems once again determined to disobey God's laws? Pray with a humble heart. Listen to the Lord and His still, small voice. Read His Word. Stay in fellowship with Christians who believe the Bible is truly the holy Word of God, not just a book of general guidelines. Come before God with a willingness to say, "I've wronged You, Lord. I'm sorry." And mean it.

The good news is that when you do repent, the Lord is gracious to forgive and put you back in intimate fellowship with Him. Repentance isn't a burden. It will lighten your load and bring joy to your soul!

Jesus, give me a meek heart. Show me my sins, then give me the courage
to confess them and receive the peace of Your forgiveness. Amen.

WHEN ALL THE WORLD *evening* FALLS APART

The Sovereign LORD is my strength; he makes my feet like the
feet of a deer, he enables me to tread on the heights.
HABAKKUK 3:19 NIV

Thank God there is hope amid your many trials. In Habakkuk, you can see that even though the hour of trouble may come, the Lord is your strength. He will not only lift you up but give you a lightness of spirit. Just like the deer. If you have ever watched a deer leap through the woods, you know that amazing nimbleness, that graceful soaring in action.

And that strength and lightness is what God offers you. Rest in that knowledge. Call on the Lord, knowing His promise is meant not only for the whole world but for you.

Holy Spirit, dwell in me fully, so when trouble comes,
I might know Your strength. Amen.

morning
BEAUTY IN TRUTH

"Every word of God is flawless."
PROVERBS 30:5 NIV

The book of Isaiah says, "The grass withers and the flowers fall, but the word of our God endures forever" (40:8 NIV). Even though God's creation is glorious, there is even more beauty in His Word, the flawless truth of God's living Word—the Bible. It has power to guide you. To comfort you. To challenge, illuminate, and convict you. To tell you of the mercy and grace of Christ, who has the power to set you free for all time.

It's the greatest book ever written, and yet the Word of God goes far beyond mere literature. It's supernatural, living, and ever whispering His truths.

*Holy Spirit, please illuminate my path with the beauty of Your truth,
and give me the courage to live it out in my daily life. Amen.*

evening
A CUP OF COMPASSION

"This is what the LORD Almighty said: 'Administer true justice; show mercy and compassion to one another. Do not oppress the widow or the fatherless, the foreigner or the poor. Do not plot evil against each other.' "
ZECHARIAH 7:8–10 NIV

The Bible offers excellent principles on how we are to live and act in this world, such as these verses in Zechariah, in which compassion seems to be the overall theme. Do you offer compassion instead of criticism? Concern instead of uninvited counsel? A listening ear rather than complaint?

Zechariah goes on to say, "But they refused to pay attention; stubbornly they turned their backs and covered their ears" (7:11 NIV). These people obviously didn't want to have a heart of compassion, and their defiant and merciless attitude was very displeasing to God.

But the good news is, you can be just the opposite. You can choose kindness and know the joy of being a blessing to others.

Lord, help me offer a cup of compassion to all those in need of it. Amen.

LAUGH AT THE *morning* DAYS TO COME

She is clothed with strength and dignity; she can laugh at the days to come.
PROVERBS 31:25 NIV

If you trust in God, He will indeed work all things for your good (Romans 8:28). You can count on it. As a Christian, you *should* count on it! That kind of trust—which is so very counter to what the world preaches—releases you from a life without hope. And it gives you the freedom to know joy even amid earthly sorrows.

Lord, please lift my head from the mire of my worries to a greater faith in You. Let me be clothed in strength and dignity, and let me so trust in You that I can laugh at the future. Amen.

THE WORST *evening* KIND OF THIEF

Be sober-minded; be watchful. Your adversary the devil prowls around like a roaring lion, seeking someone to devour.
1 PETER 5:8 ESV

The devil is the worst kind of thief, deceiver, and destroyer. He will try very hard to come in and take away all that you treasure—joy, peace, love—and leave you in a wake of confusion and anger and fear. So may we always be sober-minded. May we be watchful. Call on the Lord any time of the day or night. Rely on His perfect hand of justice, His tender mercies, and His mighty power to restore!

Lord, thank You that I can call on You day or night whenever I feel the enemy is trying to deceive me or destroy me. Amen.

morning
DELIGHT YOURSELF IN THE LORD!

*Trust in the Lord, and do good; dwell in the land and befriend faithfulness.
Delight yourself in the Lord, and he will give you the desires of your
heart. Commit your way to the Lord; trust in him, and he will act.*

PSALM 37:3–5 ESV

Name a few things that bring you delight. Is it the whiskery twitch of a bunny's nose? Is it the pure, crisp mist on an alpine slope? Perhaps the happy toast to the bride and groom? Or you might also find delight in the forgiveness between friends. All good and lovely things for you and the Lord to enjoy together.

When you stay heart-close to the Lord, you wouldn't want to do anything to mar that friendship. So you will delight in the same things. You will delight in each other. That's the way it goes with good friends.

*O Lord, I thank You that You are my dearest
and closest friend. Be ever near me. Amen.*

evening
FEELING WILD AND WEARY?

*And rising very early in the morning, while it was still dark, he
departed and went out to a desolate place, and there he prayed.*

MARK 1:35 ESV

You've gotten yourself so wearied and wild-eyed with life that you can't fall asleep at night. You can't concentrate. Right now, you can't even imagine a restful and focused life, let alone a life filled with joy.

You could always ask yourself, "Have I spent any time with God in prayer? Do I relax in the Lord's company, His sweet fellowship, His gentle corrections and challenges? His guidance and wisdom and refreshment?" As scripture reminds us, even Christ showed us how essential prayer was while He was on this earth.

There is indeed a cure for all who feel wild and weary. God is waiting.

*Lord, please help me never to see our time together as "just another thing on
my to-do list," but as precious fellowship with my dearest friend. Amen.*

A PROMISE FOR ALL SEASONS

morning

"For I know the plans I have for you, declares the LORD, plans for welfare and not for evil, to give you a future and a hope."

JEREMIAH 29:11 ESV

The older we get, the more we realize that life can have an ebb and flow like the sea. Of losses and gains, of joys and sorrows. Of laughter and tears. Of wellness and illness. Of hellos and goodbyes. These passages have parallels to the changes we witness every year in nature. There are days of summery pleasures and busy tasks. We see autumn moments of calm reflection and satisfying contentment. We come to know the bleak winter episodes of trials, grief, fear, and loneliness, as well as the many occasions of springtime growth and vitality when our spirits rise with renewed hope. No matter where we are in life, we can find joy in knowing that the Bible is full of promises from God.

Dearest Lord, thank You for supplying all my needs through the ebb and flow of life. Amen.

THE HEAVENLY SCENT OF FORGIVENESS

evening

Bearing with one another and, if one has a complaint against another, forgiving each other; as the Lord has forgiven you, so you also must forgive.

COLOSSIANS 3:13 ESV

Because of the work of Christ on the cross, we can know the clean and fragrant scent of forgiveness. No other method of heart cleansing—that the world endorses—can ever compare. To forgive in the name of Christ and to be forgiven by our Lord satisfies in ways far beyond the senses, since it is a true cleansing of the spirit.

Yes, yes, that is what we need. So, is there someone you need to forgive today? When you do, bask in that washed-clean feeling, and let it drench you in joy!

Precious Lord Jesus, who do I need to forgive? Thank You for all the times You've so generously forgiven me! Amen.

WE ARE THAT *morning* SWEET PERFUME!

*But thanks be to God, who in Christ always leads us in triumphal procession,
and through us spreads the fragrance of the knowledge of him everywhere.
For we are the aroma of Christ to God among those who are being saved and
among those who are perishing, to one a fragrance from death to death, to
the other a fragrance from life to life. Who is sufficient for these things?*

2 CORINTHIANS 2:14–16 ESV

As Christians, we are to be the winsome and beautiful and irresistible fragrance of
Christ—and no matter how busy people are, hopefully they will want to pause as we
share His love, His truth, and His life.

*Mighty God, everywhere I go, may I be part of the triumphal
procession that spreads the fragrance of the knowledge
of Your Son. In Jesus' name I pray, amen.*

DO YOU HAVE A *evening* NICKNAME?

*James son of Zebedee and his brother John (to them he gave
the name Boanerges, which means "sons of thunder").*

MARK 3:17 NIV

If the Lord gave *you* a nickname, what might it be? If you could distill the essence of
your character into several key words—or if your friends did that task for you—what
might that list look like? Does your daily walk reflect the hope and light and love and joy
of Christ? If Jesus were indeed to give you a nickname, what would you *want* it to be?

*Lord, I want to please You in every way. Help me to be a woman
of godly substance. I want to make You proud! Amen.*

morning
A GATHERING OF GOODIES

*The world of the generous gets larger and larger; the world of
the stingy gets smaller and smaller. The one who blesses others
is abundantly blessed; those who help others are helped.*

PROVERBS 11:24–25 MSG

There are any number of ways to be generous with what God has so graciously given us. And we will find that this sharing will make our world larger and larger. Granted, the blessings that come back to us might not always be material possessions. It might just be good old-fashioned joy. But who couldn't use more of that commodity?

*Lord, transform me into a bighearted soul who
loves sharing as much as gathering. Amen.*

evening
WHAT ARE YOUR JOY MAKERS?

*Come, let's shout praises to GOD, raise the roof for the Rock who saved us! Let's
march into his presence singing praises, lifting the rafters with our hymns!*

PSALM 95:1–2 MSG

When it comes to your devotions, isn't it pure joy to have an especially wondrous time with the Lord in the quietude of a solitary place? How about adding music to the glory of those moments as it suggests in the Psalms? Even if your voice is more of a croak than a croon, you can still make a joyful noise unto the Lord. He is worthy of that praise, and He will delight in your heart songs. Soon you will want to add those melodious tributes to your list of joy makers!

*Lord Jesus, I want to come into Your presence daily, worshipping
You in every way, even with shouts of joy and songs of
praise. May my praise bring us both delight! Amen.*

BAD CASE OF THE *morning* WHAT-IFS

Trust in the LORD with all your heart, and do not lean on your own understanding.
In all your ways acknowledge him, and he will make straight your paths.
PROVERBS 3:5–6 ESV

Thank God we can turn to Him when we fear the future. When bad times come, and they don't seem to want to go away, we are not to trust in our own frail understanding of the way life works. But if we trust God completely, He will make our paths straight. The Lord may not take away every trial, but He promises to be with us through every spiritual battle, every hardship. With God involved in our lives, it's not just a way to make do. It's a way to have nights of good sleep and days of real joy.

Lord, please show me how to trust You with every detail of my life. Amen.

WHEN YOU BUTT *evening* HEADS

Be humble and gentle. Be patient with each other, making
allowance for each other's faults because of your love.
EPHESIANS 4:2 TLB

As Christians, how does God want us to deal with headstrong people? The same way He expects us to live and work and play with everyone. We will need humbleness and gentleness and patience.

Sound hopeless? It is. Utterly.

But nothing is impossible with God. Only His transformative power can change the temperament of a bighorn sheep into a gentle lamb. And then you will find that joy, sweet joy, will come more easily.

Lord, I have a really hard time with _____. Please show me how to
love her as You would. And help me not to be so stubborn too! Amen.

morning
IF ONLY

*Not that I am speaking of being in need, for I have
learned in whatever situation I am to be content.*
PHILIPPIANS 4:11 ESV

You want heaven. But this fallen earth isn't heaven. So while we wait for heaven, what can we do? Pray like we mean it. Be thankful for answered prayers and the blessings that do come. And never get so caught up in the "if onlys" that we waste our lives away waiting for a perfect life. May we learn to find joy in the present and, like Paul, learn to be content in all circumstances.

*Lord, I don't want to get so caught up wanting heaven on earth
now that I forget to find joy with You every day. Amen.*

evening
THE SPRINGS OF LIFE

Keep your heart with all vigilance, for from it flow the springs of life.
PROVERBS 4:23 ESV

Today we have thousands of friends who aren't really friends and online communities that don't really offer the help and healing and personal touch of real community. We're super connected, but we're not thriving as we should.

The Bible reminds us to keep watch over our hearts. There is good reason for that. The springs of life flow from our hearts. If we allow our spirits to become a dumping ground, the springs will get contaminated. They will become poisoned and unusable.

What to do? Unplug for a while. Spend more time with God and real friends. It will be a way to find our joy again.

Lord, show me when to unplug from this modern life. Amen.

morning
REALLY TRULY FORGIVEN?

*The LORD is merciful and gracious, slow to anger and abounding in
steadfast love. He will not always chide, nor will he keep his anger forever.
He does not deal with us according to our sins, nor repay us according
to our iniquities. For as high as the heavens are above the earth, so
great is his steadfast love toward those who fear him; as far as the east
is from the west, so far does he remove our transgressions from us.*
PSALM 103:8–12 ESV

You might think, *Sometimes I don't really feel forgiven.* But faith is not so much a feeling as a commitment to God and His promises of grace. Your sins are not so unique that God decided to bypass you when He offered salvation. If you repent and ask for forgiveness, then you have indeed been forgiven. It is that simple. It is that joyful!

Embrace the truth. Live the grace. Share the news!

*Lord Jesus, thank You for washing my sins away.
I choose to believe in Your promises! Amen.*

evening
THE WEDDING AT CANA

*When the master of the feast tasted the water now become wine, and did not
know where it came from (though the servants who had drawn the water knew),
the master of the feast called the bridegroom and said to him, "Everyone serves
the good wine first, and when people have drunk freely, then the poor wine. But
you have kept the good wine until now." This, the first of his signs, Jesus did at
Cana in Galilee, and manifested his glory. And his disciples believed in him.*
JOHN 2:9–11 ESV

Jesus prepared the best for this couple in Cana, and He helped to make it a special and memorable wedding for everyone invited. Yes, Jesus is about redemption and eternal life, but He is also about providing what is best for us, including joy!

*Lord, I thank You that You offer mankind the best of
everything, including the gift of joy. Amen.*

WITH GENTLENESS *morning* COMES JOY

*To slander no one, to be peaceable and considerate,
and always to be gentle toward everyone.*
TITUS 3:2 NIV

In Galatians 5:22–23 (NIV), we are reminded, "But the fruit of the Spirit is love, joy, peace, forbearance, kindness, goodness, faithfulness, gentleness and self-control. Against such things there is no law."

Somewhere deep down we all long for more of the gentle things in life. With gentleness come the springs of joy.

*God, I pray that You will give me tenderness of heart. That I will
never slander anyone, and that I will be peaceful and considerate
and gentle in all my ways. In Jesus' name I pray, amen.*

evening YOU LACK NOTHING

*Consider it a sheer gift, friends, when tests and challenges come at you from all
sides. You know that under pressure, your faith-life is forced into the open and
shows its true colors. So don't try to get out of anything prematurely. Let it do
its work so you become mature and well-developed, not deficient in any way.*
JAMES 1:2–4 MSG

Jesus tells us that there will be trials. It is a fallen earth, not heaven. When troubles do come, you don't have to throw a party, but see what the Lord might do to use this hard situation in your life. He knows the long-term plan, while we only see tiny pieces of a puzzle. He knows how beautiful the outcome can be. He is hoping that you will grow into a woman who is so full of faith and goodness and love and joy, that you lack nothing.

*Lord, I admit I rarely see hardships as a gift. Show me how to see this life from
Your vantage point. I want You to use my trials for spiritual growth. Amen.*

morning
THE BEST PLACE TO BE

*You make known to me the path of life; in your presence there is
fullness of joy; at your right hand are pleasures forevermore.*
PSALM 16:11 ESV

But the Lord wants more from us than just to show up in a room waiting for our allotment of joy. He wants us to have a longing to truly spend time with Him, not out of obligation or with a mindset to manipulate some gift out of Him, but because we truly have a need to be with Christ because we love Him dearly.

With that attitude in mind, come rest in the Lord. In His sweet and satisfying presence, you will find fullness of joy and pleasures forevermore. It's the best place to be!

Lord, I am excited to be with You today. Amen.

evening
FOOLING OURSELVES

*But prove yourselves doers of the word [actively and continually obeying God's
precepts], and not merely listeners [who hear the word but fail to internalize its
meaning], deluding yourselves [by unsound reasoning contrary to the truth].*
JAMES 1:22 AMP

Living outside of the Lord's guidelines is a real joy killer. Wild living won't be a friend to us in the end. What might feel like pleasure for a time will morph into pain. Why would we really want to do anything that could destroy us in body and soul? It's hard to expect showers of blessings from the Lord when we are rebelliously bathing in sin.

So step boldly out into the light of God's Word. Live the truth. Taste the freedom. God will only ask us to do what will ultimately bring us what we really want—love and peace and real joy!

*Lord, forgive me. Give me the courage to do what
is right and good in Your sight. Amen.*

WHEN JOY FEELS FAR AWAY
morning

*You turned my wailing into dancing; you removed my sackcloth
and clothed me with joy, that my heart may sing your praises
and not be silent. LORD my God, I will praise you forever.*
PSALM 30:11–12 NIV

It really is okay to weep. Whether you're grieving the loss of someone dear or you're wounded deeply over a different kind of tragedy, give yourself some time to grieve, to pray, to recover. Be gentle with yourself. Rest. And then remember God's promises that He will turn your lamenting into laughter. That He will clothe you once again in joy.

*Dearest Lord Jesus, I am grieving. I see now that I cannot
recover from my loss without Your supernatural help. May Your
Comforter, the Holy Spirit, bring me relief for my aching soul.
And may I someday wake up to Your joy again. Amen.*

CUSTOM BUILT
evening

*Oh yes, you shaped me first inside, then out; you formed me in my mother's
womb. I thank you, High God—you're breathtaking!. . . I am marvelously made!
I worship in adoration—what a creation! You know me inside and out, you know
every bone in my body; you know exactly how I was made. . .how I was sculpted
from nothing into something. Like an open book, you watched me grow from
conception to birth. . .the days of my life all prepared before I'd even lived one day.*
PSALM 139:13–16 MSG

Sometimes we humans get into the mindset that we are cookie-cutter common. Well, don't you believe it! That isn't what the Bible says. You are marvelously custom-created and hand-sewn by God Himself. Not mass-produced or churned out. You, my friend, are human haute couture!

I thank You, Lord, that I am fearfully and marvelously made by You! Amen.

THE WAY WE LOVE GOD
morning

*"Teacher, which is the greatest commandment in the Law?"
Jesus replied: "'Love the Lord your God with all your heart
and with all your soul and with all your mind.'"*
MATTHEW 22:36–37 NIV

Over the years, have we discovered that we simply can't live without God's company day or night? In good times or bad? That the Lord's mercy and grace, His divine guidance and perfect love, can't come from any other source?

If you find yourself saying yes to the above, then you are not being vulnerable or weak or needy. You are being wise, for loving God with all your heart, soul, and mind is the way to grow into a woman of joy!

*Lord Jesus, I love You dearly. I thank You for who You are and
all You've done for me. May we stay forever close. Amen.*

WHEN YOU'RE ANGRY
evening

"In your anger do not sin": Do not let the sun go down while you are still angry.
EPHESIANS 4:26 NIV

God is the only One who knows what to do when our emotions run out of control. Give Christ the misunderstandings. The old baggage. The new baggage. The verbal attacks and reckless words that linger with their wounds. All of it. Place it there at His feet. And then walk away.

When you leave it there, don't revisit it. Don't drag it back. Move forward with life.

Yes, anger is easy. Forgiveness is hard. But Christ can make our burdens light. Let Him help. He's the only One who can.

*Too many times, Lord, I've gone to bed angry at someone.
Help me to reject the anger and embrace Your joy. Amen.*

morning
SOMETHING'S GOING ON

*For our struggle is not against flesh and blood, but against the rulers,
against the authorities, against the powers of this dark world and
against the spiritual forces of evil in the heavenly realms.*
EPHESIANS 6:12 NIV

If you sometimes feel like a skeptic, ask God to open your spiritual eyes even more—to be able to sense more clearly the supernatural realm. The Lord may surprise you.

Yes, the unseen world. It's there. It's real. And it's one more reason to follow Christ closely, because otherwise we are left to battle this dark world on our own. And that's not a war we can win without Christ.

*Lord, be ever near me as I struggle against the rulers, against the
authorities, against the powers of this dark world, and against
the spiritual forces of evil in the heavenly realms. Amen.*

evening
THE JOY OF BEING RESCUED

*"Suppose one of you has a hundred sheep and loses one of them. Doesn't he leave
the ninety-nine in the open country and go after the lost sheep until he finds it?"*
LUKE 15:4 NIV

Want joy? There is no greater joy than when Jesus comes to rescue you. That glorious moment of a divine embrace. So acknowledge the need. Reach out to the Lord. He's calling your name, and He wants to bring you home, to love you for all time.

Dearest Lord Jesus, thank You for the joy of being rescued! Amen.

morning
THE PERFECT GIFT

*For it is by grace you have been saved, through faith—and this is not from
yourselves, it is the gift of God—not by works, so that no one can boast.*
EPHESIANS 2:8–9 NIV

We will naturally want to offer God some lovely gifts of service simply out of gratitude for His grace, but nothing we do will get us into heaven. Nothing. What a relief! What a magnificent and completely sufficient work of grace. We can rest in that. Praise our Lord Jesus, who has done it all for us. Out of mercy. Out of love. For me. For you. . .

*Thank You, Lord, for Your sacrifice on the cross.
It means everything to me! Amen.*

evening
REASONS FOR OUR JOY!

*"In my Father's house there are many dwelling places. If it were not
so, would I have told you that I go to prepare a place for you?"*
JOHN 14:2 NRSV

When we share our faith, we don't need to lecture, but we should explain the reasons for our joy. After all, we don't represent a religion riddled and burdened with endless works and impossible strivings, but we represent the powerful promise of life eternal in Christ.

Hold fast to the truth. Let our faces reflect that hope. And may we show the world what joy really looks like!

*Dear Jesus, too many times I get so wrapped up in the world's way of seeing
life and death, I forget that there is much more beyond the confines of this
broken earth. I praise You and thank You for the hope of heaven! Amen.*

morning
EMBRACE THE QUIET

She had a sister called Mary, who sat at the Lord's feet listening to what he said. But Martha was distracted by all the preparations that had to be made. She came to him and asked, "Lord, don't you care that my sister has left me to do the work by myself? Tell her to help me!" "Martha, Martha," the Lord answered, "you are worried and upset about many things, but few things are needed—or indeed only one. Mary has chosen what is better, and it will not be taken away from her."

LUKE 10:39–42 NIV

In quiet times, you might discover the Lord's guidance, tender rebukes, and sweet encouragements. You might commune so closely that you feel His presence in the room with you. Don't run from the quiet. Embrace it. And be aware that you might be changed by the risen Savior!

Lord, may I wait in Your presence with anticipation and joy! Amen.

evening
A FORCE OF NATURE

And do not be conformed to this world [any longer with its superficial values and customs], but be transformed and progressively changed [as you mature spiritually] by the renewing of your mind [focusing on godly values and ethical attitudes], so that you may prove [for yourselves] what the will of God is, that which is good and acceptable and perfect [in His plan and purpose for you].

ROMANS 12:2 AMP

If you want to be transformed in Christ and not conformed to the world, don't forget to fellowship with the body of believers and spend time in God's Word. The Lord wants to show you what is good and acceptable and perfect!

Lord, help me to be a spiritually mature woman of God. Amen.

morning THAT BEAUTIFUL BRIDGE

That God is on one side and all the people on the other side, and Christ Jesus, himself man, is between them to bring them together.

1 TIMOTHY 2:5 TLB

Christ is our dear friend who built us a bridge to God, to heaven. He made that bridge because He loves us, and He built that bridge with His very life. We can never repay the Lord for what He did on the cross, but we can thank Him by inviting Him in for fellowship. He will be there!

Dearest Lord Jesus, thank You for being the bridge that paved my way to heaven. Amen.

evening THE FATHER OF LIGHTS

Every good thing given and every perfect gift is from above; it comes down from the Father of lights [the Creator and Sustainer of the heavens], in whom there is no variation [no rising or setting] or shadow cast by His turning [for He is perfect and never changes].

JAMES 1:17 AMP

No matter what, God still loves us and pursues us. Romans 5:8 (NIV) reminds us, "But God demonstrates his own love for us in this: While we were still sinners, Christ died for us." Yes, even while we were in our mess, mercy arrived. We don't deserve it, but God—the Father of lights and the greatest gift giver of all time—offered grace to us anyway. But as with any gift, we will need to reach out and accept it.

Thank You, God, for all the many serendipities in this life, and for the greatest gift of all—Your Son, Jesus Christ. Amen.

PASSION, NOT OBLIGATION
morning

*He answered, "'Love the Lord your God with all your heart
and with all your soul and with all your strength and with all
your mind'; and, 'Love your neighbor as yourself.'"*

LUKE 10:27 NIV

When we drag ourselves to church and sit in the back with no song in our hearts, when we hurry up with our five minutes of obligatory Bible reading, and when we serve the needy begrudgingly, it feels as though we're missing something huge. Because we are. God doesn't want us to love, worship, or serve Him out of obligation. A love that comes from coercion is no love at all. May we long for and pray for the kind of lavish love that the Lord offers to us freely. Then we can watch as our obligation turns into passion and joy.

*Lord, I don't want to just go through the motions,
but I want to love You with my whole heart. Amen.*

WHEN TO SAY NO
evening

*The apostles returned to Jesus and told him all that they had done and taught.
And he said to them, "Come away by yourselves to a desolate place and rest
a while." For many were coming and going, and they had no leisure even to
eat. And they went away in the boat to a desolate place by themselves.*

MARK 6:30–32 ESV

There are many good causes out there, but you don't have to volunteer to do all of them. You might say, "But I can't stand to disappoint people." That's a lovely sentiment, but you still have the right to say no. The enemy would like nothing better than for you to be so exhausted that you lose your zeal, your health, and your joy. Even Jesus and His disciples had to get away from the crowds so they could eat and rest. We need to do the same!

Holy Spirit, show me when to say yes and when to say no. Amen.

morning
THE GIFT OF JOY

"Don't bargain with God. Be direct. Ask for what you need. This isn't a cat-and-mouse, hide-and-seek game we're in. If your child asks for bread, do you trick him with sawdust? If he asks for fish, do you scare him with a live snake on his plate? As bad as you are, you wouldn't think of such a thing. You're at least decent to your own children. So don't you think the God who conceived you in love will be even better?"

MATTHEW 7:7–11 MSG

God wants us to know happiness, and He does offer us many good gifts throughout our lives. But we could ask ourselves a few questions along the way. For instance, "Do the desires of my heart line up with what is right and good and the will of God?" Or, "Do I expect joyful showers of blessings while I'm busy running away from God in disobedience?" Something to think about as we go before God with our requests.

Lord, thank You for Your many good gifts. Amen.

evening
THE BOOK OF JOY

Get up, my dear friend, fair and beautiful lover—come to me! Look around you: Winter is over; the winter rains are over, gone! Spring flowers are in blossom all over. The whole world's a choir—and singing! Spring warblers are filling the forest with sweet strains. Lilacs are exuberantly purple and perfumed, and cherry trees fragrant with blossoms. Oh, get up, dear friend, my fair and beautiful lover—come to me! Come, my shy and modest dove— leave your seclusion, come out in the open. Let me see your face, let me hear your voice. For your voice is soothing and your face is ravishing.

SONG OF SOLOMON 2:10–14 MSG

If you haven't read the Song of Solomon lately, you might want to once again experience this book filled with joy. It'll make your soul rise up like blossoms in springtime.

Creator God, thank You for providing such endearing writings on romance. I love reading Your holy Word. It makes my heart sing! In Jesus' name I pray, amen.

morning
A DIVINE FORGETFULNESS

Anyone who claims to be in the light but hates a brother or sister is still in the darkness. Anyone who loves their brother and sister lives in the light, and there is nothing in them to make them stumble. But anyone who hates a brother or sister is in the darkness and walks around in the darkness. They do not know where they are going, because the darkness has blinded them.

1 JOHN 2:9–11 NIV

It is hard to pray for someone while harboring ill feelings. But we can move on in love, even if it only starts with a trickle. After all, since Christ offers us what we could tenderly call a "divine forgetfulness" when it comes to *our* transgressions, it is right and good that we offer the same thing to others.

Lord, when it comes to the offenses against me, may I grow to have more of Your "divine forgetfulness." Amen.

evening
THE LIGHT OF LIFE

Again Jesus spoke to them, saying, "I am the light of the world. Whoever follows me will not walk in darkness, but will have the light of life."

JOHN 8:12 ESV

Christ lights us up and changes us, if we allow Him to. Jesus said, "I am the light of the world. Whoever follows me will not walk in darkness, but will have the light of life."

In a way, we are like living art, and our lives will never have true beauty and joy without the light of Christ. May we pray for the light—*His* light!

Thank You, Lord, for filling my life with Your light. Amen.

morning
KEEP FLOWING

*"After removing Saul, he made David their king. God testified
concerning him: 'I have found David son of Jesse, a man after
my own heart; he will do everything I want him to do.'"*

ACTS 13:22 NIV

Even though Christ is indeed perfecting us and making us more into His likeness day by day, Christians will not be perfect on this side of eternity. Even King David was far from perfect. But it didn't stop him from dancing before God. It didn't stop him from offering himself up time and time again to the service of God. It didn't stop him from becoming one of the greatest biblical heroes of all time.

Flawed vessels might have a few blemishes, but with God's help, a weak vessel can still flow with life-giving water.

*Lord, as You make me more and more into Your likeness,
help me to keep working for Your kingdom. Amen.*

evening
TAKE A JOY BREAK

*You make known to me the path of life; in your presence there is
fullness of joy; at your right hand are pleasures forevermore.*

PSALM 16:11 ESV

God wants us to enjoy this life. So take time to pause over the fullness of joy found in His presence as well as the many pleasures He provides.

Take in the breathless wonder of diamond stars strewn across a black velvet sky.

Check out the world's tiniest bird online—the bee hummingbird in all its bejeweled glory.

Feel the cooling mist off the thundering crash of ocean waves.

Come to know the sweet forgiveness between friends.

You can make your own joy list. And don't forget to take one daily or as often as needed!

*Lord, thank You for Your radiant presence, Your miracles,
and Your many creative wonders. I am in awe of You! Amen.*

morning
A CLOSE ENCOUNTER

*"If you abide in me, and my words abide in you, ask whatever you wish, and
it will be done for you. By this my Father is glorified, that you bear much fruit
and so prove to be my disciples. As the Father has loved me, so have I loved you.
Abide in my love. If you keep my commandments, you will abide in my love, just
as I have kept my Father's commandments and abide in his love. These things I
have spoken to you, that my joy may be in you, and that your joy may be full."*

JOHN 15:7–11 ESV

We need to have a close encounter with God. We need the saving grace of Christ Jesus.
In the book of John, we see such a beautiful explanation of the closeness we are longing
for. May we not only tuck these verses in our hearts, but live them daily. For abiding
in the Lord's love is knowing real joy.

Lord, our world needs a close encounter with You. Amen.

evening
WHERE I AM HEADED

Yet what we suffer now is nothing compared to the glory he will give us later.

ROMANS 8:18 TLB

As Christians, there is joy in knowing where we are headed at the appointed time by
God. To heaven. To glory. By the Lord's side forever, unfettered and no longer broken.
This life is only a mere flash compared to the boundless time of eternity.

In moments of great trial, think on these things.

*Father God, I am at the point of breaking from all my pain. Please come
to me now and help me. Please send Your Comforter, and may I never
forget the joyful place I am headed one day. In Jesus' name I pray, amen.*

morning
HOW ARE WE TO LIVE?

Pride goes before destruction, a haughty spirit before a fall.
PROVERBS 16:18 NIV

How are we to live? We need to know who we are in Christ. Precious but fallen. Saved but we are not the Savior. We have talents and gifts, yes, but they are to be used for God's glory and our shared pleasure with Him, not a private struggle toward fame.

In the confines of biblical living, we will find true freedom. And in that freedom will reside true joy.

Lord Jesus, may I run from pride and live just as You created me to live. Amen.

evening
HIS DWELLING PLACE

Now it happened that when the priests had come out of the Holy Place, the cloud filled the LORD's house, so the priests could not stand [in their positions] to minister because of the cloud, for the glory and brilliance of the LORD had filled the LORD's house (temple). Then Solomon said, "The LORD has said that He would dwell in the thick darkness [of the cloud]. I have certainly built You a lofty house, a place for You to dwell in forever."
1 KINGS 8:10–13 AMP

Solomon made a dwelling place for God, and it was truly beautiful. Now Christ has come, and He left us with His Holy Spirit. As Christians, we are a dwelling place for God—we house His presence in our innermost being.

May the world see that radiant glow of the Lord's presence in us every day!

Lord, may I be a beautiful dwelling place for Your Holy Spirit. Amen.

THE SIMPLE THINGS
morning

The LORD will indeed give what is good, and our land will yield its harvest.
PSALM 85:12 NIV

Sometimes while we're waiting on life's big majestic joys to come along, we miss the little beauties that pop up here and there. But the smallish things can also soften a hard day and gladden many a heavy heart.

Yes, the Lord will indeed give us what is good and lovely. May we always be thankful for our many blessings. We could even write them down in a little journal, and then from time to time, we could let the remembrance of them bring us great joy.

Father God, I love all the little beauties that You sprinkle throughout my day. May I not miss a single one. In Jesus' name I pray, amen.

THIS BEAUTIFUL BLUE PLANET
evening

And God blessed them [granting them certain authority] and said to them, "Be fruitful, multiply, and fill the earth, and subjugate it [putting it under your power]; and rule over (dominate) the fish of the sea, the birds of the air, and every living thing that moves upon the earth."
GENESIS 1:28 AMP

God's calling to us to be guardians of this beautiful planet is real and far from frivolous. However, the Lord has never called us to worship creation as some are doing—which is idolatry. We are instead called to be caretakers of God's beautiful earth. What a huge responsibility, but oh, such a great honor.

O Lord, show us how to watch over Your world with care. Amen.

morning
DISENCHANTMENT

*GOD, my shepherd! I don't need a thing. You have bedded me down in
lush meadows, you find me quiet pools to drink from. True to your word,
you let me catch my breath and send me in the right direction.*

PSALM 23:1–3 MSG

Take the time to breathe the fresh air and to watch the butterflies dancing through the field. Listen to the breeze as it passes through the wildflowers. Yes, enjoy God's creation. He will walk with you and talk to you. Let Him take your disenchantment and turn it into delight—for abiding in His company is everything we need for a life of joy.

*Lord Jesus, lead me beside quiet pools of water and
lush grasses. I am ready to be restored! Amen.*

evening
HE'LL QUIET YOU WITH HIS LOVE

*"The LORD your God is in your midst, a mighty one who will
save; he will rejoice over you with gladness; he will quiet you
by his love; he will exult over you with loud singing."*

ZEPHANIAH 3:17 ESV

When we are distressed or weary in this life, may we look to the Lord. He will come near and quiet us with His love. He will rejoice over us with gladness. He will exalt over us with loud singing. Imagine. The Creator of the universe. Love like that—for me, for you!

*I praise You, Almighty God, for Your love hems me in, and it restores
my soul. I love You with all my heart! In Jesus' name I pray, amen.*

morning
CHASING THE WIND

*I, the Preacher, have been king over Israel in Jerusalem. And I set my
mind to seek and explore by [man's] wisdom all [human activity] that
has been done under heaven. It is a miserable business and a burdensome
task which God has given the sons of men with which to be busy and
distressed. I have seen all the works which have been done under the sun,
and behold, all is vanity, a futile grasping and chasing after the wind.*
ECCLESIASTES 1:12–14 AMP

If we make an honest assessment of our lives, how are we doing with our human
activity? Do we love God more than the things of the world, or are we busy chasing
after what we see the world chasing after?

May we discover all the wisdom that Ecclesiastes has to offer, and may we grow
up into godly women whose lives are filled with real meaning and real joy!

*Holy Spirit, enlighten me as I read this unique
book of the Bible—Ecclesiastes. Amen.*

evening
OUR PLACE IN GOD'S FAMILY

*"You're blessed when you can show people how to cooperate
instead of compete or fight. That's when you discover who
you really are, and your place in God's family."*
MATTHEW 5:9 MSG

Do we share what we have with others? Do we choose to make the world *less* competing
and combative and *more* peaceful and godly? Have we found our place in God's family?

*Father God, in a world filled with war and violence and
hate, please make me an ambassador of Your love and
peace and joy. In Jesus' holy name I pray, amen.*

morning
OUR MANY ACTS OF WORSHIP

Wearing a linen ephod, David was dancing before the LORD with all his might, while he and all Israel were bringing up the ark of the LORD with shouts and the sound of trumpets. As the ark of the LORD was entering the City of David, Michal daughter of Saul watched from a window. And when she saw King David leaping and dancing before the LORD, she despised him in her heart.
2 SAMUEL 6:14–16 NIV

What can you do to adore and praise God for who He is and all He's doing in your life? Perhaps during your morning Bible time, you could sing a new song before the Lord. Maybe you could befriend someone at work who's friendless. Or perhaps on cold winter days, you could hand out blankets to the needy. What will your worship look like today?

Dear God, I want to worship You in all the ways that will bring You honor and joy. For Your joy is my joy! In Jesus' name I pray, amen.

evening
TO HAVE PURPOSE IS TO HAVE JOY

Don't you remember the rule we had when we lived with you? "If you don't work, you don't eat." And now we're getting reports that a bunch of lazy good-for-nothings are taking advantage of you. This must not be tolerated. We command them to get to work immediately—no excuses, no arguments— and earn their own keep. Friends, don't slack off in doing your duty.
2 THESSALONIANS 3:10–13 MSG

The Lord says in His Word that we should not eat if we do not work. Good, honest work will help us rise in the morning with hope, and it will also give us a more satisfying slumber at night.

To have purpose is to have joy.

Lord, please show me what my purpose is, and until then, may I always be willing to work. Amen.

morning
HOLD ME FAST!

*Who stood up for me against the wicked? Who took my side against evil workers?
If GOD hadn't been there for me, I never would have made it. The minute I said,
"I'm slipping, I'm falling," your love, GOD, took hold and held me fast. When
I was upset and beside myself, you calmed me down and cheered me up.*

PSALM 94:16–19 MSG

Whether your slippery slope is on a real hillside or the peril comes from another source, cling to God. Tell Him that you are slipping and falling. The Lord promises to hold you fast. To calm you and to cheer you. When life's trail becomes treacherous, and the day turns into the darkest night, God is there.

Trust Him. He won't let you down.

Lord, please help me. I'm falling. Hold me fast! Amen.

evening
WONDROUS JOY

*There were shepherds camping in the neighborhood. They had set night
watches over their sheep. Suddenly, God's angel stood among them and
God's glory blazed around them. They were terrified. The angel said,
"Don't be afraid. I'm here to announce a great and joyful event that is
meant for everybody, worldwide: A Savior has just been born in David's
town, a Savior who is Messiah and Master. This is what you're to look for:
a baby wrapped in a blanket and lying in a manger." At once the angel was
joined by a huge angelic choir singing God's praises: Glory to God in the
heavenly heights, peace to all men and women on earth who please him.*

LUKE 2:8–14 MSG

May the joy of that holy night never be forgotten. May mankind never slip into ambivalence or skepticism or make Christmas into just another commercial holiday. May we ever remember the miracle of miracles that arrived on that not-so-silent night in Bethlehem.

*Lord, I am in awe of the way You came to walk among us,
to save us, and to make us Your forever friend. Amen.*

KNOW THEM BY HEART
morning

Remember what Christ taught, and let his words enrich your lives and make you wise; teach them to each other and sing them out in psalms and hymns and spiritual songs, singing to the Lord with thankful hearts.
COLOSSIANS 3:16 TLB

When the tempter comes to lead you astray or to harm you or steal your joy, respond with the truth of the scriptures. Let the words of the Bible enrich you and make you wise. Teach the scriptures to each other. Sing them out in psalms and hymns. Know them by heart.

Jesus did.

Father God, I admit I am not very good at memorizing things, let alone passages of scripture. Please give me not only the courage to live by Your truths, but the focus and discipline to commit them to memory. In Jesus' holy name I pray, amen.

WHAT A PROMISE!
evening

Give generously to them and do so without a grudging heart; then because of this the LORD your God will bless you in all your work and in everything you put your hand to.
DEUTERONOMY 15:10 NIV

The prayers we offer up for others, the forgiveness we extend, the donations we give of our time, talent, and money—all of it—don't merely change the benefactors of our many gifts. They change us too. Just as we help others, we too are forever altered. And beyond the growth we will encounter, the Lord also reminds us that if we give generously and without a grudging heart, He will bless us in our work. What a promise. What a joy!

Lord, show me how to give and how to do it with merry gusto! Amen.

morning
A JOYFUL WALK

*Most of the crowd spread their cloaks on the road, and others cut branches from
the trees and spread them on the road. And the crowds that went before him
and that followed him were shouting, "Hosanna to the Son of David! Blessed
is he who comes in the name of the Lord! Hosanna in the highest!" And when
he entered Jerusalem, the whole city was stirred up, saying, "Who is this?"*
MATTHEW 21:8–10 ESV

When Christ came to earth, mankind proved itself to be dangerously capricious. One day people were spreading their cloaks before Jesus and crying, "Hosanna in the highest!" and soon after, people were shouting, "Crucify Him!"

As Christians, may we pray for consistency in our faith. Even when the road is rough, we can experience a steady and joyful and peaceful walk with Christ.

*O Lord, I confess that as a Christian, I haven't always been consistent.
Please forgive me and help my ways to be Your ways. Amen.*

evening
A SENSE OF JOYOUS WONDER

*Blessed be the LORD, the God of Israel, who alone does wondrous
things. Blessed be his glorious name forever; may the whole
earth be filled with his glory! Amen and Amen!*
PSALM 72:18–19 ESV

As adults, we tend to lose our sense of wonder. But as we mature, may we never forget that God is about wonder too. He has not only made a creation exploding with all things marvelous; God continues to do wonder-filled things throughout the earth and in our lives.

*Creator God, I can barely contain my awe of You and Your mighty works.
Your creation is majestic and well ordered, yet unfathomable. I praise You and
thank You. Blessed be Your glorious name forever! In Jesus' name I pray, amen.*

morning
SUCH GOOD MEDICINE!

A joyful heart is good medicine, but a crushed spirit dries up the bones.
PROVERBS 17:22 ESV

The greatest source of joy is God Himself, of course, but our Lord offers His people a plethora of joys. The wonders of creation. Friendships. Daily fellowshipping with Him. Good and meaningful work. Culinary delights. Learning and exploring. Praising God with other believers in Christ. This list really could go on and on.

Because of sin in our fallen world, there are also plenty of not-so-good things around that will crush your spirit—such as stress from worry, friendships peppered with strife, too much social media and news, addictions of any kind, or rebellion against biblical principles.

We have a choice. A heart that gathers miseries or a heart that gathers merry.

Dear Jesus, show me how to have a merry heart.
I need less gloom and more gladness. Amen.

evening
WHEN I SEE YOU AGAIN

"When a woman gives birth, she has a hard time, there's no getting around it. But when the baby is born, there is joy in the birth. This new life. . .wipes out memory of the pain. The sadness you have right now is similar to that pain, but the coming joy is also similar. When I see you again, you'll be full of joy, and it will be a joy no one can rob from you."
JOHN 16:21–23 MSG

Jesus says to His beloved, "When I see you again, you'll be full of joy, and it will be a joy no one can rob from you." Those should be some of the most comforting words ever said.

On impossible days, when you are bone tired. When you wonder what God is up to. The Bible gives us hope that surpasses all hope. Jesus says to His followers, "When I see you again."

Lord God Almighty, thank You for Your many blessings,
including the gift of joy. In Jesus' name I pray, amen.

morning
THE HOPE OF SPRING

*For we know that the whole creation has been groaning together in the
pains of childbirth until now. And not only the creation, but we ourselves,
who have the firstfruits of the Spirit, groan inwardly as we wait eagerly for
adoption as sons, the redemption of our bodies. For in this hope we were
saved. Now hope that is seen is not hope. For who hopes for what he sees?
But if we hope for what we do not see, we wait for it with patience.*

ROMANS 8:22–25 ESV

As Christians, we have the promise of being adopted as God's children, the hope of
heaven, and the redemption of our bodies. Yes, we wait with patience for the beauty
of what is to come for those who love Christ!

Lord, I am filled up to the brim with hope as I await the joys of heaven. Amen.

evening
GET SOME REST

*Then, because so many people were coming and going that they
did not even have a chance to eat, he said to them, "Come with
me by yourselves to a quiet place and get some rest."*

MARK 6:31 NIV

Are we fighting what we need—rest? Working nonstop, even on Sunday? Fussing when
we should be drifting? If we let ourselves get too exhausted, life will not go well for
us. We won't be able to work, to play, to enjoy life. Even Jesus said, "Come with me by
yourselves to a quiet place and get some rest."

*Holy Spirit, I admit I'm a workaholic at times.
Please teach me how to rest. Amen.*

morning
OH, THE MANY JOYS!

Now there was leaning on Jesus' bosom one of His disciples, whom Jesus loved.
JOHN 13:23 NKJV

When we think of religion, we may conjure up words like *stodgy, passionless, archaic, empty rituals, works, rejection, critical, rules,* and *lifeless.* Oh dear. No wonder the world wants to run the other way!

But that's not what Jesus is about. When the Lord came to us, He brought words and phrases like *refreshment, beauty, lavish love, healing touches, divine intimacy, quiet waters, dramatic rescues, sacrifice, restoration, imperishability, grace, openheartedness, glorious declarations, supernatural wonders, brilliance, singing, miracles, vanquishing the enemy, freedom from evil, rebirth, an invitation to heaven, timelessness, happiness,* and *flourish*!

May we all embrace the sweet salvation and the many joys that Christ has to offer!

O Lord, I am in awe of who You really are! Amen.

evening
SATISFYING ALL AROUND

*Everyone enjoys giving good advice, and how wonderful
it is to be able to say the right thing at the right time!*
PROVERBS 15:23 TLB

In our Christian walk, good and godly advice can be a little like that extra light to help us on our way—to keep us from stumbling around in the dark. People enjoy giving away good advice too. Ahhh, yes, just the right words at the right time. Pleasant. Valuable. Satisfying all around.

May we pray to be the givers of wise advice as well as recipients of the same gift.

*Dear God, please lead me to people who have wisdom
when giving advice, and may I always have the right words
when I speak to others. In Jesus' name I pray, amen.*

MORE FRAGILE THAN GLASS
morning

But he said to me, "My grace is sufficient for you, for my power is made perfect in weakness." Therefore I will boast all the more gladly of my weaknesses, so that the power of Christ may rest upon me.

2 CORINTHIANS 12:9 ESV

We are beloved and fallen creations who need a daily dose of grace from the true Master of the universe. We must humble ourselves and welcome the paradox at every turn—that in our weakness, Christ's power is made perfect. He is sufficient!

Lord Jesus, I admit that I am weak
and that Your grace is all I need! Amen.

DO NOT BE AFRAID
evening

Elisha answered, "Do not be afraid, for those who are with us are more than those who are with them." Then Elisha prayed and said, "LORD, please, open his eyes that he may see." And the LORD opened the servants eyes and he saw; and behold, the mountain was full of horses and chariots of fire surrounding Elisha.

2 KINGS 6:16–17 AMP

When your life feels hopeless and the road ahead impassable, these verses in 2 Kings become vital to meditate on. As followers of Christ, there is power in our prayers. Know that if you could see beyond the veil into the spiritual realm, you would be able to see all the supernatural wonders that are carried out on your behalf!

O Lord, when I become afraid, help me to remember to pray and that
You are a God with supernatural power. You are in control! Amen.

morning
LOST IN THE MINUTIAE

*" 'Love the Lord your God with all your heart and with all your soul and
with all your mind and with all your strength.' The second is this: 'Love your
neighbor as yourself.' There is no commandment greater than these."*

 MARK 12:30–31 NIV

In our walk with Christ, how many times do we get so caught up in striving that we get swallowed up in the minutiae of life?

Perhaps we need to step back and acknowledge the essentials of our faith. Now is always a good time to make those adjustments. The verses provided from Mark 12 are an excellent example of getting back to the basics. Yes, we need the whole of the Bible to live by, and yet if we love our Lord with all our heart and we love our neighbors as ourselves, would we not discover a truly wonderful Christian life? One of truth and beauty and joy?

*Lord, help me not get lost in the minutiae but stay
focused on You all through the day. Amen.*

evening
OVER THE MOON

*Light in a messenger's eyes brings joy to the heart,
and good news gives health to the bones.*

PROVERBS 15:30 NIV

Messengers can bring many kinds of wonderful and welcome news. Such as your supervisor telling you that you got that promotion you'd hoped for. Or perhaps blood test results that show no signs of a previous illness. Or maybe an anonymous gift of money to help you pay off your utility bill.

Do you know anyone who could use a message of joy today? An encouraging word of hope? A promise of good things to come?

*Holy Spirit, enlighten me today concerning who might need my assistance.
Show me the people I can touch with good news or a kind deed. Let me
be a messenger who brings joy to someone's heart! Amen.*

morning
JOY IN MERCY

"Shouldn't you have had mercy on your fellow servant just as I had on you?"
MATTHEW 18:33 NIV

At some point, you're going to have to face Matthew 18:33. Ask God to remind you of some of the times in which you jeered at other folks or when you were rude. Miraculously, some past incidences may soon arrive out of your memory banks. You will see once again how merciful God is to you when you falter or fall flat. And that tender mercy the Lord pours onto all of us is the same mercy He hopes we will pour onto others.

O Lord, please give me the supernatural strength to not
only receive mercy but offer it to others. Amen.

evening
WHAT LEADS TO REAL JOY

Distress that drives us to God does that. It turns us around. It gets us back in the
way of salvation. We never regret that kind of pain. But those who let distress
drive them away from God are full of regrets, end up on a deathbed of regrets.
2 CORINTHIANS 7:10 MSG

No matter how people run from any signs of self-reproaching guilt, they come to know it intimately.

The question from 2 Corinthians 7:10 is "What kind of sorrowful distress do we have?" If it's the worldly kind that moves us away from God, then it leads to a deathbed of regrets. But if it is godly grief, then there is good news, for it turns our hearts around and leads us back to the way of salvation and God. And, oh, how that godly sorrow leads us to real joy!

Dear God, when I commit a transgression, may I always have the godly
grief that leads to a repentant heart! In Jesus' name I pray, amen.

morning
THE LIGHT OF CHRIST

"All this will be because the mercy of our God is very tender, and heaven's dawn is about to break upon us, to give light to those who sit in darkness and death's shadow, and to guide us to the path of peace."
LUKE 1:78–79 TLB

Daybreak is a daily event, and yet the sun's light changes our world like nothing else. The radiance of our Savior's light also changes our world—His divine presence illuminating every shadowy crevice of our souls. May we forever seek out and bask in the light of Christ. For it will guide us to the path of peace. And joy!

God, thank You not only for the light of our earthly sun but for the eternal light from Your only Son, Jesus! Amen.

evening
WELCOME THE JOY!

For I am sure that neither death nor life, nor angels nor rulers, nor things present nor things to come, nor powers, nor height nor depth, nor anything else in all creation, will be able to separate us from the love of God in Christ Jesus our Lord.
ROMANS 8:38–39 ESV

This world can be a harsh landscape to navigate emotionally and in every other way. Just when you think that you are loved and thriving, it can all be snatched away.

But the one hope we can cling to is that nothing can separate us from the love of God. Unlike humanity and its reckless promises and empty vows and fickle ways, God is unchanging. He loves you. Accept His gift. Welcome that joy!

Lord, when all the world abandons me, I thank You for Your great and unfaltering love. Amen.

morning
ACKNOWLEDGING THE GIVER

*Every good and perfect gift is from above, coming down from the Father
of the heavenly lights, who does not change like shifting shadows.*
JAMES 1:17 NIV

God gives us good gifts, but sometimes we respond in the same way as some children. Our actions seem to say that we love the gifts more than we love the Giver. We don't always thank the Lord the way we should or seek His company when we want to enjoy the many gifts from His hand. But we too can change our manners in a heartbeat.

*Heavenly Father, I acknowledge that You are the Giver of all good
and perfect gifts. I thank You and praise You for them. They are
undeserved but lavish, just like Your love. May You and I always enjoy
these wonderful gifts together. In Jesus' holy name I pray, amen.*

evening
THE APPLE OF HIS EYE

*"He found him in a desert land, and in the howling waste of the wilderness;
he encircled him, he cared for him, he kept him as the apple of his eye."*
DEUTERONOMY 32:10 ESV

According to Deuteronomy, God encircles you and cares for you. You are the apple of God's eye! Really? *You? Me?* Yes! That is the God we love and serve. That is the God our souls have longed for.

So on days when the world hands you a howling wasteland, remember God's holy affections. Ponder them daily. Take them into the deepest part of you. Then allow the joy of it to shine from your heart and sing from your mouth.

Dear God, I am so happy to be the apple of Your eye. I love You too! Amen.

morning
DOING LIFE WITH GOD

In his pride the wicked man does not seek him;
in all his thoughts there is no room for God.
PSALM 10:4 NIV

God wants us to be happy but not by elbowing through life and knocking people down. The Lord wants us to do life with Him. There is an eternal difference between the two—one is holy and the other is wholly out of control. When the focus stays on us and only us, there is no room left for God. Without the Lord's daily presence, it's easy to let the world fill us with vanity and arrogance, which then leads to folly and sin.

Simply put—joy comes from doing life with God.

Lord, I want to always make room for You in my life.
In fact, I want You front and center! Amen.

evening
JOY IN HIS PRESENCE!

Through the victories you gave, his glory is great; you have bestowed on
him splendor and majesty. Surely you have granted him unending blessings
and made him glad with the joy of your presence. For the king trusts in the
LORD; through the unfailing love of the Most High he will not be shaken.
PSALM 21:5–7 NIV

No joy on earth can compare to a single moment in the presence of God. Such resplendent radiance. Such unmatched beauty. Such unfathomable mystery. Such unmerited grace. Such extravagant love. Oh yes, I am made glad with the joy of His presence!

Holy Father, I stand in awe of Your glory. You are awesome to behold.
And yet, I sense that You are not far away from me. Thank You for both
Your majesty and Your faithful attentions. In Jesus' name I pray, amen.

morning
THE GIFT OF FRIENDSHIP

But Ruth replied, "Don't urge me to leave you or to turn back from you. Where you go I will go, and where you stay I will stay. Your people will be my people and your God my God. Where you die I will die, and there I will be buried. May the LORD deal with me, be it ever so severely, if even death separates you and me."
RUTH 1:16–17 NIV

God gives us the gift of friendship. That is, other people who perhaps have similar temperaments and interests and who desire to journey through life alongside us. These friends, who help us in good times and bad, sometimes turn out to be true treasures of the heart for a lifetime. They are God's gift of joy to us.

Thank You, God, for the beautiful gift of friendship. For those good and devoted people who travel through life beside me. Amen.

evening
LIVE LAVISHLY FOR OTHERS

It is possible to give away and become richer! It is also possible to hold on too tightly and lose everything. Yes, the liberal man shall be rich! By watering others, he waters himself.
PROVERBS 11:24–25 TLB

When it comes to the talents that God has given to us, sometimes we hide those away as well for one reason or another. Over time they become a little wonky and unusable too.

Enjoying all that God has gifted us with requires a generosity of spirit. Yes, there will be chips and nicks along the way. There will be messes. It's life. But as your heart gives and pours itself out for others, it will be filled. What a joy-filled spiritual paradox!

Lord, help me to give lavishly to others, with my talents, my possessions, my life. Amen.

morning
TETHERED TO HIS HEART

*For you were straying like sheep, but have now returned
to the Shepherd and Overseer of your souls.*
1 PETER 2:25 ESV

Even as Christians, we sometimes go adrift. We forget that we cannot navigate this stormy life alone. We forget how to pray and cry in repentance. We forget how to love Him and to be loved by Him—the One who has treasured us always.

But God is the Master of helping us remember who we are in Christ. Come home to Him—come home to the joy!

O Lord, thank You for keeping me tethered to Your heart. Amen.

evening
THAT MYSTERIOUS LONGING

*He has made everything beautiful and appropriate in its time. He
has also planted eternity [a sense of divine purpose] in the human
heart [a mysterious longing which nothing under the sun can satisfy,
except God]—yet man cannot find out (comprehend, grasp) what
God has done (His overall plan) from the beginning to the end.*
ECCLESIASTES 3:11 AMP

Miraculously, eternity has been planted in our hearts—a mysterious longing that nothing can satisfy but God. We may feel that we are spinning uncontrollably in some strange terrestrial dance, but as Christians we have been made free in Christ; and with His supernatural help, we can become unbound from the unhappy confines of earthly sin. Even in the midst of what is still profound and unexplained, we can know that God has created a meaningful and joyful life for us now and for all time.

Lord, I praise You for beauty and love and purpose. Amen.

morning
GETTING TO KNOW YOU

*But do not forget this one thing, dear friends: With the Lord a day
is like a thousand years, and a thousand years are like a day.*

2 PETER 3:8 NIV

There are a number of ways to get to know the Lord better, such as being part of a Bible-believing fellowship, talking and listening to God, attending a Bible study, and going on church retreats. Psalm 23:6 (TLB) tells us, "Your goodness and unfailing kindness shall be with me all of my life, and afterwards I will live with you forever in your home." Yes, forever is in our future, and to spend it with God will be—well, pure heaven! May we enjoy getting to know the Lord's beauty and goodness and love as we wait for the glory of heaven.

*Lord, I am finding joy in getting to know You.
I love every facet about You. Amen.*

evening
TO BE MADE MERRY

*You're cheating on God. If all you want is your own way, flirting with
the world every chance you get, you end up enemies of God and his
way. And do you suppose God doesn't care? The proverb has it that
"he's a fiercely jealous lover." And what he gives in love is far better
than anything else you'll find. It's common knowledge that "God goes
against the willful proud; God gives grace to the willing humble."*

JAMES 4:4–6 MSG

God wants a happily-ever-after, and that is why He sent Christ. The Lord's honorable and self-sacrificing and splendid love is for everyone, but as with all princely offers, we must accept His beautiful proposal. Won't you say yes to the finest love your heart will ever know?

God, I accept Your proposal of love both now and forevermore. Amen.

morning
FINDING YOUR SONG AGAIN

*Serve the LORD with gladness and delight; come
before His presence with joyful singing.*
PSALM 100:2 AMP

Psalm 91:14–15 (ESV) lovingly reminds us, "Because he holds fast to me in love, I will deliver him; I will protect him, because he knows my name. When he calls to me, I will answer him; I will be with him in trouble; I will rescue him and honor him."

God loves you, and He will rescue you and help you to find your song again. Call out to Him whenever you have need. Now is always a good time!

*Lord, I don't know what went wrong, but I feel like I'm
falling to pieces. Please rescue me now. Amen.*

evening
BRINGING GOD DELIGHT

*GOD's Message: "Don't let the wise brag of their wisdom. Don't let heroes
brag of their exploits. Don't let the rich brag of their riches. If you brag, brag
of this and this only: That you understand and know me. I'm GOD, and I act
in loyal love. I do what's right and set things right and fair, and delight in
those who do the same things. These are my trademarks." GOD's Decree.*
JEREMIAH 9:23–24 MSG

God is the Creator of all things that are pleasant and beautiful and satisfying. Do we thank Him for the bounty? Do we ask Him to enjoy all of it with us? And do we ever consider how to please God—how to bring *Him* delight? Not as a way to work our way into heaven. That's impossible. But as a heartfelt thanks to the Lord for all He has done for us and because He is worthy of glory and honor and love as well as our faithful obedience. What can you do to bring God delight?

*Dearest Lord Jesus, please let me live out Jeremiah 9:24.
Make it one of my life verses. I genuinely want to please You. Amen.*

morning
A CHILD OF GOD

*Even in his own land and among his own people, the Jews, he was
not accepted. Only a few would welcome and receive him. But
to all who received him, he gave the right to become children of
God. All they needed to do was to trust him to save them.*

JOHN 1:11–12 TLB

We are all desperate to be somebody, aren't we? In fact, people will stoop to ridiculous levels to feel as though they are truly exceptional.

When you know the Lord, you no longer feel the need for these competitions. You are loved by God, and you are His child. This knowledge is so freeing that you can spend more time being the exceptional woman God created you to be. And there is no prestige or accomplishment or joy on earth that is greater than being a child of God.

Lord, I am honored to be called Your child. Amen.

evening
A SACRED MOMENT

*"Are you tired? Worn out? Burned out on religion? Come to me. Get
away with me and you'll recover your life. I'll show you how to take a
real rest. Walk with me and work with me—watch how I do it. Learn the
unforced rhythms of grace. I won't lay anything heavy or ill-fitting on
you. Keep company with me and you'll learn to live freely and lightly."*

MATTHEW 11:28–30 MSG

Maybe you feel as Job did, that the burden you carry is not your fault. Some things in this life are left as mystery. And yet we are never left alone. When you walk with Christ and cast your cares on Him, there comes a sacred moment of trust, because He is the divine Keeper of your soul. Relish the freedom of such truth. Love the Giver of such sweet liberty. Hear Him say, *"Follow Me and learn the unforced rhythms of grace."*

Lord, may I always live inside that sacred moment of trust. Amen.

morning
SPIRITUAL LANDMARKS

But grow [spiritually mature] in the grace and knowledge of our Lord and Savior Jesus Christ. To Him be glory (honor, majesty, splendor), both now and to the day of eternity. Amen.
2 PETER 3:18 AMP

After you accept Christ and you go on your life journey with Him, there can be spiritual landmarks as you go along—such as that victory over a particular sin that had once been a stronghold in your life, an enlightenment of scripture, or that new longing to be in constant communion with the Lord.

Those spiritual landmarks of growth and maturity give us hope that we are on the right path. They also give a sense of confidence and peace and joy!

Dearest Lord Jesus, thank You for the spiritual landmarks in my life that show I am growing in the grace and knowledge of You. Amen.

evening
THE GREATEST JOY OF ALL

Jesus said to her, "I am the resurrection and the life. Whoever believes in me, though he die, yet shall he live, and everyone who lives and believes in me shall never die. Do you believe this?"
JOHN 11:25–26 ESV

No matter what happens to us or how far we stray, may we always head back to the cross. It's where we can find peace. The death and resurrection of Jesus Christ for the forgiveness of sins was the most sorrowful event in history, and yet the most joyful too.

The question we are left with is the same now as it was back then. Jesus asked Martha, but He also asks you, *"Do you believe this?"*

Lord Jesus, my answer is yes. You are the resurrection and the life. I believe! Amen.

morning
I CHOOSE JOY!

*Jesus continued: "There was a man who had two sons. The
younger one said to his father, 'Father, give me my share of
the estate.' So he divided his property between them."*
LUKE 15:11–12 NIV

People are notorious for wanting what they want when they want it. We want lots of
presents from God, but we don't always desire God's *presence* in our lives. We want
our inheritance in the kingdom but not necessarily the everyday company of our Lord.
But both of these joys come together.

The story of the prodigal son has a happy ending, and it is the same ending the
Lord wants for all of us. May we all choose to go home. May we all choose the presence
as well as the presents of God. May we all choose joy!

*Lord, I'm grateful that You are a forgiving Father and that You
welcome me back home with much celebration. Amen.*

evening
PIECE BY PRETTY PIECE

*Who will transform our lowly body to be like his glorious body, by
the power that enables him even to subject all things to himself.*
PHILIPPIANS 3:21 ESV

As Christians, someday when we die, we are promised glorified bodies, but the Lord
wants to start this beautification process right now. Day by day, piece by pretty piece,
won't you let Him put His masterful touch on the mosaic of your soul? He is ready to
create something truly remarkable, something heavenly with your life.

*Every day, O Lord, I desire to become more and more like You.
Piece by piece, I want my soul to become a work of art that reflects
Your divine beauty, truth, and love. May my words elevate You
and my life exalt You. Praise be to Your holy name! Amen.*

MOURNING

*When my prayers returned to me unanswered, I went about
mourning as though for my friend or brother.*
PSALM 35:13–14 NIV

David knew where he could go for help. He knew God would see his grief and understand it. He knew God was never far from him but rather was as close as a heartbeat.
He knew he could trust God to protect him from the pain, heal his wounds, and save
his life from ruin. We can too. And like David, we can say, "My tongue will proclaim
your righteousness, your praises all day long" (verse 28 NIV).

*God, sometimes I feel as if the whole world is out to get me, even
when there might be only a few voices speaking against me. Help
me to see the truth. And help me to trust that You understand
me and will always, always be there for me. Amen.*

WOUNDS BOUND

He heals the brokenhearted and binds up their wounds.
PSALM 147:3 NIV

God not only takes delight in those who are strong and can keep on marching into
battle; He smiles into the faces of those who are filled with fear and weak with sorrow,
and yet place their hands in His. This God is the One who leans down and kisses away
the tears, who bandages up our emotional wounds, tying together the parts within
us that are broken in order to make us whole again. He is the God of bleeding hands
and feet, who knows our sorrow better than anyone else ever could.

*Healing Lord, bring me the medicine of Your love. Bind up what
is broken within me. I want to be whole in You. Amen.*

morning
WAVES

*Mightier than the thunder of the great waters, mightier than
the breakers of the sea—the LORD on high is mighty.*
PSALM 93:4 NIV

Our God is mighty—deep and wide like the ocean. Unpredictable and beyond our control. We cannot fathom Him. We cannot contain Him. We can only begin to grasp the words to describe Him. He reaches into our lives like the tides—sometimes arriving quickly and full-on, with beautiful, high, rushing waves of light. Sometimes He stretches out into our days—steady and strong and serene, teaching us peace and patience and calm.

The seas have lifted up their voice, and we have heard it. And now we can join them in their song: "The Lord, our Lord—our Lord on high is mighty."

*Sometimes, Lord, just knowing You are here, as surely as I know the
seas will come to shore, is enough to bring me peace. Amen.*

evening
NO CONDEMNATION

*There is therefore now no condemnation to those who are in Christ Jesus,
who do not walk according to the flesh, but according to the Spirit.*
ROMANS 8:1 NKJV

No condemnation. Consider those words to be your life slogan. How is your life different, or how should it be different, with the knowledge that you are free from condemnation? You never have to face hell, because Jesus faced it for you. You can know without a doubt that your life here on earth is just a dot on an eternal line, and you get to live out the rest of that line in the freedom and glory of heaven.

No condemnation. How does that knowledge shape the way you look at others? How can you extend the mercy Jesus has shown you and share the freedom of those two words with someone else today?

*Lord, I know I may get in all kinds of trouble, but praise
God that You offer me no condemnation. Amen.*

morning
UNLOVED, BELOVED

I will call Not My People, My People, and she who is Unloved, Beloved.
ROMANS 9:25 HCSB

Our God takes pleasure in exalting the humbled. He enjoys shining a spotlight on what has previously been hidden in the shadows. He makes "known the riches of His glory on objects of mercy" (Romans 9:23 HCSB). God takes the forgotten ones of the world—the broken, the unholy, the used up, the horrid, the ugly—and He remembers them, heals them, sanctifies them, restores them, and transforms them. He uses unexpected people to bring to fruition the fruits of His glory.

God can and will use you—no matter what you look like or feel like, or what your life has been like to this point. And not only will He use you to do great things in His kingdom, He will love you.

Beloved God, thank You for loving me, even when I feel unlovable. Amen.

evening
REFUGE OF DESTRUCTION

Come, see the glorious works of the LORD:
see how he brings destruction upon the world.
PSALM 46:8 NLT

How can we know that God really is God? We have to ask. We have to do research. We have to search the scriptures and see who God claims to be, what He is like, what He does, and whom He does it to. We have to keep searching and talking about Him in every corner of the world. We can meet others and tell them about Him. And then we can be still—still in the satisfaction of knowing who He is and what He wants from us.

God, please bring peace out of the destruction in our lives. Amen.

morning
DEEP LOVE

He quieted the wind down to a whisper, put a muzzle on all the big waves.
PSALM 107:29 MSG

This is our God—who humbles proud princes and sets them to wander without a home, while lifting up the oppressed and establishing them as overseers of flourishing estates. This is our God, who has a wisdom that confounds the scholars of this world and who has followers who seem foolish in their acts of kindness toward a world that rejects them.

"Good people see this and are glad; bad people are speechless, stopped in their tracks. If you are really wise, you'll think this over—it's time you appreciated GOD's deep love" (verses 42–43 MSG).

God, I want to swim in the depths of Your love and experience the stillness of Your peaceful waters. Amen.

evening
COUNT THE STARS

"Look up at the sky and count the stars—if indeed you can count them." Then he said to him, "So shall your offspring be."
GENESIS 15:5 NIV

What impossible task has God set before you? Has He asked you to count the grains of salt in a shaker or the number of times your children have said your name in the last twenty-four hours? In what ways has God been nudging you, asking you to trust Him more?

When night comes, go out and sit under the sky. Ask God where He is sending you. Talk to Him about His promises that you read in His Word. Then look up into the vast field of stars and start counting. And with every star, begin to trust God just a little bit more.

Lord, who formed the stars and set each one into the sky, thank You for Your promises. Amen.

TREASURES OF RESTLESSNESS

morning

"I have no rest; only trouble comes."
JOB 3:26 NLT

Job learned about who God is, but he also learned about himself. He learned that the bottom line to every experience we will ever have is that God is in charge. Only God. He's the only Author of our lives. He's our Creator and our King. And He is good. No matter what we think or do or say, no matter what power we think we might have, no matter how well we think we've got everything figured out, the only One who really understands the big picture is God.

Sometimes we need to be made restless before we can find true rest. Sometimes we need to be brought down low so we can know where to look for help.

You, O Lord, are everything to me. Help me remember who You are. Amen.

FREE ME

evening

Who will free me from this life that is dominated by sin and death?
ROMANS 7:24 NLT

Being a slave to our sinful nature keeps us from enjoying all the good gifts God wants us to have. But thanks be to God, He can free us. *How do I get free from myself? How do I break the cycle of sin and shame?* The answer is always Jesus. We can't do it on our own. We can't even do it together. And we can't do it just by obeying a set of laws. We must have Jesus.

"Because you belong to him, the power of the life-giving Spirit has freed you from the power of sin that leads to death" (8:2 NLT). The next time you are sitting at a red light, don't dream about getting away. Dream about getting closer to God.

Lord, free me from the hold of sin. Amen.

morning
HIDING PLACES

You are my hiding place; you protect me from trouble.
PSALM 32:7 HCSB

With God, we can be encouraged and lifted up by the joy of the Lord—and by the feeling of standing upright before Him!

God doesn't expect us to always make right choices. After all, He made us, and He has observed human behavior since the beginning. God is not surprised when we fail. So why hide? Come out, come out, wherever you are, and share your story. You'll be glad you did, and you'll help those who are listening to share their stories too.

Most holy God, please forgive all the ungodly parts of me.
I place myself in Your care. Hide me in Your love. Amen.

evening
DESIRE AND POWER

For God is working in you, giving you the desire and the power to do what pleases him. Do everything without complaining and arguing, so that no one can criticize you. Live clean, innocent lives as children of God.
PHILIPPIANS 2:13–15 NLT

Can you obey the Creator's words—the words of the One who made all things well and designed them to function together in a beautiful harmony? Can you listen to where He leads you so that your work will not be useless? Can you follow in His steps?

We *can* do all of "this." We can do these things, because the One who made us *is* working within us and through us, not just to make us capable and competent, but to make us *want* to do what pleases Him. And when we have the desire to please Him and the power to please Him, we will be able to meet the goal of pleasing Him. And then we will certainly rejoice.

Creator God, thank You for the wonderful work You perform in me! Amen.

morning
NEVER SEPARATED

For I am convinced that neither death nor life, neither angels nor
demons, neither the present nor the future, nor any powers, neither
height nor depth, nor anything else in all creation, will be able to
separate us from the love of God that is in Christ Jesus our Lord.
ROMANS 8:38–39 NIV

We all need to be reminded that we are not alone. That we are *never ever* alone. That nothing can separate us from the love of good people, and nothing can keep us away from the love of Christ. No troubles. No bumps in the night. No bad people. No illness. No persecution. No physical conditions. No mental conditions. No demons. No distance. *Absolutely nothing* can keep us from God's eternal, powerful, pure, forgiving love.

Lord, help me reach out to others and remind them
that they are never far from You. Amen.

evening
SCHEDULES

Instead, you ought to say, "If it is the Lord's will, we will live and do this or that."
JAMES 4:15 NIV

What if, instead of to-do lists, we created to-don'ts? What if we started each day by remembering all the things we would not do, could not do, except that God wills it to be so? What if we started our schedules with a thank-you note to our Father, instead of ending each day with a hurried good night to God? What if we remembered that we should make every step count for Him, because Jesus made every step on earth count for us—including each step on the way to the cross.

Lord, don't let me get so carried away with my calendar that I forget that
every day is a day You made, and I should be glad and grateful for it. Amen.

morning
LOVE COVERS

Above all, love each other deeply, because love covers over a multitude of sins.
1 Peter 4:8 niv

When you love people deeply, you become vulnerable. That doesn't mean you must subject yourself to abusive or toxic relationships. God doesn't tell us that we have to put ourselves in harm's way deliberately so that we can show love to abusers. We have to recognize that some people need to be loved in a way that helps them not to hurt others, to become better than what they are.

But loving others also means you open yourself up to the riches of deep understanding, deep intimacy, deep caring, and deep love. Love covers us when it goes deep enough. And then we learn just a bit more about the love God has for us—the love that is so deep and wide and high and long that it can cover a whole planet full of people.

God, thank You for teaching me how to love deeply. Amen.

evening
PATTERNS

*Do not conform to the pattern of this world, but be transformed
by the renewing of your mind. Then you will be able to test and
approve what God's will is—his good, pleasing and perfect will.*
Romans 12:2 niv

How in the world can we test and approve what God's will is if we don't have anything to test it against?

But we do. We have God's Word. We have the testimony of Jesus. We have the wisdom of God poured out to us through others. We have the ability to ask God about it in prayer. By doing these things, by doing what's required to test and approve what God's will is, we can renew our minds. We can get our minds following different thought patterns. We can make ourselves practice different ways of behaving. We can be transformed.

*Lord God, change me. Renew my mind. Transform
my heart. I want to know Your will. Amen.*

morning
JOY OF THE HARVEST

*He said to his disciples, "The harvest is great, but the workers
are few. So pray to the Lord who is in charge of the harvest;
ask him to send more workers into his fields."*
MATTHEW 9:37–38 NLT

Even Jesus couldn't be everywhere at once in His human form. And He knew the people would still have needs long after He had left the earth.

But He also knew that people needed to do the work. They needed to come together and serve one another. They needed to feel compassion. They needed to listen to each other's cares and share each other's sorrows. They needed to ask questions together. And then everyone would really know the joy of the harvest.

Lord, send more workers into the fields. Send me, Lord. Amen.

evening
THAT KIND OF PEACE

*And the peace of God, which transcends all understanding,
will guard your hearts and your minds in Christ Jesus.*
PHILIPPIANS 4:7 NIV

God's peace pours over us, filling us and surrounding us like a gushing stream. Even when the world looks bleak, when we can't see an answer, when we are burdened with stress and worries, God's peace can push through all of that and fill up our hearts—untangling the knots in our minds and soothing our spirits. It's the kind of sure footing we feel when we make a decision that puts us in line with His will. It's the supernatural calm we are able to cling to when storms are roaring all around us. It's the quiet confidence that allows us to step into situations that would otherwise shake us. It's the peace that we don't understand, that we can't describe, and that doesn't make sense. It's that kind of peace.

*Lord, I'm so thankful You are near me when troubles come.
Bless me with Your impossible peace. Amen.*

JUST PRAY

Is anyone among you in trouble? Let them pray.
Is anyone happy? Let them sing songs of praise.
JAMES 5:13 NIV

God's idea of good is much better than we can ever imagine. He is vastly more gracious than we have the capacity to be. He is more merciful. He is more generous. He is more faithful.

So go ahead. Are you in trouble? Pray. Are you happy? Pray and give thanks. Are you sick? Pray and ask for healing. Just pray, pray, pray.

Lord, hear my prayer. Amen.

FREELY GIVE

"Heal the sick, raise the dead, cleanse those with skin diseases, drive
out demons. You have received free of charge; give free of charge."
MATTHEW 10:8 HCSB

How amazed the apostles must have been to have been charged with delivering this gift. How thrilled they must have been to realize that they could share and share and share what they received in a kind of unending giving of a gift, enriching the world and deepening within themselves the truth of the Gospel they had been given. And so it with us—we have the amazing duty and privilege of freely sharing the Word and the love and the grace of God, over and over and over again.

Lord Jesus, let me be an unending delivery
service for the gift of Your grace. Amen.

morning
PERFECT LOVE

There is no fear in love. But perfect love drives out fear,
because fear has to do with punishment.
1 JOHN 4:18 NIV

Just like Jesus, we can love others with a love that drives out fear. We can love others even when they might reject us, or be angry with us, or insult us, or hurt us in other ways. We can still forgive and love, because we can love with the love of God. When we are firmly grounded in God's love, we don't have to worry what people may say about us or do to us. And what we find when we do love like God is that, instead of people running away from us, often they will be drawn to us. They will want to know this love too. They will want to be loved with perfect love.

Lord, I'm so glad I'm loved by You! Let me love
others the way You love me. Amen.

evening
FOR US

What, then, shall we say in response to these things?
If God is for us, who can be against us?
ROMANS 8:31 NIV

God was for us in every second of the stories of our lives, and He is for us now. He gives us everything we need and so much more than we deserve. He justifies us—forgiving us and setting things to right so that we can be freed from our lives of sin and start again.

Nothing can separate us from His love. No difficult schedules, no difficult people, no difficult financial situation, no difficult relationships. There is no bad day so awful that we cannot recover from it, because there is no bad day with God not in it.

God is for us. No one can really be against us, because no one can stand against God. Thank You, Lord.

Lord God, I am so glad You are here for me.
Thank You for being my very best friend. Amen.

morning
ROOTED

*"But since they have no root, they last only a short time. When trouble
or persecution comes because of the word, they quickly fall away."*
MARK 4:17 NIV

We become rooted by immersing ourselves in the Word of God—listening to what He has to say to us. We become rooted when we not only read His Word but live it out. We become rooted when we allow His Word to feed us every day.

We can become rooted through the generations. Maybe your family has no faith traditions in your history. Maybe you are the first in a long line to try following Christ. But now you can start your own traditions. You can become part of a family of believers and know that you have people, such as Paul and Mary and Ruth and David and Peter in your family tree. And you can pass on your faith practices to the next generation. You can make sure that they are rooted in the Word from birth.

*Lord, I want my roots to be firmly planted in
Your Word. Help me to grow. Amen.*

evening
EXPECT OPPOSITION

*Consider him who endured such opposition from sinners,
so that you will not grow weary and lose heart.*
HEBREWS 12:3 NIV

We should expect opposition. Especially at times when we've recently recovered from a bout of temptation, or when we are purposely aiming to walk the straight and narrow path. There will be bumps in the road and even whole roadblocks. Have patience. Keep pushing. Keep fighting. Keep reading God's Word. Keep praying. Keep the faith. Run the race.

Lord, I can keep going when I know You are with me. Amen.

morning
LOSING OR KEEPING

*"Anyone who loves their life will lose it, while anyone who
hates their life in this world will keep it for eternal life."*
John 12:25 niv

Do you love your life? Do you look forward to every day? What about your job? Do you hold on tightly to your work, counting every hour, checking off every achievement? Are you stashing away funds and gathering possessions? What about your family? Are you planning every moment and hanging on to each memory?

It's not wrong to enjoy our lives. But focusing too much on what happens to us in the here and now may result in our losing sight of the yet to come. And God has so much more in store for us!

*Lord, help me not to get so distracted by the nearest parts
of my life that I forget what You have promised for me.
I want to serve You well, Lord. Show me how. Amen.*

evening
STRONGER

He gives strength to the weary and increases the power of the weak.
Isaiah 40:29 niv

Thankfully we have a source we can go to when we become so tired that we find it hard to stand on truth, to act in love, and to extend grace. We can go to God Almighty, whose strength is everlasting, and who never tires of loving us. We can ask for help and for wisdom from the One who has a limitless supply of both. We can ask for refreshment and innovation from the Creator God who formed this world from end to end. When we are at our weakest, He can make us stronger. When we are without hope, He can renew our vision. When we cannot walk, He can make us fly.

Lord, I owe everything to You. Please lift me up. Make me stronger. Amen.

morning
IN GOOD HANDS

The Lord is my Shepherd [to feed, guide, and shield me], I shall not lack. . . .
Yes, though I walk through the [deep, sunless] valley of the shadow
of death, I will fear or dread no evil, for You are with me;
Your rod [to protect] and Your staff [to guide], they comfort me.
PSALM 23:1, 4 AMPC

The Father can erase your fears with a whisper. Jesus can still them with one motion. And the Holy Spirit can blow them away with one good exhale. Your Good Shepherd comes equipped with everything He needs to get you safely from one place to another.

Today and every day, remember your Shepherd. Believe He's surrounding you with every step you take. Comfort yourself with the fact that He's equipped to keep you safe, no matter how dark things seem. You, little lamb, are in good hands.

Dear Shepherd, with You, I know I'm safe no matter how dark things
get. In this truth, I find not just courage and comfort but joy! Amen.

evening
FAITH-FILLED ATTITUDE

"There's no need to fear for I'm your God. I'll give you strength.
I'll help you. I'll hold you steady, keep a firm grip on you. . . .
Because I, your GOD, have a firm grip on you and I'm not letting
go. I'm telling you, 'Don't panic. I'm right here to help you.'"
ISAIAH 41:10, 13 MSG

Your faith is what shapes your attitudes. Consider Joseph. What might have happened to him—and the nation of Israel—had Joseph not continued to believe in God when he was sold to traveling traders by his own brothers, resold into slavery, and then put into a dungeon? What if Joseph had become despondent and stopped believing God was with him, helping him, and guiding him? But Joseph did believe in the dreams God had given him. He had confidence in God. And his attitude that God would not let him down lifted Joseph up above his situations, no matter how dire they became.

Thank You, God, for being with me, helping me, and guiding me. Amen.

morning
NO MATTER

Laugh and sing for joy. Sing hymns to God; all heaven, sing out; clear the way for the coming of Cloud-Rider. Enjoy GOD, cheer when you see him! Father of orphans, champion of widows, is God in his holy house. God makes homes for the homeless, leads prisoners to freedom.
PSALM 68:3–5 MSG

One of the many great and special things about God is that He promises to stick with you through thick and thin. He's always there to back you up, bail you out, and be your advocate. No matter what comes into your life, no matter what challenge rises up before you, no matter what obstacle stands between you and your needs and desires, you never have to fear that you're alone, abandoned, or defenseless.

No matter what happens, God is with you.

Thank You, Lord God, for always being where I need You. Continue giving me Your strength and support today and every day. Amen.

evening
A SHOW OF TALENTS

"Well done, good and faithful slave! You were faithful over a few things; I will put you in charge of many things. Share your master's joy!"
MATTHEW 25:21 HCSB

Jesus made it clear that God has entrusted to each of His followers a particular talent, opportunity, or resource. And each is to be used to serve God and His people, not hidden or neglected.

Today is your day to gather up your courage and step out of your comfort zone. Consider what talents you may have been neglecting or what gifts, opportunities, or resources you have put on the back burner. Dust off that guitar. Join that nonprofit organization. Or go up into your attic and see what you have that might better the life of another.

Be faithful with what you have been given, and God will give you more.

Show me, Lord, how You would have me better use my gifts, talents, and resources for You. Amen.

TRAPPED IN DISCOURAGEMENT
morning

*I will be to you a God; and you shall know that it is I, the Lord your God,
Who brings you out from under the burdens of the Egyptians. . . . Moses
told this to the Israelites, but they refused to listen to Moses because
of their impatience and anguish of spirit and. . .cruel bondage.*

EXODUS 6:7, 9 AMPC

Although tough life experiences are inevitable for most of us, each person does have a choice as to how she or he is going to live through them. You can choose to have courage or be discouraged, to focus on your problems or God's promises.

No matter how dark your circumstances, choose to remain confident that God is with you. That His light, love, and compassion are streaming down upon you. That He will rescue you with His might and miracles.

Help me keep my eyes on Your promises and protections, Lord. Amen.

GET UP AND GO
evening

*I will trust and not be afraid, for the Lord God is my strength and
song. . . . The Lord. . .has done excellent things [gloriously]; let
this be made known to all the earth. Cry aloud and shout joyfully,
you women. . .for great in your midst is the Holy One.*

ISAIAH 12:2, 5–6 AMPC

If you want to be used by God in unique circumstances, pray—not to pull God to your will but to align your will with His. That way, when God does call, you won't be afraid. You'll just get up and go.

God, give me the courage to get up and go when You call. Amen.

morning
A FREED WOMAN

*Jesus said to her. . ."Go to my brothers and say to them, 'I am ascending to
my Father and your Father, to my God and your God.'" Mary Magdalene
went and announced to the disciples, "I have seen the Lord."*
JOHN 20:17–18 ESV

Mary had voluntarily gone to the garden, watching for and weeping for Jesus. When
others had denied Him, she proclaimed Him. When others deserted Him, she remained
near Him. When others left the empty tomb, she remained, watching, waiting, until
she met Him once more.

Because of Jesus, Mary's life was forever changed. She was no longer afraid but
trusting. No longer broken but whole. No longer a mess but a message.

*Lord, free me for You. Change my fear to trust, my brokenness
to wholeness. Make my mess a message. Amen.*

evening
KINGDOM SEEKERS

*"Do not seek what you are to eat and what you are to drink, nor be worried.
For all. . .seek after these things, and your Father knows that you need
them. Instead, seek his kingdom, and these things will be added to you.
Fear not. . .for it is your Father's good pleasure to give you the kingdom."*
LUKE 12:29–32 ESV

Jesus' cure for anxiety is to seek God. Seek His kingdom. Then all you need will be
supplied. But what does it mean to seek God's kingdom? It means to make God a priority in your life, to seek Him early in the morning through prayer and reading of the
Word. To search for His presence, wisdom, will, and way. As you do so, worries and
fears will fade away, and faith and joy will take center stage.

*Lord, in this moment, I draw near to You, seeking Your face, wisdom,
and light. Lead me where You would have me be. Amen.*

morning
SURE UNSEEN

Our life is lived by faith. We do not live by what we see in front of us. . . .
Now faith is being sure we will get what we hope for.
It is being sure of what we cannot see.
2 Corinthians 5:7; Hebrews 11:1 nlv

Consider the military conquests of Gideon, Barak and Deborah, Samson, and David; the miracles of Elijah and Elisha; Daniel in the lions' den; Shadrach, Meshach, and Abednego amid the furnace flames; the healings, prophecies, and powers of Jesus; and in the end, the amazing works of Jesus' disciples.

You too can be part of God's amazing story—if you replace your fears with faith. If you live focused on the unseen rather than the seen. If you become sure of receiving the things you hope for, certain they exist even though you cannot yet see them. Believe. And God will do something amazing.

I want to become a part of Your story, Lord.
Help me be sure of what I cannot yet see. Amen.

evening
A MIGHTY WARRIOR

"The Lord your God is with you, the Mighty Warrior who saves.
He will take great delight in you; in his love he will no longer
rebuke you, but will rejoice over you with singing."
Zephaniah 3:17 niv

If we walk through our days without God, we have every reason to be afraid. But we don't have to travel this journey alone! We have a bodyguard—as well as a spirit guard—who will never leave us nor forsake us. He is the Mighty Warrior who saves!

He takes great delight in those who love Him and stay close to Him. Surely we have nothing to fear with a hero who adores us. He loves us beyond description. He will protect us and save us. With God as our defender, we have no reason to feel afraid.

Dear Father, thank You for being the Mighty Warrior who saves.
Remind me of Your presence, and help me not feel afraid. Amen.

morning
FILLED WITH JOY

Let all who take refuge in you rejoice; let them sing joyful
praises forever. Spread your protection over them, that
all who love your name may be filled with joy.
PSALM 5:11 NLT

When we're in trouble, we can take refuge in God, and we can rejoice! We can—and will—sing His praises forever. All who love God, all who are called His children, will be filled with joy!

The reason for that joy is that we know, despite our present trouble, we have hope. We have the promise of a good future filled with love and peace, and absent from suffering and trials of every kind. Though we may not feel happy about our current circumstance, we can rejoice, because we know how our story will end.

Dear Father, I love You, and I take refuge in You. Fill me with Your joy
as I focus on the wonderful future You have planned for me. Amen.

evening
THINK ABOUT SUCH THINGS

Finally, brothers and sisters, whatever is true, whatever is noble, whatever
is right, whatever is pure, whatever is lovely, whatever is admirable—if
anything is excellent or praiseworthy—think about such things.
PHILIPPIANS 4:8 NIV

If we struggle with depression, anger, fear, or other negative emotions, we should examine what we're feeding our brains. While some issues may require a doctor's care, we can certainly move our mental health in the right direction by controlling what we think about. We can push aside those damaging beliefs and replace them with God's Word and uplifting thoughts. When we do, we'll find everything in our lives takes on a more positive hue.

Dear Father, give me strength to say no to unhealthy thoughts and
attitudes, and help me fill my mind with positive things. Amen.

morning
LOVE ONE ANOTHER

*Owe nothing to anyone except to love one another;
for the one who loves his neighbor has fulfilled the Law.*

ROMANS 13:8 NASB

When we love each other, that love comes back to us. It causes others to have good feelings about us, and they return the love. They help us when they can. It also pleases God, and He pours out His blessings on us. When we feel powerless to change our situations, we can look for ways to love other people. It may not solve all our problems, but it will certainly turn things around in the right direction.

*Dear Father, thank You for this reminder to pay my debt
of love forward. Show me who needs love today. Amen.*

evening
WAIT FOR GOD

*I waited patiently for the LORD; he turned to me and heard my cry. He lifted
me out of the slimy pit, out of the mud and mire; he set my feet on a rock and
gave me a firm place to stand. He put a new song in my mouth, a hymn of
praise to our God. Many will see and fear the LORD and put their trust in him.*

PSALM 40:1–3 NIV

Just look at all the blessings David received because he waited. First, God heard him. Then, God lifted him out of the pit. Next, He set David on a rock and gave him a firm place to stand. Finally, God put a song of praise in David's heart.

Most of God's blessings are not of the fast-food variety. Have patience, and wait for God. You'll be glad you did.

*Dear Father, teach me to wait. I know You
have good things in store for me. Amen.*

morning
DOING GOOD

*Let us not become weary in doing good, for at the proper
time we will reap a harvest if we do not give up.*
GALATIANS 6:9 NIV

Doing the right thing can be exhausting. Oh, we can all be good every once in a while. But making the right choices day after day, week after month after year, can wear us down.

However, each time we make the difficult choice to do the right thing, we create a ripple effect that will eventually come back to us, bringing in a hefty harvest of God's peace and joy and good will. Small choice by small choice, with God's help, we can create an inheritance that—in the end—will be worth the sacrifice.

*Dear Father, help me not to grow weary in doing
good. I want to honor You in all I do. Amen.*

evening
GOD AND MAN

*God is not man, that he should lie, or a son of man, that he should change his
mind. Has he said, and will he not do it? Or has he spoken, and will he not fulfill it?*
NUMBERS 23:19 ESV

God is a far cry from any human! He cannot lie. He cannot make mistakes. He cannot be anything but good. Every breath we take, every step we take, every moment of our lives, God is constantly working for our good. If He promised it, we can be certain He will deliver on that promise, no matter what.

*Dear Father, forgive me for ever doubting You. I know You
will keep all Your promises to me. I trust You, and I know
You are good. Help me relax in that knowledge. Amen.*

morning
AN UNTROUBLED HEART

"Let not your heart be troubled; you believe in God, believe also in Me."
JOHN 14:1 NKJV

"Let not your hearts be troubled." That little word, "let," implies that we have a choice. Our hearts will not remain in a troubled state without our permission. We only live in constant stress if we *allow* ourselves to live that way.

God stands ready, waiting to take our troubles. He wants us to lay them down at His feet and go on with our lives, trusting Him to take care of every detail.

Dear Father, thank You for the reminder that I do not have to be troubled.
Help me lay the difficult things of my life at Your feet. Amen.

evening
FORGIVENESS

Bear with each other and forgive one another if any of you has a
grievance against someone. Forgive as the Lord forgave you.
COLOSSIANS 3:13 NIV

Forgiveness isn't saying an action was okay. Instead, it's recognizing that the memory is a harmful one—harmful to ourselves and to our relationships with God and others—and making the choice to get rid of it. When we forgive, we release the memory or event to God to make room for good things in our own lives.

When someone hurts us, we should deal with it and get over it as quickly as we are able. Forgiveness frees us to live healthy, productive, joy-filled lives.

Dear Father, help me forgive others the way
You've forgiven me—completely. Amen.

morning
GOD'S WHISPER

*Your faithfulness, LORD, will support me. When my anxious
thoughts multiply within me, Your comfort delights my soul.*
PSALM 94:18–19 NASB

Satan wants to destroy us from the inside out. He whispers our worst fears, filling our minds with anxiety. But Satan is a liar and a loser. We don't need to listen to him. When that voice of doubt fills our heads, we need to listen closer for God's whisper. He is there, reassuring us. He is there, holding us up. He is there, comforting us and filling our souls with delight.

*Dear Father, thank You for Your loving-kindness, which gives
me strength. Thank You for delighting my soul with Your love.
Help me to hear Your voice above all others. Amen.*

evening
ALL THINGS

I can do all this through him who gives me strength.
PHILIPPIANS 4:13 NIV

Believe it or not, God loves it when we find ourselves out of our league! If we're capable of doing a job, we get the credit when it's completed. But if a task goes beyond our abilities and we call on God to help us accomplish it, He gets the glory! He lives to give love and to receive glory. When we find ourselves in an impossible situation, we can smile, knowing He will show up whenever we call.

*Dear Father, thank You for the reminder that I can do all things, not through
my own strength, but through Christ, who strengthens me. Amen.*

morning
A LIFE OF FAITH

By faith Noah, being warned by God concerning events as yet unseen, in reverent fear constructed an ark for the saving of his household. By this he condemned the world and became an heir of the righteousness that comes by faith.

HEBREWS 11:7 ESV

A life of faith requires foresight. It requires a belief in God's goodness that's even stronger than the belief in the here and now. Noah knew God loved him and that God must have His reasons for telling him to build an ark. He trusted God, and he obeyed. Because his faith was backed up with obedience, even when others called him a fool, Noah and his family were saved.

Dear Father, I trust You, and I believe in Your goodness. Help me to act in faith, even when others don't understand. Amen.

evening
OVERCOMERS

For everyone who has been born of God overcomes the world. And this is the victory that has overcome the world—our faith.

1 JOHN 5:4 ESV

God wants each and every one of His children to be winners. He wants us to be overcomers in this life. He knows we're competing both as a team and as individuals, and He longs for each of us to walk through each day as victors. He's given us everything we need to be successful in every way that's important—and the main ingredient to that success is our faith. When we trust Him, believing with everything in us that we're on the winning team, we become overcomers.

Dear Father, thank You for making me an overcomer. My faith is in You and no one else. Amen.

INHERITANCE FROM THE LORD

morning

*You know that you will receive an inheritance from the Lord
as a reward. It is the Lord Christ you are serving.*

COLOSSIANS 3:24 NIV

We serve a Master who adores us! We must never forget, no matter what humans may say or do, that God sees, and He appreciates our hard work. It is Him we serve, and He has a great reward—an impressive inheritance—waiting for us. When we feel undervalued and taken advantage of, we must remember for whom we're really working. He sees, He knows, and He cares.

*Dear Father, thank You for the inheritance You've promised me.
You know it's unpleasant to feel unappreciated. Please place people
around me who will appreciate my contributions. Amen.*

LASTING PEACE

evening

*"Peace I leave with you; my peace I give to you. I do not give to you as the world
gives. Do not let your hearts be troubled, and do not let them be afraid."*

JOHN 14:27 NRSV

God gives the kind of peace that lasts and lasts. We can take it anywhere, access it anytime. We don't have to dream about it like some elusive, distant-future vacation package. It's right here, right now. And the best part about it? God's gift of peace is free. All we have to do is trust Him.

*Dear Father, thank You for Your gift of peace. Remind me that Your
peace is there, free for the taking, any time I choose to accept it. Amen.*

morning
BEHAVING BADLY

*Whoever brings trouble to his family will be left with nothing
but the wind. A fool will be a servant to the wise.*
PROVERBS 11:29 NCV

When families live in harmony with one another, good things occur. Relationships
are healthy and strong, and love abounds. We must remember, wherever we are and
whatever we do, our actions affect those who love us most. When we choose to live
righteous, upright lives, we bring honor and blessing to our families, our relationships,
and ourselves.

*Dear Father, forgive me for bad decisions I've made
that have affected the people I love the most. Help me to
honor them—and You—with my choices. Amen.*

evening
PAYING OUT KINDNESS

*"So whatever you wish that others would do to you,
do also to them, for this is the Law and the Prophets."*
MATTHEW 7:12 ESV

When we find ourselves frustrated because others don't treat us the way we want to
be treated, we should challenge ourselves to make a game of it. How can we treat the
other person the way we'd want to be treated? Often, this type of giving attitude causes
others to soften toward us and brings about the kind actions we desire for ourselves.
Even if that doesn't happen, we will experience much more peace and joy in our lives
by paying out kindness to others.

*Dear Father, help me treat others the way I want
them to treat me, even when it's hard. Amen.*

morning
NEVER ALONE

It is better to take refuge in the LORD than to trust in people.
PSALM 118:8 NASB

In God, we have a friend like no other. He will never leave us, forsake us, or fail us. We can pour out our deepest, most shameful secrets to Him and know He will never use that information against us. He loves us with perfect love and unfailing compassion.

When we feel alone, we can ask God to send us earthly friends. But we can also know that, no matter how alone we may feel, we don't have to be lonely. We have a Friend, and we can trust Him.

Dear Father, thank You for reminding me that I can always trust You, and I'm never alone. Amen.

evening
WHO YOU ARE

"I say to you, do not be worried about your life, as to what you will eat or what you will drink; nor for your body, as to what you will put on. Is not life more than food, and the body more than clothing? Look at the birds of the sky, that they do not sow, nor reap, nor gather crops into barns, and yet your heavenly Father feeds them. Are you not worth much more than they?"
MATTHEW 6:25–26 NASB

God takes care of all His creation, from birds to fish to plants. But we are more than just His creation. We are His children! When we feel anxious, we can remind ourselves who we are and how much He loves us.

Dear Father, thank You for taking care of me. Amen.

TIME, TALENT, TREASURE
morning

*Honor the LORD with your wealth and the firstfruits from all your crops.
Then your barns will be full, and your wine barrels will overflow with new wine.*
PROVERBS 3:9–10 NCV

Giving to God feels good. It changes something within us and creates a subtle shift in our values. We realize that going out to eat or buying that five-dollar coffee every day doesn't give us the fulfillment that generosity does. Giving to God may not put us on the Fortune 500 list, but it will give us something far better—a closeness with God that cannot be matched.

Dear Father, teach me to be generous. Amen.

JOY IN EVERY MOMENT
evening

*But the Pharisees went out and conspired against him, how
to destroy him. Jesus, aware of this, withdrew from there.
And many followed him, and he healed them all.*
MATTHEW 12:14-15 ESV

When an illness conspires to destroy us and threatens to take our lives, we can respond as Jesus did. Withdraw to God, and serve others. When we fall into God, our heavenly Father will embrace us—consume us, even—with a love that surpasses understanding. When we pour our lives into serving others—even to our last breath—we forget about ourselves, our hardships, and our pain, and we find joy in every moment.

*Dear Father, I love You. I want to pour myself into
You and into others. Show me how. Amen.*

morning
THE SEVENTH DAY

*Then God blessed the seventh day and made it holy, because on
it he rested from all the work of creating that he had done.*
GENESIS 2:3 NIV

When we don't work hard, our rest isn't as fulfilling. When we don't work hard, the reward seems shallow. God rested because He was *finished.* He was *fulfilled.* He was *satisfied* with a job well done. Since we are made in His image, He wants us to know the same satisfaction and fulfillment that comes from being bone-weary after a successful, diligent workweek.

When we labor with our full energy and commitment, God blesses our efforts. He gives us rest, and that kind of rest brings contentment, gratification, and true pleasure.

Dear Father, teach me what it means to work hard. Amen.

evening
GOD'S PROTECTION

"Every word of God is flawless; he is a shield to those who take refuge in him."
PROVERBS 30:5 NIV

Trusting God is the key to receiving His protection. We all want God to keep us safe and happy, but trust can be difficult. When we fail to trust God, we drop our shields and put ourselves in peril. If we want God's protection from the enemy's darts, we must remain strong in our resolve to trust God.

*Dear Father, trust, like a shield, can be heavy and difficult. Sometimes
it's tempting to trust myself or something else, but I know that's like
dropping my shield. Help me to trust You even when it's hard. Amen.*

morning
POWERFUL STUFF

For I am convinced that neither death nor life, neither angels nor demons, neither the present nor the future, nor any powers, neither height nor depth, nor anything else in all creation, will be able to separate us from the love of God that is in Christ Jesus our Lord.

ROMANS 8:38–39 NIV

God's love won't budge an inch! No matter what situation we may find ourselves in, we can know God's love is with us. It surrounds us on all sides. When we accept Christ as our Savior, the deal is sealed. He will never, ever remove His love from us.

That's pretty powerful stuff.

*Dear Father, thank You for Your love that will
never leave me, no matter what. Amen.*

evening
MUSTARD SEED

"For truly, I say to you, if you have faith like a grain of mustard seed, you will say to this mountain, 'Move from here to there,' and it will move, and nothing will be impossible for you."

MATTHEW 17:20 ESV

We may feel that our faith is small and weak. But given a chance, it will take root and expand into something too big to be contained in our own souls. It will grow so large, in fact, that we must move outside our comfortable boundaries. If we have even a tiny amount of faith, drop it. Let it take root. Watch and see the miracles that grow from such humble beginnings.

*Dear Father, I place my tiny amount of faith in You. I trust You to cause it
to take root and grow into something strong and miraculous. Amen.*

morning
A HEAVY LOAD

"Come to me, all you who are weary and burdened, and I will give you rest. Take my yoke upon you and learn from me, for I am gentle and humble in heart, and you will find rest for your souls. For my yoke is easy and my burden is light."
MATTHEW 11:28–30 NIV

Some might say life is filled with hardship, and they would be correct. But the fact that life is long is also a blessing, because at every turn we find new opportunities, new chances, and new beginnings. With each step, God offers to take our hefty loads and replace them with tranquility, peace, and joy.

*Dear Father, I'm carrying such a heavy load right now.
Please take it from me and give me rest. Amen.*

evening
CLING TO HOPE

Bitterly she weeps at night, tears are on her cheeks. Among all her lovers there is no one to comfort her. All her friends have betrayed her; they have become her enemies.
LAMENTATIONS 1:2 NIV

Have you ever felt abandoned and forgotten? We don't need to feel that way, because God is a God of hope, and hope is the opposite of fear. Fear is a belief that something bad will happen, and hope is the belief that something good will happen. As long as we have God, we have hope, because He never, ever runs out of goodness.

Dear Father, right now it feels like nothing will ever be better. Yet I will cling to the belief that You have good things in store for my life. Amen.

morning
HEAVEN ON EARTH

*One thing have I asked of the LORD, that I will seek after: that I
may dwell in the house of the LORD all the days of my life, to gaze
upon the beauty of the LORD and to inquire in his temple.*
PSALM 27:4 ESV

While we can't duplicate heaven on earth, that should always be our goal. When we speak gently, when we love boundlessly, when we do all we can to live at peace with those in our household, we create a little haven, a piece of heaven on earth. Showing love and acceptance to those who don't live up to our standards is hard. . .yet that's what God does every time He looks at us.

*Dear Father, help me create a bit of heaven on
earth. I want to love like You love. Amen.*

evening
BE AN ENCOURAGER

Encourage one another.
HEBREWS 10:25 NLT

God wants to take us to a place beyond ourselves. He wants us to live on a higher plane. When we surrender to His will for our lives and say, "I can't do it, God, but I know You can," He works miracles. He changes our hearts, and He often changes the hearts of those around us. Often, that change begins with an encouraging word to another person, even when it's the last thing we want to do. When we encourage others, God begins a cycle of love that will come back to us many times over.

Dear Father, help me be an encourager! Amen.

morning
ALL MY NEEDS

*And my God will supply all your needs according
to His riches in glory in Christ Jesus.*
PHILIPPIANS 4:19 NASB

When we have a need, we should tell God about it, and then leave it with Him. Our lives become a beautiful, exciting treasure hunt when we make our requests known with full confidence that He'll deliver. He is God. He will provide. And when He does, it will be more than we need.

*Dear Father, forgive me for worrying about my needs.
I know You will provide, and I trust You. Amen.*

evening
BLESSINGS, NOW AND THEN

*He brought them forth also with silver and gold: and there
was not one feeble person among their tribes.*
PSALM 105:37 KJV

God wants to bless us today. He sent His Son, Jesus, so we could have abundant life. But the blessings of eternity are so much greater than anything we can imagine in the here and now. When God doesn't choose to answer our prayers for more money or replenished health, He's not ignoring our requests. He's just answering them differently. When we join His presence in heaven, we will have silver and gold, and there will not be one feeble person among us.

*Dear Father, thank You for the blessings You give me in this life.
Remind me of the blessings that await me in eternity. Amen.*

SURROUNDED BY COMFORT
morning

Praise be to the God and Father of our Lord Jesus Christ, the Father of compassion and the God of all comfort, who comforts us in all our troubles, so that we can comfort those in any trouble with the comfort we ourselves receive from God.

2 CORINTHIANS 1:3–4 NIV

We are God's messengers on this earth. Because He cares for us so tenderly, He wants us to turn around and care for others. We are to offer comfort and compassion to people who are hurting. When we do that, the blessings are twofold. The people we comfort receive a taste of God's goodness, and we are comforted as well! God knows that when we focus our hearts on caring for others, we forget our own troubles for a time.

*Dear Father, thank You for Your comfort. Help
me comfort others in need. Amen.*

CONFIDENCE IN THE PROVIDER
evening

"But blessed is the one who trusts in the LORD, whose confidence is in him. They will be like a tree planted by the water that sends out its roots by the stream. It does not fear when heat comes; its leaves are always green. It has no worries in a year of drought and never fails to bear fruit."

JEREMIAH 17:7–8 NIV

We all go through times of financial drought. These are the times we have more money going out than coming in. During a drought, our first instinct is often to worry and stress about the future.

But blessed are those who trust in the Lord, who've made the Lord their hope and confidence. Who needs the rain when we have God? When we are firmly positioned in Him—and in His Word and His promises—we have a source that goes deep and will never run dry.

*Dear Father, when it comes to my finances—and everything else
in my life—I place all my hope and confidence in You. Amen.*

morning
HIGHER WAYS

We work hard with our own hands. When we are cursed,
we bless; when we are persecuted, we endure it.
1 CORINTHIANS 4:12 NIV

God's ways are higher than our ways. Though His wisdom may seem unnatural, it will always lead to more peace and more satisfaction in our lives. God sees everything, and He will take vengeance on the unjust. He doesn't want us to concern ourselves with that. He wants us to return hate with love. He wants us to return cruelty with kindness. And God, who knows all, will reward our consistent hard work and purity of heart, and bring about much better justice than we could imagine.

Dear Father, please help me to work hard and show humility.
I trust You to take care of injustice as You see fit. Amen.

evening
STAYING CLOSE

The LORD is close to the brokenhearted and saves those who
are crushed in spirit. The righteous person may have many
troubles, but the LORD delivers him from them all.
PSALM 34:18–19 NIV

God's Word never promises an easy life. Trouble will follow us, whether we live for God or not. We are assured, however, that if we follow God, and if we live for Him, He will never leave us to trudge through our hardships alone. When we feel lonely, we can simply breathe in. His presence is right there, filling every breath, pounding with every heartbeat. He will walk with us each painful step of the way, and He will deliver us to a place of hope and joy and peace.

Dear Father, thank You for staying close to me.
Help me feel Your presence. Amen.

morning
CHRIST IS FOR US

You, Lord, took up my case; you redeemed my life.
LAMENTATIONS 3:58 NIV

Though circumstances may threaten to overwhelm us, we can relax, for God is both lawyer and judge. He loves us. He is always for us, never against us. It doesn't matter what kind of trouble we're in or how we got into our current situation. He has our ultimate good as His goal, and He works tirelessly to bring about His beautiful purpose in our lives.

Dear Father, thank You for this reminder that You are my advocate. You have taken up my case, and You are working right now on my behalf. I trust You, and I know that somehow You will redeem this situation for my good and for Your purpose. Amen.

evening
HEART-GIVING

Give generously to them and do so without a grudging heart; then because of this the LORD your God will bless you in all your work and in everything you put your hand to.
DEUTERONOMY 15:10 NIV

God doesn't need our money. He *wants* our hearts. When we take joy in whatever we give to God, He is delighted. When we give generously to Him, with love and excitement over the gift, He will bless us.

Dear Father, I may not have much to give, but I want to give everything I can. I love You. Amen.

morning
DRAW NEAR. . .

*Let us then with confidence draw near to the throne of grace, that
we may receive mercy and find grace to help in time of need.*
HEBREWS 4:16 ESV

When our faith needs strengthening, all we need to do is draw near to God. We'll find the confidence we need, along with every bit of mercy and grace to see us through each day, when we stand as close as we can to our Father.

We draw near by reading His Word, praying, and listening for His response. When we consistently do those things, we'll find our faith is strong, and we feel the peace and inner joy He promised.

*Dear Father, forgive me for ever leaving Your side. I want to draw near to
You. Thank You for always welcoming me into Your presence. Amen.*

evening
GOOD THINGS

*That is why we labor and strive, because we have put our hope in the living
God, who is the Savior of all people, and especially of those who believe.*
1 TIMOTHY 4:10 NIV

When we have Christ, we have hope. We have the internal assurance that no matter how bad things get, good things are on the way! God loves us, and He is always working on our behalf to give us hope, peace, and joy. And at the end of it all, we will have eternal life in His presence.

Because of this hope, we can keep going. We can keep working, striving, and pressing on. No matter what happens today, we can know beyond doubt that good things are on the way.

*Dear Father, thank You for the promise of
good things. Thank You for hope. Amen.*

morning
THE POWER OF "IF"

*Jesus replied, "Listen to the truth. If you do not doubt God's power
and speak out of faith's fullness, you can also speak to a tree and it will
wither away. Even more than that, you could say to this mountain,
'Be lifted up and be thrown into the sea' and it will be done. Everything
you pray for with the fullness of faith you will receive!"*

MATTHEW 21:21–22 TPT

If you choose to believe in the Lord's promise and embrace His authority in your
situation, and *if* you command in His name, your faith has the capacity to shift things.

Pray with fervor when you need God's help, and then decide to believe God hears
you and will show up. Why? Because your faith matters to the Father, and He will
bless you for it.

*Father, please increase my faith in the power of "if," believing that it allows
me to tap into Your strength and power. In Jesus' name I pray, amen.*

evening
YOU'RE INVITED

*Now on the final and most important day of the Feast, Jesus stood,
and He cried in a loud voice, If any man is thirsty, let him come to
Me and drink! He who believes in Me [who cleaves to and trusts in
and relies on Me] as the Scripture has said, From his innermost being
shall flow [continuously] springs and rivers of living water.*

JOHN 7:37–38 AMPC

In this crazy world, how wonderful to know we have a God who sees us right where
we are. How amazing to commune with a God who offers to quench a thirst that only
He can satisfy. When you choose to cling to God, trust His will and ways and rely on
Him for the outcome. You will find peace, strength, and wisdom.

*Father, what a privilege to be called into a relationship with You! Thank You
for inviting me into community. I energetically say yes, and I ask that You help
me believe in Your promises and trust in them. In Jesus' name I pray, amen.*

morning
PRAYING WITH GREAT FAITH

*I pray with great faith for you, because I'm fully convinced that the
One who began this gracious work in you will faithfully continue the
process of maturing you until the unveiling of our Lord Jesus Christ!*

PHILIPPIANS 1:6 TPT

What if the words you spoke about a difficult circumstance revealed no reservation, and instead pointed to the unwavering trust you had in God? What if you shut down any skeptical or worrisome thoughts by opening the Bible to belief-building scriptures? You know, even a small step in the direction of faith yields big results in God's economy. And every time you say yes and believe, the Lord will honor it.

*Father, help me be the kind of woman that prays with great faith. Give
me the courage to trust in You when something seems impossible. I
know the Word says You always keep Your promises, but sometimes
doubt creeps in. Help my unbelief. In Jesus' name I pray. Amen.*

evening
YOUR RESPONSE IS FAITH

*"This is how much God loved the world: He gave his Son, his one
and only Son. And this is why: so that no one need be destroyed; by
believing in him, anyone can have a whole and lasting life."*

JOHN 3:16 MSG

Friend, faith is your response to God's selfless gift of His Son. You don't need a boatload of belief to walk this out. You don't have to be a pillar of faith or have your life cleaned up. There's nothing you can do to make yourself sinless. It's not up to you to earn your way into heaven. What is required of you is enough faith to believe Jesus gave His life at the Father's request to erase your sin. That small *yes* is a seed of faith He will grow daily.

*Father, thank You for Jesus. I'm so grateful I don't have
to find a way to earn an eternity with You. Help my faith
continue to grow in You! In Jesus' name I pray, amen.*

morning
WHAT WILL THEY SAY ABOUT YOUR FAITH?

And now the time is fast approaching for my release from this life and I am ready to be offered as a sacrifice. I have fought an excellent fight. I have finished my full course with all my might and I've kept my heart full of faith.
2 TIMOTHY 4:6–7 TPT

You only get one shot at this, and life really is just a breath. This is the time to let your light shine so God is glorified by your words and actions. What better legacy to leave those you love than one of steadfast faith? You get to choose what kind of inheritance you pass on. Let's choose to be women who will be remembered for their excellent fight, for finishing the race set before us, and for having a heart full of faith.

Father, help me be so full of faith that I will be able to influence others for You. In Jesus' name I pray, amen.

evening
THE POWER THAT BRINGS THE WORLD TO ITS KNEES

Every God-born person conquers the world's ways. The conquering power that brings the world to its knees is our faith. The person who wins out over the world's ways is simply the one who believes Jesus is the Son of God.
1 JOHN 5:4–5 MSG

If you are a child of God—if you've asked Jesus to be your personal Lord and Savior—then you are a force to be reckoned with. You're backed by the God of creation who has made a way for victory through the death of His Son on the cross. It's your belief in Him that gives you strength and might to weather the storms of life. It may be rough at times, but you won't be defeated if you trust God through it. So chin up, buttercup, because your faith enables you to win against anything the world throws your way.

Father, thank You for making a way to find victory in a world bent on trying to destroy. I am choosing to stand in that power today! In Jesus' name I pray, amen.

morning
RIGHT IN THE MIDDLE

*I pray that God, the source of all hope, will infuse your lives with
an abundance of joy and peace in the midst of your faith so that
your hope will overflow through the power of the Holy Spirit.*
ROMANS 15:13 VOICE

Be encouraged by this verse from Romans. It shows us that we can pray for God's help when we find ourselves in the messy middle. As we continue to put one foot of faith after the other, taking the next step toward reconciliation, we can ask God to infuse us with abundance. You can ask for joy, peace, and hope. And it's your belief in His ability—be it big or small—that opens the door for the Holy Spirit to flood you with exactly what you need to keep going.

*Father, I'm right in the middle of a hard season and in desperate need of
encouragement that things will get better and I will get through it. Please
infuse me with Your hope, joy, and peace. In Jesus' name I pray, amen.*

evening
HOW TO FIGHT THE GOOD FIGHT

*Timothy, don't let this happen to you—run away from these things! You are a
man of God. Your quest is for justice, godliness, faithfulness, love, perseverance,
and gentleness. Fight the good fight of the faith! Cling to the eternal life you
were called to when you confessed the good confession before witnesses.*
1 TIMOTHY 6:11–12 VOICE

We are to pursue and serve the Lord with our lives. We're to trust Him to grow the fruit of the Spirit in us so we can love those around us. And we are to trust God, building our faith in His will and ways every day. These are the ways we fight the good fight, friend! This is how we point others to God in heaven!

*Father, let me never give up pursuing Your will in my life. And bless me
with the desire to love You with all my heart. In Jesus' name I pray, amen.*

morning
A BEAUTIFUL FUTURE

"For I know the plans I have for you," says the Eternal, "plans for peace, not evil, to give you a future and hope—never forget that. At that time, you will call out for Me, and I will hear. You will pray, and I will listen. You will look for Me intently, and you will find Me."
JEREMIAH 29:11–13 VOICE

Every morning, welcome the Lord into the details of your day. Ask for an increase in faith to hear and see Him. Invite God into your hopelessness and fear, and share your deepest concerns. Tell Him you need encouragement to know He hasn't forgotten you. And maybe ask God to remind you of the value you hold in His eyes. We all need reassurance that He is trustworthy and that He has plans for our beautiful future.

Father, help me trust You with what's ahead, knowing Your heart for me is always good. In Jesus' name I pray, amen.

evening
CONSISTENT FAITH

And Jesus, replying, said to them, Have faith in God [constantly].
MARK 11:22 AMPC

At the end of the day, all you really have is the Lord. You may have a great support system who loves you dearly, but they are not your savior. You might have a full calendar to keep your mind occupied, but that can't heal your heart. Remember that you have God, and He is always in your corner. When you choose to constantly trust Him with anything and everything, you will have all you need to walk out this life well.

Father, sometimes I feel overwhelmed with my life, and I try to fix it myself. I rely on me. And it's later that I remember You. Forgive me for that, and help me run to You first. In Jesus' name I pray, amen.

morning
PEACE FOR TRUSTING

You will keep the peace, a perfect peace, for all who trust in You, for those who
dedicate their hearts and minds to You. So trust in the Eternal One forever,
for He is like a great Rock—strong, stable, trustworthy, and lasting.
ISAIAH 26:3–4 VOICE

The Lord will never leave you hopeless or helpless when you need Him. God is a stabilizing force when the ground under you begins to shake with worry or fear. He is faithful to fulfill every promise and stand by you through every messy moment. Even more, God's unwavering love for you is forever and for always. Your faith in Him unlocks endless gifts and blessings. He is always ready and able to help.

Father, what a relief to know that You will reward my trust
in You with peace for me. In Jesus' name I pray, amen.

evening
DEEPLY ROOTED

Happy are those who trust in the LORD, who rely on the LORD. They will
be like trees planted by the streams, whose roots reach down to the water.
They won't fear drought when it comes; their leaves will remain green.
They won't be stressed in the time of drought or fail to bear fruit.
JEREMIAH 17:7–8 CEB

If you surrender control and trust the Lord instead, you will find happiness. Your roots of faith will go down so deep that nothing will sway you. Happiness and joy cannot be stolen, because they're firmly planted in your heart. Be it in a valley or on a mountaintop, in abundance or in lacking, you won't be on an emotional roller coaster. It's God's hand through your faith that will keep you steady.

Father, help me trust in You above all else. Grow my roots of faith
deep in the soil of Your goodness! In Jesus' name I pray, amen.

TRUSTING HIM OVER *morning* THE WORLD

*See those people polishing their chariots, and those others grooming their
horses? But we're making garlands for GOD our God. The chariots will
rust, those horses pull up lame—and we'll be on our feet, standing tall.*

PSALM 20:7–8 MSG

Anchor your faith to the Lord. Let Him be what you hold on to when life throws a
curve ball. God is always dependable and trustworthy and will never fail you. He is
faithful every day and in every way. And when you believe His promises to save and
heal, you won't be let down.

*Father, help me remember the world has nothing reliable for me
to hold on to. Give me the right perspective, so I don't put my hope
in things that cannot deliver. I want to trust You over the world.
I want my faith to rest in You alone. In Jesus' name I pray, amen.*

evening FAITH SUPPORTED

*Meanwhile, the moment we get tired in the waiting, God's Spirit is right alongside
helping us along. If we don't know how or what to pray, it doesn't matter. He
does our praying in and for us, making prayer out of our wordless sighs, our
aching groans. He knows us far better than we know ourselves, knows our
pregnant condition, and keeps us present before God. That's why we can be so
sure that every detail in our lives of love for God is worked into something good.*

ROMANS 8:26–28 MSG

Your faith is supported—always has been and always will be. Consider it a group
effort with heaven. And no matter the size of your faith, the Holy Spirit makes up the
difference. Let this truth seep into the nooks and crannies of your heart when you feel
like your faith isn't good enough.

*Father, thank You for the Holy Spirit being
active in my life! In Jesus' name I pray, amen.*

AN INVITATION TO KNOW HIM BETTER

morning

*He who deals wisely and heeds [God's] word and counsel shall
find good, and whoever leans on, trusts in, and is confident
in the Lord—happy, blessed, and fortunate is he.*
PROVERBS 16:20 AMPC

When you let the Bible guide your steps, your faith grows deep roots as you learn about the God you serve. Heeding the counsel in its pages enriches your life on every level. And it not only pleases the Lord, but it brings you a lasting happiness able to withstand even the toughest storms that may come your way. Let faith be your driving force as you navigate the challenges of life.

*Father, thank You for the Word. I'm so grateful to have a tangible
reminder of Your faithfulness. Let it be my go-to resource for righteous
living, the place I find truth and instruction every time I open its
pages. Use it to grow my faith! In Jesus' name I pray, amen.*

UNCHANGING

Jesus the Anointed One is always the same: yesterday, today, and forever.
HEBREWS 13:8 VOICE

How wonderful to know that God is the same yesterday, today, and will be tomorrow, providing stability. It means that His love for you isn't conditional. His plans for your life aren't shakable. His ability to intervene isn't affected by anything or anyone. His sovereignty can't be removed. And God's mood is unaffected by the state of the world. It means you can anchor your faith in the Lord with confidence, knowing He is trustworthy in every aspect of your relationship with Him.

*Father, thank You for providing stability in an ever-changing world.
Thank You for being a safe place for my heart. In Jesus' name I pray, amen.*

morning
STARTING WITH FAITH

Make me hear of Your faithful love in the morning, for I trust in You.
Teach me how I should walk, for I offer my soul up to You.
PSALM 143:8 VOICE

We all know that what you do in the morning sets the tone for the day. It matters. And when you get right with God before the busyness starts, you are making the wise choice of setting yourself up for goodness! It's a decision to activate your faith as a shield of protection for what the day may bring. And the Lord will honor that decision in ways you can't even imagine! Rise and shine and choose to start with faith.

Father, remind me as I wake up each morning to get my
heart right with You. In Jesus' name I pray, amen.

evening
BOLD AND FREE

My purpose in writing is simply this: that you who believe in God's Son will
know beyond the shadow of a doubt that you have eternal life, the reality and
not the illusion. And how bold and free we then become in his presence, freely
asking according to his will, sure that he's listening. And if we're confident
that he's listening, we know that what we've asked for is as good as ours.
1 JOHN 5:13–15 MSG

Friend, go ahead and dream big. Boldly ask for what your heart desires. No request is too large, too small, or too weird. You can have confident faith that God hears your prayers. He is always listening. And because He knows what's best for you, He responds accordingly. Your job is to ask away and then trust His answer is the best, because the Lord's heart for you is always good.

Father, thanks for the freedom to pray bold
and big! In Jesus' name I pray, amen.

morning
UNSHAPED BY THE WORLD

*Don't become so well-adjusted to your culture that you fit into it without even
thinking. Instead, fix your attention on God. You'll be changed from the inside
out. Readily recognize what he wants from you, and quickly respond to it. Unlike
the culture around you, always dragging you down to its level of immaturity,
God brings the best out of you, develops well-formed maturity in you.*

ROMANS 12:2 MSG

For us to walk out our faith in God. . .for us to discern what His will is for our life. . .we
have to keep our hearts turned toward Him. We must train our minds to stay focused
on His promises. And when we do, we'll know what is good and pleasing to the Lord,
and it will bring out the best in us.

*Father, I want only You to have influence over
my life. In Jesus' name I pray, amen.*

evening
HIS PROMISE IN THE STORMY SEAS

*When you face stormy seas I will be there with you with endurance and calm;
you will not be engulfed in raging rivers. If it seems like you're walking through
fire with flames licking at your limbs, keep going; you won't be burned.*

ISAIAH 43:2 VOICE

Know without a doubt God is closer than your next breath. And it's His presence that
will give you endurance for the stormy waters and a sense of calm as you navigate
through them. God promises that you won't get caught in the undertow of the struggles
you're facing. You won't get pulled underwater because of your problems. Instead, He
will reward your faith by making sure you have everything you need to come out the
other side with joy, hope, and strength.

*Father, I am so thankful for Your availability. What a gift to know no
matter what I'm facing, You've got me. In Jesus' name I pray, amen.*

morning
MORE THAN ENOUGH

*Yahweh is my best friend and my shepherd. I always have more than enough.
He offers a resting place for me in his luxurious love. His tracks take me
to an oasis of peace near the quiet brook of bliss. That's where he restores
and revives my life. He opens before me the right path and leads me along
in his footsteps of righteousness so that I can bring honor to his name.*

PSALM 23:1–3 TPT

The psalmist chose to trust God. Seeing Him as a friend and shepherd gave him faith to follow His leading, and they experienced rest, peace, bliss, restoration, revival, and a sweet relationship along the way. He had more than enough to convince him of God's trustworthiness. Why not let the Lord be your guide?

*Father, please be my shepherd and leader. Sustain and restore me each
day, showing me how to live in a right relationship with You. Guide me as I
navigate the challenges and joys coming my way. In Jesus' name I pray, amen.*

evening
ROLL YOUR WORKS

*Roll your works upon the Lord [commit and trust them wholly
to Him; He will cause your thoughts to become agreeable to His
will, and] so shall your plans be established and succeed.*

PROVERBS 16:3 AMPC

When your dreams include a desire to hear God's leading, the Word says He will supernaturally cause your thoughts to match up with His will. You won't go rogue, satisfying the fleshly hopes of your humanity. Instead, you will let the Lord transform your plans to align with His will, and He will then establish them and bring success. This is faith in action!

*Father, there are so many ideas for my future that I'm chewing on
but will now bring them to You for direction. Give me the ears to hear
Your voice. Thank You for being interested, and for helping me solidify
and secure them with Your favor! In Jesus' name I pray, amen.*

VICTORY ON THE *morning* OTHER SIDE

*Blessed [happy, spiritually prosperous, favored by God] is the man
who is steadfast under trial and perseveres when tempted; for when
he has passed the test and been approved, he will receive the [victor's]
crown of life which the Lord has promised to those who love Him.*

JAMES 1:12 AMP

When you're steadfast and persevere in those hard moments, holding on to your belief that you can make it through with the Lord's help, you'll find a blessing waiting. Knowing God is for you and working all things for your good creates happiness. Faith makes you favored by Him. And your unwavering trust comes with a promise of victory on the other side.

*Father, I appreciate that You offer incentives to those who
choose to trust You in the hard moments. I love knowing my
obedience is not only recognized, but also rewarded. Help me
see the bigger picture of faith. In Jesus' name I pray, amen.*

WHITE KNUCKLE *evening* YOUR FREEDOM

*At last we have freedom, for Christ has set us free! We must always cherish
this truth and firmly refuse to go back into the bondage of our past.*

GALATIANS 5:1 TPT

God is challenging you to white knuckle the freedom you've received. Sometimes we have to hold it with all we've got. We have to believe it's ours for the taking, activating our faith to access His strength so we can walk it out. What a beautiful gift you've been given. Don't let anyone—not even yourself—take it away.

*Father, thank You for the gift of freedom through Your Son. Too
often I forget, or I feel unworthy of it, so I choose to stay trapped in
my fear and insecurities. It keeps me from living my best life, and I
lose out on experiencing Your goodness. Give me courage to fully
accept the freedom You have for me! In Jesus' name I pray, amen.*

morning
A FAITH-BUILDER

Let the words from the book of the law be always on your lips. Meditate on them day and night so that you may be careful to live by all that is written in it. If you do, as you make your way through this world, you will prosper and always find success. This is My command: be strong and courageous. Never be afraid or discouraged because I am your God, the Eternal One, and I will remain with you wherever you go.

JOSHUA 1:8–9 VOICE

The Lord's desire is to walk through life with you. Reading His Word helps you recognize His will and plan created just for you. The more you know God, the stronger and more courageous you'll feel, because His promises will be on your heart.

Father, thank You for encouraging me to know Your Word in my heart. It's power-packed with faith-building encouragement. . . just what I need. In Jesus' name I pray, amen.

evening
HE WILL ALWAYS BE THERE

So who can separate us? What can come between us and the love of God's Anointed? Can troubles, hardships, persecution, hunger, poverty, danger, or even death? The answer is, absolutely nothing. As the psalm says, On Your behalf, our lives are endangered constantly; we are like sheep awaiting slaughter. But no matter what comes, we will always taste victory through Him who loved us.

ROMANS 8:35–37 VOICE

Here's good news for a broken heart: There's nothing you can do to make God break up with you. You're incapable of making Him walk away. Whether you're a hot mess or all put together, you're adored. And when you think you don't fit in, remember you're perfect in His eyes. Ask Him for the faith to believe it.

Father, what a relief to know there's nothing I can be or do that will separate me from You. In Jesus' name I pray, amen.

morning
TRANSFERRED AND GUARANTEED

Our faith in Jesus transfers God's righteousness to us and he now declares us flawless in his eyes. . . . What incredible joy bursts forth within us as we keep on celebrating our hope of experiencing God's glory!

ROMANS 5:1–2 TPT

How cool is it that when you choose to believe Jesus is the Son of God and died for your sins, that act of belief transfers the righteousness of God onto you? In other words, your faith has made you flawless to the Father.

In a world filled with heartache and pain, let this be a source of joy. Grab hold of these promises and let them fuel your hope. Embrace your faith so you can find peace and comfort no matter what may come your way.

Father, I love that my choice to believe in Jesus opens up a beautiful life of faith for me. Help me live in that victory every moment of every day, trusting You to meet my needs. In Jesus' name I pray, amen.

evening
THE DOMINO EFFECT

Even in times of trouble we have a joyful confidence, knowing that our pressures will develop in us patient endurance. And patient endurance will refine our character, and proven character leads us back to hope. And this hope is not a disappointing fantasy, because we can now experience the endless love of God cascading into our hearts through the Holy Spirit who lives in us!

ROMANS 5:3–5 TPT

Notice the domino effect in today's verse as one choice builds on the next. When you decide to go all-in with the Lord, something beautiful happens. He promises to use everything in your life for His glory and your benefit. He wastes no opportunity to grow you into the faith-filled woman He created you to be. And if you'll allow it, pressures result in endurance that will refine your character and lead you back to hope.

Father, what a privilege to have You constantly refining me and my faith. Thank You! In Jesus' name I pray, amen.

morning
BOLD PRAYERS

*LORD, part your skies and come down! Touch the mountains so they
smoke! Flash lightning and scatter the enemy! Shoot your arrows and
defeat them! Stretch out your hand from above! Rescue me and deliver
me from deep water, from the power of strangers, whose mouths
speak lies, and whose strong hand is a strong hand of deception!*
PSALM 144:5–8 CEB

Can you imagine the confidence a prayer like this would take? Friend, you don't have to pray soft and sweet prayers using flowery words. Your prayers don't have to follow a formula or sound lofty. You have the freedom to pray bold prayers full of passionate pleas. You can share what is on your mind. And you can ask for anything. God already knows the depths of your heart, but He wants to hear from you. Take that step of faith and talk to the Lord with complete transparency. Nothing you say or share will ever change the way He feels about you.

*Father, thank You for letting me be honest
with You! In Jesus' name I pray, amen.*

evening
SOMETHING TO SING ABOUT

*For God's Word is something to sing about! He is true to his
promises, his word can be trusted, and everything he does is reliable
and right. The Lord loves seeing justice on the earth. Anywhere
and everywhere you can find his faithful, unfailing love!*
PSALM 33:4–5 TPT

The promises of God are worth humming a tune or singing at the top of your lungs. They are worthy of our trust, because the Word tells us of His reliability. In other words, God will do what He says He will do. The Lord is just, which means He is fair—which means His promises and commandments apply to everyone. We're equally loved and favored. And knowing this helps to grow our faith as we choose to believe God Himself is faithful and trustworthy.

*Father, let me sing Your goodness every day. Let Your promises always be on
my lips. Thank You for being faithful and kind. In Jesus' name I pray, amen.*

morning
BENEFITS OF LOVING BIG

*When you live a life of abandoned love, surrendered before
the awe of God, here's what you'll experience: Abundant life.
Continual protection. And complete satisfaction!*
PROVERBS 19:23 TPT

Let the Lord feel your abundant appreciation for all He's done. Make sure He knows the depths of your reverence for who He is. Be quick to share God-moments with others, giving Him due credit for intervening. Don't let a day pass without sharing your thankfulness as He meets your every need, every time. This will not only set you up for blessings, but it will also supernaturally increase your faith. Remembering His goodness trains us to trust He will do it again.

Father, I see the ways You've intersected with my life, and I am so grateful for it. I love You big, and I wanted to make sure You knew it. I don't just love You for what You've done. I love You for who You are. In Jesus' name I pray, amen.

evening
SLEEP LIKE A BABY

You will sleep like a baby, safe and sound—your rest will be sweet and secure. You will not be subject to terror, for it will not terrify you. Nor will the disrespectful be able to push you aside, because God is your confidence in times of crisis, keeping your heart at rest in every situation.
PROVERBS 3:24–26 TPT

God is here with you, ready to hear what's heavy on your heart. He knows every detail about those things keeping you stirred up. He understands the complexity of them and how they intersect with your life. Even more, God has the ability to calm your anxious heart and comfort you. Tell Him what's bothering you, and then sleep like a baby.

Father, it's the middle of the night when I can't shut my mind off. In my fear, I predict horrible outcomes and endings that leave me feeling hopeless and fearful. Please comfort me. In Jesus' name I pray, amen.

morning
YOU ARE KNOWN

*For You shaped me, inside and out. You knitted me together in my
mother's womb long before I took my first breath. I will offer You my
grateful heart, for I am Your unique creation, filled with wonder and
awe. You have approached even the smallest details with excellence; Your
works are wonderful; I carry this knowledge deep within my soul.*
PSALM 139:13–15 VOICE

Friend, since He has been a hands-on God to you from the start, it should bolster your confidence in who He can be for you today. It should make your faith in Him blossom. It should shatter every barrier that keeps you from fully trusting God's hand in your life. You are known and loved. Invite Him into the details of today.

*Father, I'm so grateful You know every detail of me. You took
time to create me. Let that increase my faith and build a beautiful
relationship of trust in You! In Jesus' name I pray, amen.*

evening
BE BLESSED

*Blessed are the meek and gentle—they will inherit the earth. Blessed are those
who hunger and thirst for righteousness—they will be filled. Blessed are the
merciful—they will be shown mercy. Blessed are those who are pure in heart—they
will see God. Blessed are the peacemakers—they will be called children of God.*
MATTHEW 5:5–9 VOICE

When you choose to be gentle, seek righteous living, show mercy, or purpose to be pure and try to live at peace whenever possible, extraordinary blessings occur. Go back and reread the verses from Matthew 5 to see what each choice yields. Which one affirms you the most? Which one challenges you the most? Then talk to God about it.

*Father, what a great reminder that obedience comes with a blessing.
Thank You for rewarding the things that matter the most instead of
the things of little value to the Kingdom. You are a blessing to me!
Help me be a blessing to others! In Jesus' name I pray, amen.*

morning
LIVING DIFFERENTLY

*Let all bitterness and wrath and anger and clamor [perpetual animosity,
resentment, strife, fault-finding] and slander be put away from you, along with
every kind of malice [all spitefulness, verbal abuse, malevolence]. Be kind and
helpful to one another, tender-hearted [compassionate, understanding], forgiving
one another [readily and freely], just as God in Christ also forgave you.*
EPHESIANS 4:31–32 AMP

A byproduct of faith is a desire to live and love differently. It's setting aside the ways
you used to operate and embracing the ways of God. It's an intentional decision to see
the world through the lens of love and grace. How do you get there? Start by investing
time in your relationship with the Lord. That's where heart transformation begins.
Then continue to choose God's way—like in today's verse—every chance you get.

*Father, I am committed to growing in my relationship with You. I want my
words and actions to point to You in heaven. In Jesus' name I pray, amen.*

evening
THE CONNECTION BETWEEN
OUR HEART AND OUR WORDS

*If you put yourself on a pedestal, thinking you have become a role model
in all things religious, but you can't control your mouth, then think
again. Your mouth exposes your heart, and your religion is useless.*
JAMES 1:26 VOICE

If we are full of love, we will speak lovely things. If we're full of faith, it will show in
our words. If we're full of compassion, it will be evident in how we respond. There is a
weighty connect between our heart and our words, and it should serve as the catalyst
to deepen our relationship with the Lord.

*Father, I know my time with You has direct results in how I live. Help
me make quiet time a priority so I can be filled with Your love. Give me
a pure heart so my words will reflect it. In Jesus' name I pray, amen.*

morning
ON THE WAY

*While I was still in prayer, Gabriel, the man I had seen in the earlier
vision, came to me in swift flight about the time of the evening sacrifice.
He instructed me and said to me, "Daniel, I have now come to give you
insight and understanding. As soon as you began to pray, a word went
out, which I have come to tell you, for you are highly esteemed."*
DANIEL 9:21–23 NIV

Wherever you need encouragement, boldness, resources; whatever your desires, thoughts, troubles—you name it—God knows your heart. Don't hold back. Approach your Father in openness and humility. You are greatly loved. Say these words to yourself: *I am greatly loved.* Rest in His love. Rest in the knowledge that He is awesome enough to answer prayers before they are prayed.

*Father, fill me with assurance in the silence that
You have been and are at work. Amen.*

evening
FOR OUR GOOD

*And we know that in all things God works for the good of those who
love him, who have been called according to his purpose.*
ROMANS 8:28 NIV

God is a big God; He has big plans. With our eyes focused on Him, we aren't so likely to see life centered in and revolving around us, but rather coming from God and for His glory. We aren't so likely to forget the One who commands the whole picture. All of what God has in mind for His children we can't begin to fathom, but we can begin to have faith that what He has in mind is good.

So even while being battered by the winds, don't lose sight of the horizon. Blue sky is hidden behind those stormy clouds, just waiting for God to reveal it.

Lord, increase my faith that You are working all things for good. Amen.

morning
THE PITS

So when Joseph came to his brothers, they stripped him of his robe—the ornate robe he was wearing—and took him and threw him into the cistern.

GENESIS 37:23–24 NIV

Looking back, you see God's hand in your life. Through the good and bad, and sometimes *very* bad, you can pinpoint where you were headed and how God was shaping you each moment. The trouble is seeing while you're in the middle of life, in the pit. With the walls towering around you, the sky only a patch overhead, how can you imagine something better *beyond*? It takes faith. Have faith that God is present. Have faith that He is at work, even when you can't see Him moving. He has shown Himself faithful over the centuries and won't change now.

God, even in the pit I will have faith. Please hold my faith steady when it wavers. Keep my eyes focused on You until I can see. Amen.

evening
FIRST AND FOREMOST

Christ Jesus came into the world to save sinners—of whom I am the worst. But for that very reason I was shown mercy so that in me, the worst of sinners, Christ Jesus might display his immense patience as an example for those who would believe in him and receive eternal life.

1 TIMOTHY 1:15–16 NIV

Maybe you believe there's no way you can be an example to others. If that's the case, think about these words of Paul: "Think of what you were when you were called. Not many of you were wise by human standards; not many were influential; not many were of noble birth. But God chose the foolish things of the world to shame the wise; God chose the weak things of the world to shame the strong. God chose the lowly things of this world and the despised things—and the things that are not—to nullify the things that are" (1 Corinthians 1:26–28 NIV). God called you, He redeemed you, and now He chooses to use you for His glory.

Lord, may my life, like Paul's, be proof that You save. Amen.

morning
UPHILL

"May the LORD our God be with us, as He was with our fathers. May He not leave us nor forsake us, that He may incline our hearts to Himself, to walk in all His ways, and to keep His commandments and His statutes and His judgments, which He commanded our fathers."

1 KINGS 8:57–58 NKJV

We *can* triumph over the flesh, but we need to rely on God—first for leading us to follow, then for empowering us to follow through. Our outward following and victory result from His leading and power within.

Whatever uphill battles we face, let's not start pedaling without going to God. The One who draws our hearts close to Himself will be by our side giving us the extra boost we need to reach the summit and sweet reward.

God, I know You're calling me to walk in Your ways—please help me obey. Amen.

evening
POTTER AND CLAY

You, LORD, are our Father. We are the clay, you are the potter; we are all the work of your hand.

ISAIAH 64:8 NIV

Alone, we would never produce the beautiful vessel God has in mind. We can't. We aren't the potter. But as clay in the Potter's hand, our lives become new. As we yield to Him, He daily fashions us into His daughters. Even when the pot looks like a lump on the wheel, we never need to doubt the Potter's skill. He envisions the end before He begins. He softens, molds, and smooths with precision, and He won't leave the pot unfinished.

Father, forgive me when I wander from Your ways. I hear You calling. Please draw me back to You, as clay ready to be shaped. Amen.

morning
WHERE GOD LEADS

*But Ruth replied, "Don't urge me to leave you or to turn back
from you. Where you go I will go, and where you stay I will stay.
Your people will be my people and your God my God."*
RUTH 1:16 NIV

At the outset, Ruth didn't know where following would lead. Even at the end of her life, she likely didn't know how God would use her faithfulness to bless countless others. She had to take each day, one after the other, trusting God to take care of the rest. Wherever God has us today, and wherever He might lead us tomorrow, one thing is certain: He is present and active. And He can do great things with our willingness to stick close to Him.

*Lord, I don't know what will happen as I take these next steps in
faith, but I trust You to do wonderful things through me. Amen.*

evening
WITH HIS HELP

*And next to him was Shallum the son of Hallohesh, leader of half
the district of Jerusalem; he and his daughters made repairs.*
NEHEMIAH 3:12 NKJV

Church families today sometimes undertake what seem like monumental tasks. We send missionaries to areas firmly resistant to the Gospel. We raise large amounts of money to plant churches. We minister to communities facing unimaginable crisis.

What monumental task is before you and your church today? Begin by asking God to work through you. God is just as mighty as He was in Nehemiah's day, and as we join together with fellow believers, He works through us to achieve even the impossible.

*God, You know what we are setting out to do. Be with us. Work
through us. May we accomplish big things in Your name. Amen.*

morning
PRESS ON!

*Not that I have already obtained all this, or have already arrived at my goal, but
I press on to take hold of that for which Christ Jesus took hold of me. Brothers and
sisters, I do not consider myself yet to have taken hold of it. But one thing I do:
Forgetting what is behind and straining toward what is ahead, I press on toward
the goal to win the prize for which God has called me heavenward in Christ Jesus.*

PHILIPPIANS 3:12–14 NIV

What is God doing in you today? Where can you shift your attention from the rearview
mirror and instead look forward and press on? If forgetting the past and pursuing
Christlikeness seems too daunting, remember: Ultimately God is our means, and He is
our reason. It is Christ's work on the cross that redeems us fully. It is Christ's work in
us that produces righteousness. We owe our present and future to Christ, and through
Him we can live lives unburdened by the past.

*Lord, remind me that You are always greater than my sin,
that You are the source of my success. Help me press on. Amen.*

evening
RIGHT ON TIME

*But do not forget this one thing, dear friends: With the Lord a day is like a
thousand years, and a thousand years are like a day. The Lord is not slow in
keeping his promise, as some understand slowness. Instead he is patient with
you, not wanting anyone to perish, but everyone to come to repentance.*

2 PETER 3:8–9 NIV

God today is the same God as then. In all these years, He has not been idle. He is shaping
our days with precision. And what He has promised, He will bring about. Meanwhile,
this waiting period has purpose. God is not late, but patient. He gives His children
time to come to Him. Let's model our heavenly Father and not grow impatient; let's
use this time to share what God has done and what He continues to do.

*God, I'm eternally grateful that You waited long enough for me to
turn to You. I pray that many more would do the same. Amen.*

morning
PROVE IT

God is greater than our hearts, and he knows everything. Dear friends,
if our hearts do not condemn us, we have confidence before God.
1 JOHN 3:20–21 NIV

On days when you feel less than confident about your salvation, look to your love. Where do you see love manifested? In acts of kindness, big or small. In compassion, even for those who hate you. In the pull to reach out to others. . . All flow from a heart that is His. Still unsure? Rest in the words of 1 John: *"God is greater."* He is greater than our doubts. He knows our hearts and who belongs to Him. "God's solid foundation stands firm, sealed with this inscription: 'The Lord knows those who are his' " (2 Timothy 2:19 NIV).

God saves, and the proof is in our love.

God, my confidence is a little shaky today. But I believe in Jesus and how He
saves me. Remind me, please, of all the ways my life reflects Your love. Amen.

evening
SURE-FOOTED

For who is God besides the LORD? And who is the Rock except our God?
It is God who arms me with strength and keeps my way secure. He makes
my feet like the feet of a deer; he causes me to stand on the heights.
PSALM 18:31–33 NIV

If the path ahead of you seems precarious, focus instead—as David did—on all the ways that God makes His children secure. Need protection? God is our shield. Overwhelmed? Find refuge in Him. See no way out? He is our deliverer. Think all hope is lost? God is salvation. Feeling unsteady? Stand firm on the solid rock. God, who is like no other, will equip us and steady us, making our feet secure even on the roughest paths.

God, You are one of a kind, worthy of endless praise. I'm heading up a steep
trail right now. With each step, plant my feet firmly on the rock. Amen.

morning
STAY AWHILE

*"Martha, Martha," the Lord answered, "you are worried and upset
about many things, but few things are needed—or indeed only one.
Mary has chosen what is better, and it will not be taken away from her."*
LUKE 10:41–42 NIV

Paul once wrote, "I think that all things are worth nothing compared with the greatness
of knowing Christ Jesus my Lord" (Philippians 3:8 NCV). What "nothings" distract us
from getting to know Jesus? Where do we funnel our energy to the exclusion of quiet
moments at His feet? We have much to gain from choosing the good portion. And what
we gain, we'll never lose.

*Lord, I'm distracted. A time of stillness with You is the last thing on my
mind. Forgive me. Nothing is of greater value than You. Amen.*

evening
THOSE HE LOVES

*My child, do not reject the LORD's discipline, and don't get
angry when he corrects you. The LORD corrects those he
loves, just as parents correct the child they delight in.*
PROVERBS 3:11–12 NCV

Everything God does is aimed at restoration. Ever since the Fall, God has been bringing
us back to communion with Him. Even in His discipline—the correction that seems to
tear us down—God's goal is to build us up. "Blessed is the one you discipline, LORD,"
the psalmist said (Psalm 94:12 NIV). We have so much to gain as we allow the Lord's
discipline to do its work. Let's not reject His blessing.

*Lord, those You love, You correct. From now on, I choose
to focus on the love behind the discipline—on the way
You are doing something beautiful in me. Amen.*

morning
PORTRAIT OF A WOMAN

Who can find a virtuous woman? for her price is far above rubies.
PROVERBS 31:10 KJV

What describes the Proverbs 31 woman? Words like *dependable, savvy, diligent, strong, openhanded, fearless, joyous,* and *caring.* Her crowning glory? Reverence for God. She is a woman of faith, which brings her praise. If you look, you can see aspects of her reflected back at you in the mirror. And as you seek God each day, you'll see her more and more.

God, please work in me so that I have the heart of a virtuous woman. Amen.

evening
WHAT'S THE PLAN?

In their hearts humans plan their course, but the LORD establishes their steps.
PROVERBS 16:9 NIV

The next time you make plans, keep these instructions in mind: "Now listen, you who say, 'Today or tomorrow we will go to this or that city, spend a year there, carry on business and make money.' Why, you do not even know what will happen tomorrow. What is your life? You are a mist that appears for a little while and then vanishes. Instead, you ought to say, 'If it is the Lord's will, we will live and do this or that' " (James 4:13–15 NIV). Place God first before the plan. Include Him in the process. You'll find that when you partner with God, you succeed (Proverbs 16:3).

*Father, I have so many plans! Today I hand them over
to You. May Your will be done, not mine. Amen.*

morning
LOOKING AHEAD

*"Forget the former things; do not dwell on the past. See, I am doing
a new thing! Now it springs up; do you not perceive it? I am making
a way in the wilderness and streams in the wasteland."*

ISAIAH 43:18–19 NIV

Looking back over your life, where have you seen God work mightily on your behalf? Where can you say, "Remember when God. . ."? Memories of God's faithfulness are beautiful blessings. Gain confidence from all God has done. Allow His track record to build up your faith. *But* don't stop looking forward. Keep your eyes trained on how God is working in you today. . .and tomorrow. Anticipate the "new thing" He is doing, because greater things are yet to come.

*God, when I survey the life I've lived so far, I can see Your fingerprints
all over it. Reveal to me all the new things You are doing too. Amen.*

evening
CAUSE FOR BOASTING

*But he said to me, "My grace is sufficient for you, for my power is
made perfect in weakness." Therefore I will boast all the more gladly
of my weaknesses, so that Christ's power may rest on me.*

2 CORINTHIANS 12:9 NIV

Paul's view of weakness wasn't limited to its downside. The weakness itself wasn't enjoyable, but Paul saw the potential for God's power to work through him in his weakness. God told Paul, and He tells us today, that His power "is made perfect in weakness." The weaker we are, the more plainly we see how powerful God is to use even our weaknesses to His glory. Our God is mighty, and that's a reason to boast.

*God, I hate being weak. But when I feel small, I'm reminded of just how
big You are. Use my weaknesses to show off Your strength. Amen.*

morning
THE LONG WAY AROUND

When Pharaoh let the people go, God did not lead them on the road through the Philistine country, though that was shorter. For God said, "If they face war, they might change their minds and return to Egypt." So God led the people around by the desert road toward the Red Sea. The Israelites went up out of Egypt ready for battle.

EXODUS 13:17–18 NIV

We may wish we'd reach wherever we're headed faster. We may not even know where we're going. But once the journey is over, what a joy to look back and see God's mastery and care in action. Every road traveled, each experience, trials and all, has purpose. Even on the most winding path, we can have faith that God has a destination in mind, and He will make sure we get there.

God, I'm amazed by how You got me from where I was to where I am. Thank You for the masterful way You guide me. Amen.

evening
FOCUS!

Set your minds on things above, not on earthly things.

COLOSSIANS 3:2 NIV

In heaven, we'll be transformed, perfected. Until then, we strive to model our Savior as best we can. The earth will always be full of distractions and pitfalls, but with minds focused on "things that are above," we are filled with God's power that shapes us as His daughters day by day. Don't look down. Keep your eyes focused on heaven.

Lord, when I take my eyes off You, I falter. So why do I let myself lose focus so easily? Please help me set my mind on things above. Amen.

morning FRUITFUL

But the fruit of the Spirit is love, joy, peace, forbearance, kindness, goodness, faithfulness, gentleness, and self-control. Against such things there is no law.
GALATIANS 5:22–23 NIV

What is a Christian like? She's loving—showing the kind of love Christ showed. She's joyful—possessing a sense of well-being from God no matter the circumstance. She's peaceful—resting in the calm of knowing God. She's patient—long-suffering through hardships. She's kind—treating others with care and concern. She's good—displaying the holiness fitting for one of God's children. She's faithful—proving herself trustworthy, devoted. She's gentle—having a spirit of meekness. She's self-controlled—taming the flesh while pursuing godliness.

However small the harvest, the Holy Spirit is producing what we could not produce alone. May it be our prayer that we bear more and more of that good fruit.

Holy Spirit, I see the fruit You yield in my life. It's my desire to bear a bounty of good fruit—so much that others see me and say, "That's a Christian!" Amen.

evening TIMES INFINITY

"Do not judge, and you will not be judged. Do not condemn, and you will not be condemned. Forgive, and you will be forgiven. Give, and it will be given to you. A good measure, pressed down, shaken together and running over, will be poured into your lap. For with the measure you use, it will be measured to you."
LUKE 6:37–38 NIV

The One who has pardoned an unpayable debt continues to forgive us when we disobey. Even with the best intentions, we will still fail time and again; and time and again we can ask our Father's forgiveness without crossing our fingers that He'll forgive. He will. Hardening our hearts and refusing to offer forgiveness does not honor God's grace, and He won't overlook our stinginess, a scenario that Jesus illustrated in His parable of the unforgiving servant (Matthew 18:23–35). But when we forgive generously, limitlessly, as God does, we will get back an equal measure.

Father, may my forgiveness point the way to Yours. Amen.

morning
TAKE A LOOK AROUND

The heavens declare the glory of God; the skies proclaim the work of his hands.
PSALM 19:1 NIV

There's no better place to look for reassurance of God's presence and power than nature. Can we see the intricacy of a snowflake, the hues of a sunset, or the lush growth of plants without imagining a Creator? Can we hear the boom of thunder, the rush of waves, or the silence of a vast night sky without thinking of Someone higher than ourselves? God's creation is shouting. The same almighty God at work in nature is at work in us.

God, in my modern life, I've lost something of You. Even if it's only a few minutes, I want to set aside time every day to hear what Your creation has to say. Amen.

evening
QUENCHED

The LORD will guide you always; he will satisfy your needs in a sun-scorched land and will strengthen your frame. You will be like a well-watered garden, like a spring whose waters never fail.
ISAIAH 58:11 NIV

God provides a constant source of life-giving water to the believer. Jesus declared, "Whoever believes in me, as Scripture has said, rivers of living water will flow from within them" (John 7:37–38 NIV). God's living water both grants eternal life in heaven and supports spiritual life on earth through the Spirit. We as believers need water to grow just as we need air to breathe. Perhaps this truth is most obvious when we're in a dry spell. It's then that we cry out like the psalmist, "As the deer pants for the water brooks, so pants my soul for You, O God. My soul thirsts for God, for the living God" (Psalm 42:1–2 NKJV).

When you're thirsty, return to the Source. Dip deeply into God's Word.

Holy Spirit, fill me to the brim with living water. Amen.

morning
PERSISTENTLY PERSISTENT

*Jesus told his disciples a parable to show them that
they should always pray and not give up.*
LUKE 18:1 NIV

God wants us to approach Him with our needs. And it's okay to be persistent, like the blind beggar along the road outside Jericho who called out to Jesus for mercy. Even though the crowds rebuked him, he called out the same words again; and Jesus responded, restoring his sight. Or like the Canaanite woman who sought healing for her daughter. At first Jesus remained silent; then He turned her down. But the woman asked again. This time Jesus answered, "Woman, you have great faith! Your request is granted" (Matthew 15:28 NIV).

Go ahead. Ask Him one more time.

*Father, thank You for listening to my every request. Even in the
asking, You are building my faith. So I'll keep asking. Amen.*

evening
DIE TO LIVE

*"Whoever finds their life will lose it, and whoever
loses their life for my sake will find it."*
MATTHEW 10:39 NIV

When we choose Christ over self, when we forsake the world to follow Him, we gain abundant life now and eternal life to come. "Most assuredly," said Jesus, "unless a grain of wheat falls into the ground and dies, it remains alone; but if it dies, it produces much grain. He who loves his life will lose it, and he who hates his life in this world will keep it for eternal life. . .and where I am, there My servant will be also. If anyone serves Me, him My Father will honor" (John 12:24–26 NKJV).

*Lord, You've given me true life through the cross—life for
my soul now and in eternity. Every day, show me more
of what it means to lose my life for You. Amen.*

morning "SHEPHERD ME!"

*The LORD is my shepherd. . . . Yea, though I walk through
the valley of the shadow of death, I will fear no evil: for thou
art with me; thy rod and thy staff they comfort me.*

PSALM 23:1, 4 KJV

Each of us believers is one of the Lord's flock. He knows us individually, calling us by name, and cares for us beyond anything we could imagine. He is our Good Shepherd, and we will not fear even the valleys because He is with us—guarding and guiding, shepherding us through life. "Now may the God of peace, who through the blood of the eternal covenant brought back from the dead our Lord Jesus, that great Shepherd of the sheep, equip you with everything good for doing his will, and may he work in us what is pleasing to him" (Hebrews 13:20–21 NIV).

*Lord, when I face my fears, please remind me that I don't face them
alone. You, my Good Shepherd, walk before me. Amen.*

evening A LESSON IN HUMILITY

*Humble yourselves, therefore, under God's mighty
hand, that he may lift you up in due time.*

1 PETER 5:6 NIV

God is continually working in your life. When, in His sovereignty, He brings you through challenging times, don't resist His mighty hand—He's using even the rough moments for your good and His glory. Instead, "give your[self] completely to God. . . . Humble yourself in the Lord's presence." And in due time "he will honor you" (James 4:7, 10 NCV).

*God, I don't like where I am right now, but I won't fight what You're doing in
my life. I choose to humble myself before You so that You can lift me up. Amen.*

morning
"FOR GOD SO LOVED"

For God so loved the world, that he gave his only begotten Son, that whosoever believeth in him should not perish, but have everlasting life.
JOHN 3:16 KJV

The heavenly Father's love is indeed vast. And its extent is something God is forever revealing to our hearts. Paul's prayer for the Ephesians was "that out of his glorious riches he may strengthen you with power through his Spirit in your inner being, so that Christ may dwell in your hearts through faith. And I pray that you, being rooted and established in love, may have power, together with all the Lord's holy people, to grasp how wide and long and high and deep is the love of Christ, and to know this love that surpasses knowledge" (Ephesians 3:16–19 NIV). How much does God love us? As wide as Christ's outstretched arms on the cross. From heaven to earth and back.

Father, I love You so much. Thank You for the reminder that You love me much more. Amen.

evening
CONTENTED

Be content with what you have, because God has said, "Never will I leave you; never will I forsake you."
HEBREWS 13:5 NIV

The kind of contentment Paul wrote about has nothing to do with how much or how little a person owns but everything to do with the One who satisfies. In a passage on God's provision, Paul told believers, "I have learned in whatever state I am, to be content: I know how to be abased, and I know how to abound. Everywhere and in all things I have learned both to be full and to be hungry, both to abound and to suffer need. I can do all things through Christ who strengthens me" (Philippians 4:11–13 NKJV). Paul could be content trusting in God's presence to get him through times of plenty and need. He could be content resting in the God who met his deepest longings. He could be content knowing that what God gave was enough.

God, where You are, no matter what else fills my life, I will be content. Amen.

MAKING EVERYTHING BEAUTIFUL
morning

Your beauty should come from within you—the beauty of a gentle and quiet spirit that will never be destroyed and is very precious to God.
1 PETER 3:4 NCV

When the Lord sent Samuel to anoint the next king of Israel, He told Samuel, "Do not consider his appearance or his height. . . . The LORD does not look at the things people look at. People look at the outward appearance, but the LORD looks at the heart" (1 Samuel 16:7 NIV). It didn't matter if David was impressive physically; God was peering inside, to his heart. He's still gazing on our hearts, and if our focus is the outer shell, we'll miss it. While we expend a good deal of energy on the surface, trying to make the outer shell more beautiful, God is working within. He is making us beautiful in ways that won't become clear and won't be complete until heaven.

*God, when I pick apart what You've created,
give me eyes to see as You do. Amen.*

BE A DOER
evening

*But whoever looks intently into the perfect law that gives
freedom, and continues in it—not forgetting what they have
heard, but doing it—they will be blessed in what they do.*
JAMES 1:25 NIV

James wrote, "Do what God's teaching says; when you only listen and do nothing, you are fooling yourselves. Those who hear God's teaching and do nothing are like people who look at themselves in a mirror. They see their faces and then go away and quickly forget what they looked like. But the truly happy people are those who carefully study God's perfect law that makes people free, and they continue to study it. They do not forget what they heard, but they obey what God's teaching says. Those who do this will be made happy" (James 1:22–25 NCV). Did you catch that last part? The hearer who obeys "will be *made* happy." God honors obedience. He blesses those who choose to heed His direction.

God, through Your Spirit, help me hear and obey. Amen.

morning
KEEP UP THE GOOD WORK

*Let us not become weary in doing good, for at the proper
time we will reap a harvest if we do not give up.*
GALATIANS 6:9 NIV

Believers are not to grow weary of doing good. Paul told the church in Corinth, "Do not let anything move you. Always give yourselves fully to the work of the Lord, because you know that your work in the Lord is never wasted" (1 Corinthians 15:58 NCV). Whatever we do for God has value. Even at the end of days when the good we do seems to be for naught, we have reason to call on our Strength and keep up the good work.

*God, energize me to do the good things You've prepared for me.
Doing good is never in vain—You will use Your people's good
works for Your glory and reward them in heaven. Amen.*

evening
FIRST THINGS FIRST

Take delight in the Lord, and he will give you the desires of your heart.
PSALM 37:4 NIV

"Seek first his kingdom. . .and all these things will be given to you as well" (Matthew 6:33 NIV). We see the same pattern throughout the Bible. "Humble yourselves before the Lord, and he will lift you up" (James 4:10 NIV). "Commit your works to the LORD and your plans will be established" (Proverbs 16:3 NASB). "Delight yourself in the LORD, and He will give you the desires of your heart (Psalm 37:4 NASB). Whatever our hopes, dreams, or wishes, the pursuit of them must come second to God in our hearts. And when we put Him first, we discover a miraculous truth: He meets our every need and our every desire.

*God, You know my heart's desire, what I long for. Even if it materialized
this very moment, it wouldn't be enough. But with You filling my
heart to the brim, everything else falls into place. Amen.*

GOING HOME

Jesus replied, "Anyone who loves me will obey my teaching. My Father will love them, and we will come to them and make our home with them."
JOHN 14:23 NIV

Our Lord is in heaven this very minute readying our eternal home. He told the disciples, "Do not let your hearts be troubled. You believe in God; believe also in me. My Father's house has many rooms; if that were not so, would I have told you that I am going there to prepare a place for you? And if I go and prepare a place for you, I will come back and take you to be with me that you also may be where I am (John 14:1–3 NIV). One day, we'll be going home. In the meantime, we have another promise—that God will make a home in us, preparing us for that day when we will be forever at home.

Lord, I know You are with me. And I know You will have a home waiting for me in heaven. Amen.

UNBURDENED

"Come to Me, all who are weary and burdened, and I will give you rest. Take My yoke upon you and learn from Me, for I am gentle and humble in heart, and YOU WILL FIND REST FOR YOUR SOULS."
MATTHEW 11:28–30 NASB

To receive Christ through faith means a cessation of endlessly, and futilely, working toward righteousness. It means rest in the grace of God. And it means an easy yoke. "Take My yoke upon you and learn from Me," Jesus tells us. When we take Christ's yoke, far from finding a demanding taskmaster, we find a gentle and humble Lord to guide us. We find a God whose commandments are not burdensome (1 John 5:3) and who cares about us so much that we can cast our burdens on Him (1 Peter 5:7). We find rest for our souls.

Lord, I was tired and burdened before I met You, but You brought relief from the heavy load I could not bear. Thank You for that soul-deep, abiding rest that comes only through You. Amen.

morning
AT PEACE

*Put into practice what you learned from me, what you heard and
saw and realized. Do that, and God, who makes everything work
together, will work you into his most excellent harmonies.*
PHILIPPIANS 4:9 MSG

At the close of one of his epistles, Paul said, "Rejoice in the Lord always; again I will say, rejoice! . . . The Lord is near. Do not be anxious about anything, but in everything by prayer and pleading with thanksgiving let your requests be made known to God. And the peace of God, which surpasses all comprehension, will guard your hearts and your minds in Christ Jesus" (Philippians 4:4–7 NASB). God is near, so tell Him with gratitude for all He does, what's worrying you. His peace will empty you of doubt and fear while filling you with the knowledge that God is working everything together in perfect harmony.

*God, I'm uneasy and uncertain. Please take the worry and replace
it with calm. You are at work, so I am at peace. Amen.*

evening
SUPERFOOD

How sweet are thy words unto my taste! yea, sweeter than honey to my mouth!
PSALM 119:103 KJV

Jeremiah wrote, "When your words came, I ate them; they were my joy and my heart's delight" (Jeremiah 15:16 NIV). And Ezekiel described his encounter with the Lord like this: "And he said to me, 'Son of man, eat what is before you, eat this scroll; then go and speak to the people of Israel.' So I opened my mouth, and he gave me the scroll to eat. . . . So I ate it, and it tasted as sweet as honey" (Ezekiel 3:1–3 NIV). The prophets did not actually eat the parchment and ink that displayed God's words; their ingesting was symbolic of taking in the Word and allowing it to work in them. When we study the Bible, chewing on its words and internalizing them, we experience lasting benefits. God's Word sustains us and grows us.

God, I will eat Your words daily so that I am nourished. Amen.

morning
NO PEEKING!

*God has given them a desire to know the future. He does everything just right
and on time, but people can never completely understand what he is doing.*
ECCLESIASTES 3:11 NCV

God has purposely made us with eternity in our hearts (Ecclesiastes 3:11). God, though, is still sovereign over the *when* and *what*. Solomon, in his wisdom, came to understand this truth well: "I've also concluded that whatever God does, that's the way it's going to be, always. No addition, no subtraction. . . . That's so we'll quit asking questions and simply worship in holy fear" (Ecclesiastes 3:14 MSG). But remember: God is full of goodness and faithfulness. We can trust Him to do all things "just right and on time." We can worship Him in wonder of His mastery of all that is—as we wait for the story to unfold, without knowing what's going to happen next.

*God, help me to rest in You, content that You know
and control every page and the ending. Amen.*

evening
GLORY TO GOD

*But we have this treasure in earthen vessels, that the excellency
of the power may be of God, and not of us.*
2 CORINTHIANS 4:7 KJV

God's Word compares our earthly lives to earthen vessels. In biblical times, clay pots were common; people used them every day, and they were easily broken. We may wonder why our lives are like these plain, breakable pots. If God wants to declare His glory, why not make us shining golden vases? But God's glory shines brightest when He does miraculous things through jars of clay. Paul wrote, "We have this treasure from God, but we are like clay jars that hold the treasure. This shows that the great power is from God, not from us" (2 Corinthians 4:7 NCV). The pot that is nothing alone highlights the treasure.

These unfinished, fragile vessels point directly to the Master working through us.

God, use this life of mine—this jar of clay—to display Your glory. Amen.

HE'S CALLING

*And those he predestined, he also called; those he called, he
also justified; those he justified, he also glorified.*
ROMANS 8:30 NIV

God's calling is a wondrous thing if you think about it. God determined, before the foundation of the world, the ones He would call; the ones He calls He makes right with Himself, and those He makes right He will one day glorify in heaven. Until that day, the Lord calls to our hearts like a shepherd to sheep: "He calls his own sheep by name and leads them out. When he has brought out all his own, he goes on ahead of them, and his sheep follow him because they know his voice" (John 10:3–4 NIV). Truly, we'd recognize it anywhere.

*Lord, You called me to Your fold, and You call to me each day.
Please keep my heart open to hear Your voice. Amen.*

WHAT IT TAKES

*So Christ himself gave the apostles, the prophets, the evangelists,
the pastors and teachers, to equip his people for works of
service, so that the body of Christ may be built up.*
EPHESIANS 4:11–12 NIV

Fill in the blank: It takes a _____ to raise a child. If you answered *village*, you got it. Who's your "village"? Through whom is God working to help raise you, His child? Think about the individual people—from pastors to teachers to fellow church members—whom God has placed in your life to speak His truth. Pray for them. Thank God for them.

*God, You have blessed my life with godly men and women to guide me.
Their words and actions help me grow, and their presence reminds
me of how You are present in my life in so many ways. Thank You,
God. Please be with them as they do Your good work. Amen.*

morning
LOOKING AND LISTENING

I have not stopped giving thanks for you, remembering you in my prayers.
I keep asking that the God of our Lord Jesus Christ, the glorious Father, may
give you the Spirit of wisdom and revelation, so that you may know him better.
I pray that the eyes of your heart may be enlightened in order that you may
know the hope to which he has called you, the riches of his glorious inheritance
in his holy people, and his incomparably great power for us who believe.
EPHESIANS 1:16–19 NIV

As we read His Word, God uses His Spirit to bring sight and hearing to our hearts; He is helping us understand more and more of His truth according to His immeasurable power—"the utter extravagance of his work in us who trust him" (Ephesians 1:19 MSG). May Christ's command be our desire: "Whoever has ears, let them hear" (Matthew 11:15 NIV).

God, thank You for giving me eyes to see and ears to hear; thank You for
shedding light on Your Word and imparting understanding to my heart.
Please be with me and work in me each time I read the Bible. Amen.

evening
BY NAME

He telleth the number of the stars; he calleth them all by their names.
PSALM 147:4 KJV

Our names are dear to God, forever in His sight and always in His mind. Possibly the least-favored parts of the Bible to read are those filled with lists of names. But even if our eyes cross and our brains lose track of all those names, God knows each one and the face behind it. He has compiled an even longer list of names too. If you are a believer, God calls your name, and He has written it in the Lamb's book of life (Revelation 21:27).

God, You spoke the world into existence, and yet You speak
my name. Thank You for knowing me personally, for calling
me to You. I praise Your name, God of my life! Amen.

morning
INCREASING LUMINOSITY

The path of the righteous is like the morning sun,
shining ever brighter till the full light of day.
PROVERBS 4:18 NIV

"In the past you were full of darkness," Paul wrote to believers, "but now you are full of light in the Lord. So live like children who belong to the light. Light brings every kind of goodness, right living, and truth" (Ephesians 5:8–9 NCV). With light to guide our way, we can "learn what pleases the Lord" (Ephesians 5:10 NCV). And so our paths become brighter and brighter as we glow with increasing righteousness, as our hearts shine brighter and brighter with God's truth, until we can be no brighter one day in glory.

God, You brought me out of darkness into light. Thank You for the
promise that even when darkness floods this world, my path will only
get brighter. Use Your light in me to light the way to You. Amen.

evening
SOAR!

But they that wait upon the LORD shall renew their strength;
they shall mount up with wings as eagles.
ISAIAH 40:31 KJV

Where is God when another day or another step seems unbearable? Where He always is. With us. Waiting to support our weight as we fall back on Him. "Do you not know? Have you not heard?" Isaiah wrote. "The LORD is the everlasting God, the Creator of the ends of the earth. He will not grow tired or weary, and his understanding no one can fathom. He gives strength to the weary and increases the power of the weak. Even youths grow tired and weary, and young men stumble and fall; but those who hope in the LORD will renew their strength. They will soar on wings like eagles; they will run and not grow weary, they will walk and not be faint" (Isaiah 40:28–31 NIV).

Lord, be my strength, be my power so that I can go on. Amen.

morning
"MY PLEASURE!"

*"The LORD your God is with you, the Mighty Warrior who saves.
He will take great delight in you; in his love he will no longer
rebuke you, but will rejoice over you with singing."*

ZEPHANIAH 3:17 NIV

It was with joy in mind and not sadness, willingly and not begrudgingly, that our Lord died and rose again to give us life through faith in Him: "Looking unto Jesus, the author and finisher of our faith, who for the joy that was set before Him endured the cross, despising the shame, and has sat down at the right hand of the throne of God" (Hebrews 12:2 NKJV). And it is with joy and not cheerlessness, wholeheartedly and not halfheartedly, that He works in us today and will one day bring us into His presence.

*God, I can't believe it! You reign over the universe, yet You
delight in me. May You be my delight too. Amen.*

evening
DIG DEEPER

*As newborn babies want milk, you should want the pure and simple
teaching. By it you can mature in your salvation, because you
have already examined and seen how good the Lord is.*

1 PETER 2:2–3 NCV

God's Word is rich and living. We can study it for a lifetime and never exhaust all it has to say. But how often do we stop at a sip when we should gulp? How often are we content with an appetizer when we should dig into the meat course? If you aren't digging in, do so! Every sip and bite of the Word has the potential to work in us; just think of what deep Bible study can do. Not sure where or how to begin? Pick a book, pick a chapter. Read, then repeat. Read until the words fill your head, remembering that the One who wrote the words also whispers to your heart.

*God, be with me as I delve into Your Word.
Use it to grow me and develop me. Amen.*

morning
UNCHANGING

"I the LORD do not change."
MALACHI 3:6 NCV

"I AM WHO I AM," God told Moses (Exodus 3:14 NCV). The New American Standard Bible notes that the "I AM" of Exodus 3:14 is "related to the name of God, *YHWH*. . .which is derived from the verb *HAYAH, to be.*" God is. Stretch your mind as far as it can go backward or forward in time, and even beyond that point, God is. He says, "I am the Alpha and the Omega. . .who is, and who was, and who is to come, the Almighty" (Revelation 1:8 NIV). What does that mean for us? In our yesterdays, todays, and tomorrows, and into eternity, we are never without the unchanging One who is.

God, You always were, always are, and always will be. I bow to
You, and I thank You for always working in me. Amen.

evening
WHEN HE CUSHIONS THE CRUNCH

The Lord is merciful and gracious, slow to anger
and plenteous in mercy and loving-kindness.
PSALM 103:8 AMPC

God shows up in unexpected ways in our lives often enough that we know He can do anything. Other times we feel the effect of the way He created our world—the laws of physics are in force, and they hold true. And the fallenness of creation ensures that negative results are, many times, the norm. But sometimes He steps in and reroutes the path of the storm or cushions the impact of the crash or smooths away the contours of the tumor—and we remember, once again, that all things bow to His will. That's our unexpectedly merciful Father.

Heavenly Father, I praise You for the ways You show up
in unexpected mercy in my life. Most of all, I thank You
for the mercy I've received through Jesus. Amen.

NOT STRAIGHT LINES
morning

You number my wanderings.

PSALM 56:8 NKJV

One of the pleasantries of driving on a country road are the landmarks—old school buildings, white wood-sided churches, faded barns, glorious farmhouses, vintage roadside parks, and historical sites. They're stories in visual form. Behind every one of them is a tale of life, love, and learning, of hardship, sacrifice, and joy. Someone cared enough to carve out a place to live, a place to share with others, a place with meaning.

And these unexpected vignettes are what God uses in our spiritual journey too. When you feel like you can't find the "yellow brick road" to Oz, God may be letting you wander a bit so He can teach you wonderful, unexpected things along the way.

*Heavenly Father, I know I can trust Your leadership. If I
follow Your voice, You will get me to the place I need to be
and teach me new things along the way. Amen.*

LET THE FLOWERS BLOOM
evening

*For behold, the winter is past; the rain is over and gone.
The flowers appear on the earth, the time of singing has come.*

SONG OF SOLOMON 2:11–12 ESV

We can choose to make our future brighter as we base our decisions, not on our feelings, but on the realization that God has called us to make choices that encourage growth in our spiritual lives. We can deliberately choose to put our hope in God even when we aren't feeling hopeful. We can purposefully clear away the weeds and let the flowers poke through.

God calls us to open our eyes to the season of flowers. Let it come when it's time. Don't stay in the rain. Listen, the birds are starting to sing.

*Dear Father, I'm glad You understand the seasons in our lives. Thank You
for bringing me through a difficult time. Now I turn to the time for flowers
and ask You to help me cultivate joy again in my life. In Jesus' name, amen.*

DISCOVER YOUR TOOLS
morning

*Tell Priscilla and Aquila hello. They have been my
fellow workers in the affairs of Christ Jesus.*
ROMANS 16:3 TLB

When we answer God's call, He goes beyond what we expect. He takes what we offer and expands and multiplies it, just as Jesus did with a little boy's lunch one day.

What do you have to give today to do God's will? A computer screen? Diaper bag? Homework? Teacher's desk? Stethoscope? File drawer? Canning jars? Home business?

Use the tool God has given you for today. Has He put before you an opportunity to serve in a new way? Pray and try. You may grow in ways you'd never believe. And the record of what you do may inspire someone else.

*Lord, take the ways I know I can serve and the unexpected
ways You're going to show me, and let me use them for
Your glory. Grow me today as I follow You. Amen.*

EVERY LITTLE DETAIL
evening

If riches increase, set not your heart upon them.
PSALM 62:10 KJV

When trouble comes and money gets low and the bank accounts look skinny, we have to remember that our security is not in that, but in Christ. Whether our nation or our families flourish or lag economically, He is the Source of our stability. He is able, out of His great riches, to supply what we need today and every day. After all, that's what He'll be doing for eternity for those who love Him—taking care of every little detail. We can trust Him to do that for us today too.

*Lord, I proclaim that You are Master of my life and my money.
Today I have unexpected financial needs. I bring them to You and
trust that You can take care of every detail. In Jesus' name, amen.*

morning
GOD OF THE UNEXPECTED

Then Martha, as soon as she heard that Jesus was coming, went and met Him, but Mary was sitting in the house. Now Martha said to Jesus, "Lord, if You had been here, my brother would not have died."

JOHN 11:20–21 NKJV

Who expected the Messiah in a cow's crib? Or angels heralding shepherds? Or the Life-giver hanging on a cross? The empty tomb on a chilly morning? These are the unexpected imprints of our God, His signature in our world. If He can do all this, we can trust Him. His response to your need may surprise you, but so will His grace. And someday you'll see a plan so exquisite, it will take your breath away.

Heavenly Father, You work in unexpected ways. You see my unexpected tears, and You respond to them according to Your great plan. I trust You today. In the name of Your Son, I pray. Amen.

evening
A FRIEND WHO IRRITATES

Do not rejoice when your enemy falls, and do not let your heart be glad when he stumbles.

PROVERBS 24:17 NKJV

Jesus took time for all people—the clean, the dirty, the legal, the criminal, the wealthy, the poor, the healthy, the ill, the fun to be around, and the shunned. He calls us to do the same. You may discover that you like other people more than you thought you could. You might be surprised with an unexpected friendship with someone you thought you couldn't stand.

God, it's difficult to be nice to this person I'm thinking of right now. Give me grace to go out of my way to be friendly. Help me to celebrate her good news and pray for her troubles. Show me how to get to know her better so I can understand who she really is. In Jesus' name, amen.

morning
USED TO BE A FRIEND

And Samson's wife was given to his companion, who had been his best man.
JUDGES 14:20 ESV

We are called by Jesus to love our enemies. This doesn't mean, of course, that we must conjure up warm fuzzies for a person who has damaged a marriage or has hurt us in some other destructive way; but it does mean that we "love" them by not enacting vengeance on them ourselves. We are not to make them pay. God will do that. And He has much better ways to keep track of what's going on.

When a friend unexpectedly acts in an unfriendly way, the hurt is real. In those moments, we must rely on the strength of our God who never betrays and whose steady love can uphold us in any surprise.

Father God, I've been hurt by someone who was supposed to be my
friend. I need Your grace so that I can forgive and not seek vengeance.
I ask for strength and peace and hope. In Jesus' name, amen.

evening
HEAVENLY FRIENDS

Do not forget to entertain strangers, for by so doing
some have unwittingly entertained angels.
HEBREWS 13:2 NKJV

God has His hosts ready at a second's notice if He wills to use them in your life. You are never out of His thoughts or His reach. Someday He might send a heavenly helper to aid you in a moment of crisis; and if He does, it will be Him working out His plan for you out of His love. No one is more present in our unexpected moments that our great God, who "makes his angels spirits, and his servants flames of fire" (Hebrews 1:7 NIV).

Heavenly Father, You are the commander of the hosts of heaven.
Thank You for sending them to earth when You have a task for them to
complete. I may never realize I have seen one of them, but I know I can
trust You if ever I need the assistance of a heavenly friend. Amen.

morning
A RUTH OPPORTUNITY

But Ruth replied, "Don't urge me to leave you or to turn back from you. Where you go I will go, and where you stay I will stay. Your people will be my people and your God my God."
RUTH 1:16 NIV

Perhaps you have extended family members who are very different from you. Today, accept Ruth's challenge and look for ways to bond with them in healthy ways. Of course, one should never forsake God for pagan worship or adopt practices that violate His laws. But within those boundaries, why not see how you can surprise them with unexpected overtures of friendship? And who knows? It might open their hearts to Christ if they don't already know Him.

Heavenly Father, thank You for creating different people groups on the earth. You have included some of them in my family. I want to reach out to them and surprise them with friendship that goes beyond mere tolerance. I'm asking for wisdom as I look for those opportunities today. In Jesus' name, amen.

evening
A PERSON OF REST

I have calmed and quieted my soul, like a weaned child with its mother; like a weaned child is my soul within me.
PSALM 131:2 ESV

You may get the chance to provide a moment of rest for someone. Our world is filled with people who are jostled by every kind of stress one can imagine. Maybe an encounter with you, filled with the Holy Spirit, could cause them to consider letting God rule. After all, if He can quiet you so you bring rest to others, He can use that rest to be a witness.

Lord, I'm glad for the promise of rest. Like the psalmist, I want to choose purposefully to be calm and quiet. And I want to bring unexpected rest to others. In Jesus' name, amen.

morning
LONELINESS TURNED
TO LAUGHTER

*You have turned for me my mourning into dancing; you have
loosed my sackcloth and clothed me with gladness.*
PSALM 30:11 ESV

These are things we can be joyful about even when alone. Celebrating the triumphs of
our God is always appropriate—alone or with others. And it can include laughter. The
book of Exodus records how Moses and Aaron's sister, Miriam, led the Israelites in a
joyous celebration after the Lord brought them through the Red Sea. "Then Miriam. . .
took a tambourine in her hand, and all the women went out after her with tambou-
rines and dancing. And Miriam sang to them: 'Sing to the LORD, for he has triumphed
gloriously; the horse and his rider he has thrown into the sea'" (Psalm15:20–21 ESV).

Our God specializes in turning the negative into positive. If we focus on Him and His
power, we can be surprised by the joy He brings to our hearts and the life we feel in our spirits.

Jehovah God, I trust You. Amen.

evening
LAUGHING AT IMPOSSIBILITIES

*And Sarah said, "God has made laughter for me; everyone who hears will
laugh over me." And she said, "Who would have said to Abraham that
Sarah would nurse children? Yet I have borne him a son in his old age."*
GENESIS 21:6–7 ESV

Sarah was old, and her womb was withered. Dead. She didn't expect to birth a child.
And she certainly didn't expect to laugh. But she did both.

What are you hoping for that seems impossible? Can you believe that God might
bring it to pass? Can you imagine that someday you might be laughing in delight at
the fulfillment of a promise? It might seem just as impossible, but God can do the
impossible. "Is anything too hard for the LORD?" (Genesis 18:14 ESV).

*Jehovah God, I ask You to be at work in all the impossibilities
about which I am praying. You can do anything! Amen.*

morning
VICTORY

When the LORD brought back the captivity of Zion, we were like those who dream. Then our mouth was filled with laughter, and our tongue with singing. Then they said among the nations, "The LORD has done great things for them." The LORD has done great things for us, and we are glad.

PSALM 126:1–3 NKJV

Someday God will set this world free from the curse of sin, and Satan will be cast into eternal fire. The victory of God's kingdom will be complete, and we will reign with Christ forever. Only the Father knows when that day is coming, but we are secure in the knowledge that it is a specific date on His timetable. And when that unexpected and glorious day arrives, we will have joy like we've never had it before.

Heavenly Father, You rejoice every time a spiritual captive is set free by Your power. You hold all future events in Your hands. Today I want to live with the anticipation of Your final victory. Amen.

evening
HIS NAME IN THE NIGHT

I remember Your name in the night, O LORD.

PSALM 119:55 NKJV

In the night, we need power. Power to rest, power to rejuvenate, power to relinquish all things into the Almighty's hands.

In Psalm 119, verse 55, the writer recommends an action we can use to fight our overwhelming weakness as the daylight fades and dusk approaches.

We can remember His name:

Jehovah—Provider	Jesus—Savior	Prince of Peace
Lord—Sovereign	Almighty God	King of kings
Messiah—Promised One	Everlasting Father	Friend

In every unexpected nighttime moment, His name has the comfort we seek. And His power is revealed, if we choose to believe in Him.

Lord Jesus, You are Life and Peace and all I need tonight. I trust the power in Your name for the unrest in my heart. Amen.

morning
PRECIOUS EXPRESSIONS

A word fitly spoken is like apples of gold in settings of silver.
PROVERBS 25:11 NKJV

You may not think of it this way, but every morning when you wake up, God is sending you a note. The sun shining outside your window, the oxygen circulating in your bedroom, the birds chirping on the branches, the people who populate your day—these are the expressions of love He puts in your life.

Sometimes God sends something out of the ordinary; sometimes it's just the blessedness of an uneventful routine. Look for His message in your life today.

Father, Your heart of love overwhelms me. Thank You for showing Your love to me in so many ways. I want to pass it on to others. In Jesus' name, amen.

evening
POWER OF A VOICE

She, supposing Him to be the gardener, said to Him, "Sir, if You have carried Him away, tell me where You have laid Him, and I will take Him away." Jesus said to her, "Mary!" She turned and said to Him, "Rabboni!" (which is to say, Teacher).
JOHN 20:15–16 NKJV

Mary Magdalene had twice received unexpected joy. The first was when Jesus cast seven spirits from her (Luke 8:2), and the second was when He cast away her despair on Easter morning.

Perhaps you too need to hear the power of Jesus' voice. Today voices everywhere are creating fear and anxiety and dread. But His voice brings freedom and joy.

Heavenly Father, thank You for sending Your Son to speak peace to our world. Thank You for the power of His voice and the power of His resurrection that triumphs over everything. Like Mary, I worship You today. Amen.

morning
STARTLING DELIVERANCE

*By faith Moses, when he was born, was hidden for three
months by his parents, because they saw that the child was
beautiful, and they were not afraid of the king's edict.*
HEBREWS 11:23 ESV

Did Jochebed know that the princess went to the river to bathe? Did she intend for
Moses to be found? It's very possible. She stationed her daughter there as a sentinel,
to keep tabs on what happened. Miriam had probably been instructed in what to say,
but who could have guessed that it would turn out so beautifully?

What new thing has God brought into your life that seems negative and dangerous?
What is He telling you to do to help His plan move forward? Weave a basket? Stand
guard?

Step out in faith and do it. Deliverance comes in unexpected ways.

*Dear Father, thank You for the surprising ways You bring deliverance to our
world. Help me follow what You have for me to do today. In Jesus' name, amen.*

evening
THE WONDER OF FORGETFULNESS

The chief cupbearer did not remember Joseph, but forgot him.
GENESIS 40:23 ESV

Sometimes we feel like God has forgotten. We see ways that things could work out. Surely
Joseph did too as he passed day after day in the prison, going about his routines, wondering
if today might be the day his name would be called and he would be summoned. Surely he
was tempted to despair, as month rolled into month and one year into two. But God had
not forgotten him, and the moment of release had already been marked in His calendar.

So it is with us. Never doubt that God is at work every second, every minute, every
day, every month, every year. What looks like a curse may instead be a blessing. God
remembers you, and at the right time, release will come.

*Dear heavenly Father, I know I can trust You just like Joseph
did. You were with him, and You will be with me. Thank You
for watching over everything that concerns me. Amen.*

morning
REWARDS OF WILLINGNESS

*One who heard us was a woman named Lydia, from the city of Thyatira,
a seller of purple goods, who was a worshiper of God. The Lord opened
her heart to pay attention to what was said by Paul. And after she was
baptized, and her household as well, she urged us, saying, "If you have
judged me to be faithful to the Lord, come to my house and stay."*

ACTS 16:14–15 ESV

It's true: A willingness to share what we have results in rewards. At times, we have
probably been reluctant to share our homes or our resources or our time—and for a
variety of reasons, not all of them selfish. But when we make the sacrifice and open up
our palms in good ways, God can take the blessings we have and bring others to Him.

*Dear Lord, help me to recognize when I need to offer help, and
give me a willing heart. In the name of Jesus, amen.*

evening
REWARD OF FAITH

*Now there was one, Anna. . .a widow of about eighty-four years, who
did not depart from the temple, but served God with fastings and prayers
night and day. And coming in that instant she gave thanks to the Lord,
and spoke of Him to all those who looked for redemption in Jerusalem.*

LUKE 2:36–38 NKJV

Anna served God continually in the temple, night and day, with fasting and prayer.
Perhaps she didn't want to miss the Promise. Perhaps she couldn't bear the thought
of being absent on the day when the Christ child appeared. So she came continually.
And she waited. . .through days and months and years.

A woman's life is filled with seasons of waiting. And having faith while we wait is
challenging. Days turn into weeks, and it seems our prayers are unanswered and our
hopes are for nothing. Remember Anna. Remember her faith. Remember her reward.

*Dear heavenly Father, as I wait in faith, help me hold
to Your promise and never let it go. Amen.*

morning
REWARD OF TEARS

*Those who sow in tears shall reap in joy. He who continually
goes forth weeping, bearing seed for sowing, shall doubtless
come again with rejoicing, bringing his sheaves with him.*
PSALM 126:5–6 NKJV

We don't hear a lot about soul-winning, but it is still very close to God's heart. Proverbs 11:30 NKJV tells us that whoever wins souls "is wise." God wants all of the people of the earth to know about His love for them and His plan to redeem them. You and I need to be open to being "tear sowers." There is no greater joy than seeing a new life in Christ begin.

*Dear God, You are not willing that anyone perish in eternity
without You. Today, show me how I can sow in tears and
reap in the joy of a soul harvest for You. Amen.*

evening
PRECIOUS TIME

*Look carefully then how you walk, not as unwise but as wise,
making the best use of the time, because the days are evil.*
EPHESIANS 5:15–16 ESV

We all have them—the little bits of time in and around our main events of the day— fifteen minutes here, five minutes there. Before an appointment, in between clients— time in the hourglass that goes unused.

In a spiritual sense, we need to make use of that precious time, because every bit of it is a gift from God. We must not just spend time making our own lives better; we should be looking around for the good we can do for others, especially as it relates to ministering to the needs of their souls.

It's amazing how much one can accomplish in a little bit of time. What can you do today?

*Dear Father, thank You for the gift of time. I have twenty-
four hours in my day just like everyone else. Help me to use
those hours wisely and well. In the name of Jesus, amen.*

morning SECURE

Strength and dignity are her clothing, and she laughs at the time to come.
PROVERBS 31:25 ESV

This woman can laugh at the future, not in a mocking, foolish, irresponsible way but in a trusting, joyful way. She knows that God holds everything in His hands and that He has the final say. She doesn't have to try to figure everything out when she trusts the One who knows all. "He has made everything beautiful in its time. Also, he has put eternity into man's heart, yet so that he cannot find out what God has done from the beginning to the end" (Ecclesiastes 3:11 ESV).

Father in heaven, You hold all things in Your hands, and You made everything, including me. Today I trust You for my future, and I find my strength and dignity in following Your purpose. Amen.

evening RELATIONSHIP

"Many women have done excellently, but you surpass them all." Charm is deceitful, and beauty is vain, but a woman who fears the LORD is to be praised.
PROVERBS 31:29–30 ESV

To fear the Lord is to acknowledge His sovereignty and live with reverence for His authority over us. A woman who does this understands much about her purpose in the world. She is listening for the voice of her God and trying to reflect Him in everything she does. That is why she does things excellently. That is why her relationship with Him is more vital than earthly beauty or charm. The outer beauty perishes, but the inner beauty is unfading (1 Peter 3:4).

Heavenly Father, my understanding of You and my relationship with You shape the woman I am. Give me grace this day to live in Your light and love. Amen.

morning
REWARD

Give her of the fruit of her hands, and let her works praise her in the gates.
PROVERBS 31:31 ESV

Better than fireworks or applause or trophies, the words "Well done" are an eternal reward.

The godly woman will have no greater joy than to hear words of commendation from her Lord. Maybe they will be something like these words from Jesus' parable: "Well done, good and faithful servant. You have been faithful over a little; I will set you over much. Enter into the joy of your master" (Matthew 25:21 ESV).

*Dear heavenly Father, someday I will stand before You, and I
want You to be pleased with how I reflected You on earth. Help me
to live my life with eternity in view. In Jesus' name, amen.*

evening
UNMERITED GRACE

*Then Job answered the LORD and said, "I know that You can
do all things, and that no plan is impossible for You."*
JOB 42:1–2 NASB

After a season of suffering and unjust criticism, Job listened in awe as God revealed His wisdom and power. The Lord rules over all His creation, yet He cares about each person.

It is truly difficult not to complain when the Lord allows us to be subjected to tragedies or hardships. But by trusting His ultimate control, we learn to lean on His everlasting arms. When we feel like we can't take another step, He will carry us and sustain us. God is always with us.

Unwarranted calamity reveals God's mercy to us, His unmerited grace.

*Almighty and powerful God, we trust in You to bring us through
our difficult times. Wrap us in Your loving arms. Amen.*

morning
SOLACE OF HUMOR

Laughter cannot mask a heavy heart.
When the laughter ends, the grief remains.
PROVERBS 14:13 TLB

A distressing loss leaves a hole in our hearts, as well as our lives. Sharing amusing stories softens the edges of that painful cavity. But when the laughter fades, sadness returns. As we continue to recount our memories, the roles of sadness and laughter gradually reverse. Then we can visualize God's hand in the situation, and our torment-ing "if only" thoughts slowly diminish.

If we let Him, the Lord will provide the cheerfulness we need to heal our aching hearts. We will laugh and smile and feel joyful again. . .soon. With God, it's possible.

Gracious God, please comfort our heavy hearts. Give us laughter in our
tears, joy in our sorrow, and hope in Your loving embrace. Amen.

evening
HOPE ABOUNDS

Now may the God of hope fill you with all joy and peace in believing,
so that you will abound in hope by the power of the Holy Spirit.
ROMANS 15:13 NASB

Treating our fellow men and women with love and respect, regardless of their ethnicity or beliefs, carries out the principles of brotherly love that Jesus taught. When we are strong, we help the weak. From our surplus, we provide for the needy. We feed the hungry and tend to the sick or injured. We share the message of Jesus Christ with the hopeless. God's love shines through us so that we illuminate the path to Him.

And as we give of ourselves, our hope abounds.

God of our hope, thank You for granting opportunities to show Your love
through our giving. Let our joy and peace through You bring hope to others.

morning
ROCK OF SAFETY

*From the ends of the earth, I cry to you for help when my heart
is overwhelmed. Lead me to the towering rock of safety.*
PSALM 61:2 NLT

We might experience moments when we think God says, *"Oh, not you again! What do
you want now?"* That is a human response to repetitious cries for help, but not our
heavenly Father's. His loving-kindness is part of His flawless character. He delights in
our prayers and supplications as much as He treasures our obedience to Him.

Seek Him, and you will find Him. Ask, and it will be answered for you.

*Father God, You are with us in our most disheartened moments as well
as our most joyous occasions. Quick to forgive and slow to anger, You
answer our prayers and lead us to the towering rock of safety.*

evening
APPROACHABLE GOD

*On the day I called, You answered me;
You made me bold with strength in my soul.*
PSALM 138:3 NASB

Each answered prayer emboldens us to come to God more frequently. Upon waking
every morning, we can greet the Lord with thanksgiving for a new day and for watching
over us during the night. We ask Him to bless our food at mealtimes. A news report
will prompt us to pray for people we don't know or to praise Him for a good outcome
in a life-threatening situation. As we prepare for bed, we can say, "Good night," and
thank Him for all we accomplished that day.

Through the sacrifice of His only begotten Son, God has made Himself approach-
able. We are His children, and He delights in our bond with Him.

*Heavenly Father, we thank You for answering our prayers and praise You
for making it possible for us to come to You anytime, day or night. Amen.*

morning
OUR CONSOLATION

"Then I would still have this consolation—my joy in unrelenting
pain—that I had not denied the words of the Holy One."
Job 6:10 NIV

In all his suffering, Job remained faithful to the Lord. Despite his friends' apathetic charges against his character, he held tight to his belief that God would relieve him of his blight, either by healing or by death.

When we are in the middle of an impossible adversity such as a natural disaster, sickness, or the death of a loved one, the only stability is in our foundational trust and belief in the Lord. Our faith in Him will be our consolation as He lovingly guides us through hardship.

Loving Father, as we suffer unrelenting pain or emotional anguish,
let us find joy in our faithfulness to You and Your holy words.

evening
RESCUE MISSION

For He rescued us from the domain of darkness, and transferred us to the kingdom
of His beloved Son, in whom we have redemption, the forgiveness of sins.
Colossians 1:13–14 NASB

When our circumstances bring us low, we can find joy in the good news of Jesus Christ. Our belief in Him means this mortal life will be the only hell we will experience. Without Him, this life would be the only heaven we would know. There is no better rescue mission than being saved from the darkness of Satan's clutches and delivered into the eternal kingdom of Christ.

O precious Father God, You alone have rescued us from the domain of
darkness through Christ Jesus. We now have the assurance that You are
with us even now and will protect us from our earthly adversaries.

morning HOLY SPIRIT

Watch over your heart with all diligence, for from it flow the springs of life.
PROVERBS 4:23 NASB

What do we harbor inside us—evil thoughts or goodness? Do springs of life flow through us, or do we find a dried-up dust bowl?

When images of those who have hurt us in the past come to mind and lead to anger, we know the thoughts are not from God. He wants us to enjoy His peace. Our inner Sentry, the Holy Spirit, reminds us to pray for those people and praise God for His everlasting love.

Loving Father, help us set up Your Sentry to guard our hearts and thoughts from Satan's seeds of bitterness. Amen.

evening READ, STUDY, PRAY

Watch yourselves so you don't lose what we have worked for, but that you may receive a full reward.
2 JOHN 8 HCSB

We often weary ourselves arguing with misguided men and women about God's truth. They use Bible verses out of context or extrabiblical writings to spread their rotten apples. To those who are weak in faith, these deceivers sound convincing. The best way we can discern and affirm God's true message is to read and study His Word and pray every day. Then we will enjoy the blessings of His abiding grace, mercy, and peace.

Gracious God, we trust in You and Your holy Word to help us guard against persuasive false teachers. Amen.

morning
MESSAGE OF HOPE

Our hearts ache, but we always have joy. We are poor, but we give spiritual riches to others. We own nothing, and yet we have everything.
2 CORINTHIANS 6:10 NLT

We find contentment in recognizing the true value of God's riches, not the world's. Money and possessions don't last. All the *things* we care about today could be gone tomorrow. But nothing can take away our joy in the everlasting love of the Father, our intimate relationship with Jesus Christ, and the prudent guidance of the Holy Spirit. These eternal possessions are far greater than material wealth.

Like Paul, let us faithfully share God's kingdom and righteousness with the lost right now, for we live for the life to come.

O Lord, the God of our salvation, bless us with Your joy so that we may find contentment in sharing Your message of hope with others. Amen.

evening
FLOURISH

He who trusts in his riches will fall, but the righteous will flourish like the green leaf.
PROVERBS 11:28 NASB

The temptation to trust in material assets to save us is a powerful lure to overcome. But money really doesn't buy happiness, nor can it bribe death. It is a temporary gift in this mortal world.

Whether we're wealthy, poor, or in the middle, God is our Provider. The only riches we can count on to last forever are God's love, His mercy, and His gift of eternal life. Putting our trust in Him, we will flourish in His righteousness.

O God, our bountiful Father, everything belongs to You. We trust in You for all our provisions.

morning
NEW HOPE

*So be truly glad! There is wonderful joy ahead, even
though the going is rough for a while down here.*

1 PETER 1:6 TLB

The proof of our faith is evident as we persevere in joy, knowing that our trials are temporary. We too have that same inheritance of God's eternal love, dispelling the darkness forever when He calls us home.

The dawn's light of joy awaits us at the end of the dark tunnel of our suffering. Every new day provides fresh hope for us as we serve our mighty God.

*O God, our Father, Your promise that our heavenly inheritance
has been firmly fixed brings us joy and strengthens our faith
as we persevere through our worldly troubles. Amen.*

evening
NEVER ALONE

*Therefore, since we have been declared righteous by faith, we have peace with God
through our Lord Jesus Christ. We have also obtained access through Him by faith
into this grace in which we stand, and we rejoice in the hope of the glory of God.*

ROMANS 5:1–2 HCSB

We can confidently face any trial or difficulty in the assurance that we have direct access to the Lord. We are not alone. The Holy Spirit takes every step with us as our Guide, Conscience, and Comforter.

Our loving Father will bring all of His purposes for us to fruition at His discretion. Since we are part of this ongoing process of trials and joys, we take pleasure in the blessing of peace with God.

*Gracious God, let us find comfort in knowing we have peace with You in
every situation we encounter. We rejoice in the hope of Your glory. Amen.*

morning
A NEW TAPESTRY

*And we know that God causes everything to work together for the good of
those who love God and are called according to his purpose for them.*
ROMANS 8:28 NLT

The ups and downs of each experience create a new pattern for a new tapestry. We will adorn our mansions in heaven with beautiful wall hangings created by God. We won't see the dark threads as our heartaches, but as essential portions that add depth to the finished image.

As we wind our way through all our circumstances—the good, the bad, and the mundane—we have the hope of God's promise to work everything out for His glory.

*God, our loving Father, we relinquish our impossible
moments to You—to weave them in with Your blessings for
us. We treasure Your glorious handiwork. Amen.*

evening
JOY IN DISTRESS

*You have seen me tossing and turning through the night.
You have collected all my tears and preserved them in your
bottle! You have recorded every one in your book.*
PSALM 56:8 TLB

God gives His loving attention to every aspect of our suffering, from a single tear to our most devastating heartache. He takes into account every offense, every betrayal, and every loss we endure. He knows our pain. He knows the worries that keep us awake at night. And He holds us in His loving arms.

In David's lament psalm, he pleaded for God's help, acknowledged His continuing presence in his life, and offered praise. Following David's example, we can find joy in our distress through God's kindhearted love. He's got our backs—and our tears.

*Father God, calm our tossing and turning. Give us Your comfort in our
weeping. We place our broken hearts into Your tender embrace.*

morning
POWERFUL ALLIANCE

No one has ever seen God; if we love one another, God remains in us, and His love is perfected in us. By this we know that we remain in Him and He in us, because He has given to us of His Spirit.
1 JOHN 4:12–13 NASB

The Holy Spirit guides us back to the Lord when we stray. He comforts us in our suffering. He reveals God's wisdom to us when we study His Word. He prays for us when we're deeply grieved or distressed and can't find the words. He helps us with our difficult decisions. He prompts us to forgive those who have hurt us with their words or deeds. He encourages us to love one another as Christ loves us. And He shares our joy when God blesses us in abundance. What a powerful alliance we have in abiding with Him!

We love You, Lord. Let us show others our love for You through the abiding Holy Spirit. Amen.

evening
PERMANENT RELIEF

For the creation was subjected to futility, not willingly, but because of Him who subjected it in hope; because the creation itself also will be delivered from the bondage of corruption into the glorious liberty of the children of God. For we know that the whole creation groans and labors with birth pangs together until now.
ROMANS 8:20–22 NKJV

Adam's fall from grace subjected all creation to the penalty of his sin. The whole earth and all it contains are pregnant with the destructive impact of one man's rebellion. As we approach the final days, our trials and tribulations increase. We run the gamut of emotions with each dilemma.

God has planned for the relief of every tribulation. We wait eagerly for His fulfillment of our hope in the resurrection of our bodies.

Then God's joy will replace our tribulations.

Almighty God, we put our trust and hope in You.

morning
REWARDS IN HEAVEN

Therefore I ask you not to become discouraged about my tribulations in your behalf, since they are your glory.
EPHESIANS 3:13 NASB

When we suffer for doing good, or serving others, let us not lose heart. We are storing up wonderful rewards in heaven.

Let us not lose heart when trials come because of everyday burdens. Our life here is fleeting. Tribulations will not follow us into eternity when the Lord calls us home in His time.

Thank You, Lord, for reminding us not to lose heart during our tribulations. We have Your promise of future joy and comfort. Amen.

evening
SONGS OF PRAISE

"Great and marvelous are your works, O Lord God, the Almighty. Just and true are your ways, O King of the nations. Who will not fear you, Lord, and glorify your name? For you alone are holy. All nations will come and worship before you, for your righteous deeds have been revealed."
REVELATION 15:3–4 NLT

Repeat today's song of thanksgiving and praise from the book of Revelation.

The words of wonder and admiration will turn your heart to praise. Every sentence is an intentional focus on God—and His mighty works! This song is a joyful celebration of His infinite power and wisdom—and His righteousness!

Aren't you blessed to know the one and only Miracle-Worker, Truth-Teller, and Promise-Keeper? You are blessed indeed!

Promise-Keeper, I am so blessed to have a growing relationship with You. Please refocus my thoughts. I want to think less of myself and more of You every day. I praise You! Amen.

morning
PROOF OF VICTORY

*"Nevertheless do not rejoice in this, that the spirits are subject to you,
but rather rejoice because your names are written in heaven."*
LUKE 10:20 NKJV

We face spiritual battles all day, every day as we serve on the mission field in our specific calling. Preaching from a downtown corner, leading a children's Sunday school class, writing books and articles—to name a few—spread God's Word. He records our names in heaven as we work for Him. This is proof of our victory.

*Lord of heaven and earth, we rejoice in knowing our names are recorded
as Your servants. We are encouraged to continue our fight in the battle.*

evening
CONTENTMENT

*True godliness with contentment is itself great wealth. After
all, we brought nothing with us when we came into the world,
and we can't take anything with us when we leave it.*
1 TIMOTHY 6:6–7 NLT

What brings real peace and joy? Contentment. The importance of this spiritual discipline can't be overlooked. For contentment coupled with godliness equals "great wealth." Why? Because when we live in a state of gratitude, trusting God will supply all we need, we realize just how immensely blessed we are. Paul writes, "Teach those who are rich in this world not to be proud and not to trust in their money, which is so unreliable. Their trust should be in God, who richly gives us all we need for our enjoyment." (1 Timothy 6:17 NLT).

Do you feel anxious, always striving for the next thing, for more? Pause. Rest. Rely on God's unending strength and love.

*Father, calm my heart and help me to live every day,
grateful for Your surpassing goodness to me.*

morning
A BOUNTIFUL END

*Then the angel of the LORD appeared to the woman and said
to her, "Behold now, you are infertile and have not given
birth; but you will conceive and give birth to a son."*
JUDGES 13:3 NASB

When our productivity slows to a stop, we often feel barren. Maybe our business loses money or health problems reduce our usefulness. The Lord can provide a bountiful end to our desolate season, even if the remedy seems chaotic or exasperating. God, in His sovereignty, will use it to bring about His purpose for our lives. Step back and watch Him move.

*Father God, let us remember Your sovereignty to work
Your glory through any situation and any person. Amen.*

evening
THE LORD REMEMBERS

Yet the chief cupbearer did not remember Joseph, but forgot him.
GENESIS 40:23 NASB

Though being forgotten by man may have discouraged Joseph, the Bible records no complaints. In fact, Joseph seemed to have trusted the Lord so thoroughly that, no matter what, he knew the Lord was always with him.

People forget their promises to us, but the Lord remembers His until the end of time.

*O Lord our God, thank You for Your everlasting presence in our
lives—in our prosperity as well as in our distress. Amen.*

morning
THE GREAT HEALER

He heals the brokenhearted and binds up their wounds.
PSALM 147:3 NKJV

Both grief and despair continue until we adapt to an altered lifestyle. Easier said than done by ourselves. But with the help of Almighty God, small steps toward healing physically, emotionally, and spiritually are possible. When we yield our sorrow to the Lord, He heals our broken hearts and binds our wounds.

God in heaven, You are the Great Healer. We give our pain, our sorrow, and our wounds to You and accept Your love, compassion, and mercy in return. Amen.

evening
CULTURE OF LOVE

Help us, O God of our salvation, for the glory of thy name: and deliver us, and purge away our sins, for thy name's sake.
PSALM 79:9 KJV

The Lord provided a new nation for the early settlers of America to worship Him. Our forefathers, through the inspiration of the Holy Spirit, established a republic to ensure the people of their God-given rights. More recent officeholders, either by choice or negligence over the years, have allowed corrupt government officials to dismantle those liberties. As we unconsciously pushed God's love away, Satan's hatred crept into the land. How can we turn the culture of hate into brotherly love? Only through prayer and godly behavior.

O God of our salvation, we lift up our nation in prayer for a revival of Your love through us. Deliver us from Your enemies, and cleanse us of our evil ways. Amen.

morning
WILLING OBEDIENCE

*And Hannah answered and said, No, my lord, I am a woman
of a sorrowful spirit: I have drunk neither wine nor strong
drink, but have poured out my soul before the LORD.*

1 Samuel 1:15 kjv

God delivered Hannah from a position of shame to one of respect. She conceived and named the baby Samuel, which means "name of God." After holding her son, nursing him, and watching him grow, take his first steps, and speak his first words, she kept her vow. Hannah gave Samuel to Eli, the Levite priest, at the temple. How difficult it must have been to keep her promise.

The Lord honored Hannah's sacrifice and gave her five more children to love.

When we think we have nothing left within us to offer the Lord, He will provide His gift through our own obedience to Him.

*Heavenly Father, open our hearts to be
sacrificially obedient to Your calling. Amen.*

evening
SHARING TRUTH

*"Be strong and very courageous. Be careful to obey all the law
my servant Moses gave you; do not turn from it to the right or
to the left, that you may be successful wherever you go."*

Joshua 1:7 niv

We might have family members and friends who don't share our desire to know and obey God's Word. Their flippant, contrary attitudes frustrate us when we try to lead them to the Promised Land, our heavenly future. But as we read and study the Bible, we find the courage and strength to persist in sharing the truth so they can enter the family of God.

*Loving God, we need Your strength and encouragement to obediently
lead others from their wanderings and into our Promised Land. Amen.*

morning
UNFATHOMABLE PEACE

*May you have more and more of His loving-favor and peace as
you come to know God and our Lord Jesus Christ better.*

2 PETER 1:2 NLV

Christ's shed blood washed away the stains of our immorality and rebellion. Knowledge of His Word helps us maintain self-control and resist temptations. Walking in His righteousness, we show brotherly kindness and love to each other. We are quick to forgive and eager to help.

Holding fast to these qualities in our daily lives draws us closer to the Lord. We will disappoint Him from time to time because we still struggle against fleshly desires. In those times, He offers His mercy when we humbly lay our failings at the foot of the cross. During both harmony and hardship, He fills us with His unfathomable peace.

*Loving Father, please multiply Your grace and peace in us
as we make every effort to know You more intimately.*

evening
OVERCOMERS

*And hope does not disappoint, because the love of God has been poured
out within our hearts through the Holy Spirit who was given to us.*

ROMANS 5:5 NASB

Disappointment comes from many sources, like a broken promise, a rained-out summer vacation, or the latest gadget that doesn't live up to our expectations.

By seeking God's blessing when we face challenges, we overcome. As we press on, we develop perseverance and strength of character. Our hope emerges through our stalwart and faithful moral fiber.

People, places, and things are certain to fail us, but we can always count on our hope in the Lord to carry us past the disappointment.

*Gracious heavenly Father, we exult in the hope of Your glory as
we carry on through life's disappointing moments. Amen.*

morning
HE FINDS US

He asked them, "What are you discussing so intently as you walk along?" They stopped short, sadness written across their faces.
LUKE 24:17 NLT

Discouragement weighs us down. How often do we walk along in sorrow, unaware that the Lord is with us on our journey? If we seek Him in our distress, He finds us. If we ask Him to show us the way, He will direct our paths.

Jesus reveals Himself to us in many wonderful ways. And He won't vanish. He's here within us to stay.

Heavenly Father, we praise You for making it possible for us to walk with You in all our journeys. Let our hearts be glad and rejoice in Your faithful presence.

evening
SET FREE

Who executes justice for the oppressed; who gives food to the hungry. The LORD frees the prisoners.
PSALM 146:7 NASB

God feeds us, not only with body-nourishing sustenance, but also with His soul-nourishing Word. Jesus said that we will live not by bread alone but by every word that proceeds out of the mouth of God. The food we eat fills us for the moment, but God's Word lasts forever.

God liberates us from the prison of hopelessness. Held captive by the sin of Adam, we were doomed to separation from God. But He provided the sacrificial blood of Jesus Christ, which set us free to spend eternity in His glorious embrace. Only God could make this possible.

We praise You, O God, for Your everlasting provisions. Amen.

morning
IN EXPECTATION

*For He has not despised nor scorned the suffering of the afflicted; nor has He
hidden His face from him; but when he cried to Him for help, He heard.*
PSALM 22:24 NASB

Through all his grievances and afflictions, David faithfully petitioned God for relief
from his plight. He praised and honored the Lord in expectation of an answer. Many of
his prayers included a confession of sin, in which he took responsibility for his strife.
God heard and answered.

When we suffer various afflictions, let us come to the Lord with expectation. As
children of the living God, we should be confident that our prayers soar to Him. He
hears, and He answers.

*Our loving Father, we praise You for Your loving-kindness. Forgive us
where we have failed You, and deliver us from our afflictions. Amen.*

evening
SUFFICIENT GRACE

*Concerning this I pleaded with the Lord three times that it might leave
me. And He has said to me, "My grace is sufficient for you, for power
is perfected in weakness." Most gladly, therefore, I will rather boast
about my weaknesses, so that the power of Christ may dwell in me.*
2 CORINTHIANS 12:8–9 NASB

It's easy for us to fall into the snare of pride and boasting when our efforts bring others
to Christ. Our focus veers from working in ministry for the Lord to satisfaction in our
achievements. Paul claimed his "thorn" kept him from self-exaltation.

Even though he implored God three times to remove the source of his misery, the
answer remained the same: Rely on God's sufficient grace. When neither prayer nor
medical science can remedy our pain, perhaps the Lord is using it for His good purpose.

*Merciful Father God, grant us Your grace and mercy as we humbly
serve You, whether in pain or in contentment. Amen.*

morning
HE IS FAITHFUL

Great is his faithfulness; his loving-kindness begins afresh each day. My soul claims the Lord as my inheritance; therefore I will hope in him. The Lord is wonderfully good to those who wait for him, to those who seek for him.
LAMENTATIONS 3:23–25 TLB

God looks at our hearts then distributes His judgments and blessings accordingly. When we come to Him in humble repentance, we can count on His faithfulness to forgive us. Through His loving-kindness, He restores us as a new day, fresh with opportunities to serve Him. No matter how dismal our circumstances might be, God is faithful to us.

Merciful God, great is Your faithfulness! As Your loving children, we put our hope in You for our blessings and disciplines. Amen.

evening
RIGHT PATHS

Trust in the LORD with all your heart, and do not rely on your own understanding; think about Him in all your ways, and He will guide you on the right paths.
PROVERBS 3:5–6 HCSB

We serve an incomparable God, a doting Father, who loves us with an everlasting love. Through our faith in Jesus Christ, we have fellowship with Almighty God. He won't shove us to the side, no matter how gigantic or miniscule our challenge may be. Nothing is too big or too small for Him. He will give us clear instructions to remove the obstacles and will guide us through for His purposes.

O Lord, remind us to trust in You first when impossible situations overwhelm us. We will follow Your guidance to the right paths.

morning
OUR SHEPHERD

*Yea, though I walk through the valley of the shadow of death, I will fear
no evil: for thou art with me; thy rod and thy staff they comfort me.*
PSALM 23:4 KJV

We are the sheep of the Lord's pasture. When our predators close in on us, we look to our Shepherd for protection. God defends us against their vicious attacks with His rod of righteousness.

When we roam away from the flock and into the path of our enemy, God guides our wayward feet back to the safety of His fold with the staff of His holy Word.

We find peace and comfort in the assurance of His ever-present help.

*O God, our Good Shepherd, we praise You and
give thanks for Your protection. Amen.*

evening
POSITIVE PERSPECTIVE

"Vanity of vanities," says the Preacher, "All is vanity."
ECCLESIASTES 12:8 NKJV

A positive perspective is the beginning of contentment. We recognize and take pleasure in what God has provided, trust in His control, and faithfully seek His kingdom and righteousness.

God teaches His three key principles of life: His efforts are wonderful, our mortal life is an adventure, and death is a door to eternity with Him.

*O Lord, we will praise You and give thanks in all times,
in our youth and old age, in our troubles and tranquility.
For we live in the blessed contentment of You.*

morning
TRUST FOR TODAY

*"So do not worry about tomorrow; for tomorrow will worry
about itself. Each day has enough trouble of its own."*
MATTHEW 6:34 NASB

Jesus points out that even birds are content to let God feed them. He created them with an internal trust-in-Him feature. Flowers never say, "I have nothing to wear." God cares about the well-being of His wildlife—and even more so about ours. Let us be content with each day, giving it a chance to generate new opportunities for us.

Living one day at a time doesn't mean we can shirk our responsibility to prepare for the future. Preparation today holds back tomorrow's troubles.

File yesterday in memories. Trust the Lord today!

*Our loving Father, every day You give us is a blessing.
Let us be content and grateful to You for each one. Amen.*

evening
PERSEVERE

*"And so I tell you, keep on asking, and you will receive what you ask for. Keep on
seeking, and you will find. Keep on knocking, and the door will be opened to you."*
LUKE 11:9 NLT

Jesus noted that an earthly father wouldn't substitute a snake for a fish or a scorpion for an egg when responding to his child's request. We have no reason to question our heavenly Father's intentions. If we seek Him with all our heart, we will find Him.

God loves and values us. Let us persevere in our prayers and thanksgivings, waiting expectantly for God to open His door to us.

*Abba Father, we come to You with a heart of gratitude and
hope, confident that You hear and answer our prayers.*

morning WINNING

*For whoever is born of God overcomes the world; and this is
the victory that has overcome the world: our faith.*

1 JOHN 5:4 NASB

The apostle John says that relying on the Holy Spirit to guide us lessens the burden to keep God's commandments. Our obedience leads to a deeper fellowship with our heavenly Father, as well as our family in Christ. This strong bond weakens our sin nature and gives us the spiritual strength to adhere to a life that delights God.

Our love for Jesus grows our faith, and our faith increases our love for Him in perpetuity. We show God's love in us when we support each other during weak moments and rejoice together in the Lord's blessings.

We will overcome the world, though it hates us, with our faith in our Lord and Savior, Jesus Christ.

*Beloved God, we praise You for our victory over
the world. Let us strive to please only You.*

evening CALMING OUTLOOK

*Let the peace that comes from Christ rule in your hearts. For as members
of one body you are called to live in peace. And always be thankful.*

COLOSSIANS 3:15 NLT

We let God's love shine through us in our words, deeds, and manners. How can we not rejoice in every opportunity to serve our Lord each day as we share such a wonderful bond of unity with each other? Our Christian love has taken root and continues to grow within us.

When we allow the peace that comes from Christ to rule our hearts, then compassion, gentleness, and forgiveness come through us naturally. And we are always thankful for that calming outlook.

*Merciful God, we praise You and thank You for the eternal peace of
Christ, which rules in every circumstance of our lives. Amen.*

morning
BECAUSE OF WHO HE IS

God proves His own love for us in that while
we were still sinners, Christ died for us!
ROMANS 5:8 HCSB

God loves us, not because of who we are, but because of who He is. We were helpless, ungodly beings who did nothing to deserve His love. And yet, He poured out His love within our hearts through the Holy Spirit, which bonded us to Him when we believed in Christ as our Savior. We cannot fathom a love so powerful.

Almighty God, we cannot fathom the depth, endurance, or power of Your
love for us. We can only thank You by sharing it with others. Amen.

evening
BIRTHRIGHT

The Spirit Himself testifies with our spirit that we are children of God,
and if children, heirs also, heirs of God and fellow heirs with Christ, if
indeed we suffer with Him so that we may also be glorified with Him.
ROMANS 8:16–17 NASB

What greater witness do we have to attest to our heavenly inheritance than God Himself? The Holy Spirit indwells us at the moment of salvation, and then He claims us as His children. When we suffer, He suffers with us. When we rejoice, He rejoices with us. Being born again into the family of God, we have the assurance that we will never endure hardships alone. As fellow heirs with Christ, we will also share in His glory. We will take part in the rich blessings of His kingdom.

This gives us hope for the near future, as God nurtures us in this mortal life, and the eternal future—where we will be with Him forever.

Gracious and loving Father, thank You for the blessing of
being Your heirs through our Savior, Jesus Christ.

MUSTARD SEED FAITH
morning

Without faith it is impossible to please God, because anyone who comes to him must believe that he exists and that he rewards those who earnestly seek him.
HEBREWS 11:6 NIV

Noah pleased the Lord because he trusted His word. He had never seen a flood, yet he built the ark and rounded up the animals. Abraham passed God's test by offering up Isaac. His promised son with Sarah was the only route to the Messiah. Abraham believed so profoundly that God would fulfill His promise, he didn't hesitate to obey.

If we consider the great cloud of witnesses and their depth of faith, we might feel insignificant. But these were ordinary people like you and me.

Jesus said nothing would be impossible for us if we have faith the size of a mustard seed. Even this faith pleases God. As mustard seeds grow into huge trees, so our faith will mature.

Our God in heaven, we put our faith and trust in You. Amen.

CAN'T YOU HEAR HIM WHISPER?
evening

He says, "Be still, and know that I am God."
PSALM 46:10 NIV

No matter what happens, if we're in close step with Jesus, we won't be so frantic, our spirits won't be riddled with terror. What we need to do is to be still and know that He is God. Know that He is still in control, even though we think the bad news is in control. It's not. God is.

Life would be more peaceful, more focused, more infused with joy if we were already in the midst of communion with God when troubles come.

Can't you hear Him whisper to you, *"Be still, and know that I am God"*?

Lord, help me to want to spend time with You every day of my life—in fair weather as well as stormy. Amen.

RECONCILED RELATIONSHIPS
morning

*God. . .reconciled us to Himself through Christ
and gave us the ministry of reconciliation.*
2 CORINTHIANS 5:18 NASB

As God-followers, you and I have been reconciled ourselves through the sacrificial death of Christ. We have been brought into a restored relationship with our Creator. We can now enjoy the benefits of being part of His family. And we have been given the responsibility of telling others about these benefits. As we interact with friends and coworkers, let's not neglect to tell them that there is good news about the most important relationship they could ever have—one with Christ, who reconciles us to the Father through His cross.

*Dear God, thank You for letting Jesus go to the cross so that
I could have a relationship with You. Help me to share this
good news with others today. In Christ's name, amen.*

THE FLOWER FACTORY
evening

The flowers are springing up, the season of singing birds has come.
SONG OF SOLOMON 2:12 NLT

God manages an authentic flower factory. He is the designer and sustainer of it all. He puts the blooms to bed in the fall and wakes up the seeds in the spring. He watches over the ground through the frosts and smiles as the sun warms the earth again. And, of course, He sends those "April showers" to speed up the growing process.

Without Him, nothing grows. Jesus came to give us "a rich and satisfying life" (John 10:10 NLT). And He also grows people. Just as the flowers spring up with new life, He offers us opportunities to sink our roots down into His grace and bloom even more beautifully.

*Lord, I'm delighted with the beauty of the flowers of spring. I want
to reflect Your glory like they do. Please work in my life and let
the beauty of Jesus shine through me. In His name, amen.*

morning
SIMPLE JOYS

So I decided there is nothing better than to enjoy food and drink and to find satisfaction in work. Then I realized that these pleasures are from the hand of God.
ECCLESIASTES 2:24 NLT

Why is it that we get so bogged down in our modern way of life? Our advances in technology give us more gadgets to manage; our commitment to wellness and fitness and good teeth brings more and more health appointments to our schedules; our desire to raise fully prepared children adds lessons and sports to the family calendar. . . When you add social events and church attendance and more, there isn't a lot of time or mental energy left for delighting in simple joys. But that's what we all crave at the end of the day, isn't it?

Let's commit to work toward the goal of relishing the simple things. After all, they are pleasures from the hand of God.

Lord, thank You for the delights of family and home. Show me how to use my time wisely so I may fully enjoy them. Amen.

evening
THIS IS THE DAY THAT THE LORD HAS MADE. . .AND I JUST MESSED UP!

This is the day which the LORD has made; let us rejoice and be glad in it.
PSALM 118:24 NASB

Have you ever wondered how a perfectly good day can get so messed up?

When things go wrong, how can we fix the day?

We can turn to our God who is the essence of redemption. Since He sent Jesus to redeem our souls, He is able also to redeem even the smallest earthly concern. Coming to Him for mercy is the first step in righting the wrong. Exchanging our failure for His grace reminds us that all is not lost. The day is His, after all, and He offers the hope we need to live it through to the end.

Father God, thank You for Your abundant mercy and constant grace. Redeem my failures today, and help me not to repeat them. In Jesus' name, amen.

A MOMENT TO CONSIDER
morning

"And why are you worried about clothing? Notice how the lilies of the field grow; they do not labor nor do they spin. . .yet I say to you that not even Solomon in all his glory clothed himself like one of these."
MATTHEW 6:28–29 NASB

Jesus used the lilies of the field to demonstrate how the Father provides. He doesn't compare one to another; He created them all and delights in the beauty of each. And how foolish it would be for the flowers to measure themselves against each other! After all, the field isn't theirs and the glory isn't their own. It all belongs to Him. Today, let's trust the Gardener and His individualized care. After all, the lilies do.

Father, I am Yours; let me honor You with what I wear and resist the temptation to compare myself with others. In Jesus' name, amen.

ARE YOU AWARE OF STRESS?
evening

*You will keep in perfect peace all who trust in you,
all whose thoughts are fixed on you!*
ISAIAH 26:3 NLT

We're all aware that stress is widespread and affects us in many ways. And stress management is difficult to implement. Taking a vacation only helps a few weeks out of the year. Relaxing on the weekend only increases the anxiety of Monday morning. . . . Yes, stress is a problem, and it is here to stay.

For Christians, stress seems to fly in the face of Jesus' promise of peace and abundant joy. Yet the peace He gives keeps the stress from destroying us. He keeps the threads of our sanity from unraveling. But He expects us to do what we can to help ourselves. Take a good look at your schedule and your routines, and ask God for wisdom so you can appropriately manage your stress.

God, grant me the serenity to accept the things I cannot change, courage to change the things I can, and wisdom to know the difference. Amen.

THE GOD OF *morning* THE TREES

*Out of the ground the LORD God caused to grow every
tree that is pleasing to the sight and good for food.*
GENESIS 2:9 NASB

A tree is a remarkable symbol of life and beauty. The many species remind us of the variety in people. The tree's resilience in many types of weather makes us remember that the inner life is what keeps it going and the source of that life is nutrition that it draws up from its roots. The shade of a tree shows us that we can contribute to the comfort of others. The many uses of the wood and bark of trees hint that even in death, there is purpose and beauty.

The genius behind the tree is, of course, our Creator God. Genesis tells us that He caused every kind of tree to grow. And it is God who can make us as beautiful and resilient as one of them. Now *that* is something to celebrate!

Dear God, thank You for the gift of trees. In Jesus' name, amen.

A FRESH *evening* START

*"See, I am doing a new thing! Now it springs up; do you not perceive it?
I am making a way in the wilderness and streams in the wasteland."*
ISAIAH 43:19 NIV

As we trust in God, He will make us into new creatures. That's not something we can do ourselves. Our pasts can't hold us back. While Satan loves to remind us of our past and the mistakes we've made, God is turning the wilderness of our lives into beautiful growth with His living water. Remember to trust God for the changes He is making in you and to thank Him for His unfailing love.

*Heavenly Father, we thank You that Your love never runs
out on us. Thank You for covering our sins with the blood of
Your Son and giving us new life every day. Amen.*

THE WARRIOR *morning* SINGS

"The LORD your God is with you, the Mighty Warrior who saves.
He will take great delight in you; in his love he will no longer
rebuke you, but will rejoice over you with singing."
ZEPHANIAH 3:17 NIV

We sing worships songs to God, but have you thought about His joy over you being so great *He* bursts out into song? Or maybe He sings you a sweet lullaby like a parent does to a small child. Next time you sing a worship song, think about what kind of song God would sing about you. Let that fuel your worship of Him and deepen your relationship with the One who loves you so greatly.

Heavenly Father, it is almost too much for us to comprehend that
You, the Creator of the universe, could sing about us. We want to
understand that, even in just the small way our minds can handle.
Show us Your love, and help us to love You more deeply. Amen.

THE GOOD *evening* SHEPHERD

He tends his flock like a shepherd: He gathers the lambs in his arms and
carries them close to his heart; he gently leads those that have young.
ISAIAH 40:11 NIV

One way we can get to know God better is to spend time studying each of His characteristics. This evening's verse shows us a loving Shepherd, gently tending His vulnerable lambs, carrying those who can't walk. The Bible often uses the image of the good shepherd to describe our relationship with God. A good shepherd provides everything the sheep need: food, water, rest, protection, and care.

If you struggle with seeing God as loving you deeply and caring for every detail of your life, meditate on scriptures that show God as the Good Shepherd and ask Him to reveal this part of Himself to you.

Heavenly Father, thank You for being the Good Shepherd.
Your love for me is far more than I could ever imagine. Amen.

morning
WHERE GOD'S WILL BEGINS

*Do not conform to the pattern of this world, but be transformed
by the renewing of your mind. Then you will be able to test and
approve what God's will is—his good, pleasing and perfect will.*
ROMANS 12:2 NIV

Many people like to characterize God as a killjoy, the One who has the list of do's and
don'ts. But at the end of Romans 12:2, you see that God's will for us is good, pleasing,
and perfect. Is that something you can say about the last movie you saw? When we
follow God's will for our lives, it is the path that is the best one for us. God's instructions are intended to help us and keep us from harm. And it starts with our thoughts.

*Dear God, please help us to check what we are putting into
our minds. So much can seem harmless. Help us to thirst
after those things that draw us closer to You. Amen.*

evening
JOY IN TRIALS

*Consider it pure joy, my brothers and sisters, whenever you face
trials of many kinds, because you know that the testing of your
faith produces perseverance. Let perseverance finish its work so
that you may be mature and complete, not lacking anything.*
JAMES 1:2–4 NIV

Nothing that happens on earth will take away our heavenly reward and the joy we will
have in heaven. With Christ, the fruit of our trials can be growth, maturity, peace, and
the fruit of the Spirit instead of despondency, discouragement, depression, and hopelessness. Ask God for wisdom for the next step. Draw close to Him. Let perseverance
finish its work to increase your maturity. Take real steps of obedience and faith, because
the key to joy is obedience.

*Lord, as hard as it is, help us to find joy in the difficult things that
come our way, because we know You have given us the ultimate
victory. And in the process we can become more like You. Amen.*

RUN YOUR RACE IN *morning* COMMUNITY

*Let us draw near to God with a sincere heart. . . . Let us hold unswervingly
to the hope we profess. . . . And let us consider how we may spur one
another on toward love and good deeds, not giving up meeting together,
as some are in the habit of doing, but encouraging one another.*

HEBREWS 10:22–25 NIV

This section of Hebrews is closely related to Psalm 40:9–10, which talks about sharing with our community how God has saved us, how He has helped us, and how He loves us and is faithful. When we share with each other how God is working in our lives, we are encouraged on our journey. This kind of sharing deepens our faith in God and gives us hope. Take advantage of the community God has placed you in on your journey of faith.

*Dear God, sometimes it's hard to make time for church and small
groups in our busy schedules. Help us realize how vital other
believers are in our journey of faith. Remind us to share with
each other what You have been doing in our lives. Amen.*

THE CHOICE TO *evening* BE CHEERFUL

A cheerful look brings joy to the heart; good news makes for good health.

PROVERBS 15:30 NLT

King Solomon, inspired by God, penned this divine wisdom over three thousand years ago. Researchers today know that a positive attitude affects both the length and the quality of one's life. Attitude plays a big role in winning over disease. Attitude is also a choice.

When faced with challenges, choose to stand up straight and smile. Feel the blessings in a positive attitude.

*Lord, I pray that in every situation in my life,
You point me to praise and the positive. Amen.*

morning
I WAS SORT OF BLIND, BUT NOW I SEE!

"But blessed are your eyes because they see, and your ears because they hear."
MATTHEW 13:16 NIV

When Jesus walked on earth, He healed many from physical blindness. He also recognized those whose spiritual blindness kept them from seeing and hearing the truth of His words. Some decided, despite of His teachings, that Jesus was a threat to their investments, business, or positions. Jesus applauds those whose spiritual eyesight is 20/20. He spotlighted the disciples, whose hearts and lives were changed because of Jesus. They saw. They heard. They believed.

We have the treasure of God's Word, which gives us clear vision from here all the way to heaven.

Lord, thank You for Your truth and direction each day. Amen.

evening
PRAISE TO THE WOMEN!

After this, Jesus traveled about from one town and village to another, proclaiming the good news of the kingdom of God. . . . These women were helping to support them out of their own means.
LUKE 8:1, 3 NIV

In Jesus' time, women had few rights and little importance. Yet Jesus included them in His ministry: The women learned from Master Rabbi Jesus; they helped support the ministry. They fed the followers with meals from scratch. When Jesus disappeared from the tomb, the disciples doubted, but the women were the first to see the risen Jesus, and they believed Him to be the Messiah.

Though some may say, "You're only a woman," think of Jesus' take instead: *"You're important enough to share in My kingdom!"*

Jesus, thank You for giving women importance and respect on earth and in heaven. Amen.

morning
DON'T GIVE UP! GOD
SEES YOUR POTENTIAL

*"The LORD does not look at the things people look at. People look
at the outward appearance, but the LORD looks at the heart."*
1 SAMUEL 16:7 NIV

Our Creator sees more of our hearts and potential than anyone on earth. Just as He saw a king in David—while his siblings might have thought of him as only a pesky little brother—God sees the best of what we can be. He believes in us.

When it comes to believing what others believe we can and can't accomplish, trust in God instead and soar without limits!

Heavenly Father, thanks for my skills and the way You lead me in using them.

evening
COINCIDENCE OR GOD?

The old has gone, the new is here!
2 CORINTHIANS 5:17 NIV

God can make you a new person and set you on an astonishing path. His vision for your life and potential is limitless. No matter where you have been or what you have done, God makes you new and clean when you accept Jesus. He also can guide you to break through the barriers of fear to accomplish new achievements and goals.

If He can transform the worst of humans, what can He do with you? Anything!

Lord, light the path ahead that You have planned for me.

morning
EXUDE ENCOURAGEMENT

Let us consider how we may spur one another on toward love and good deeds, not giving up meeting together. . .but encouraging one another.
HEBREWS 10:24–25 NIV

Encouragement promotes growth and confidence. Everyone benefits from words that lift and nourish. Everyone needs encouragement to hurdle the negatives that hit them in words, situations, and relationships. Look for the gifts in others. Compliment others on the things they do well, their progress, and their achievements. Give others the vision God sees in them. Sincere words can change a life. God will show you how.

Lord, give me the words of encouragement others need. Amen.

evening
SEEKING ADVICE

The LORD says, "I will guide you along the best pathway for your life. I will advise you and watch over you. Do not be like a senseless horse or mule that needs a bit and bridle to keep it under control."
PSALM 32:8–9 NLT

In the hurried lives we live, it's easy to fall into a routine and switch over to autopilot. You could say that we become similar to the mule in this scripture—putting hardly any thought into our days and simply being guided by chaos and distraction.

God has more for us. If we take the time to seek out His counsel, He will advise us. He will guide us along the best pathway for our lives and watch over us. He will give us purpose, and our lives will be filled with adventure and divine encounters.

Lord, forgive me for being so busy. Help me to slow down and seek Your counsel. I want to walk this journey of life with You.

A PERSISTENT *morning* LOVE

"O Israel," says the LORD, "if you wanted to return to me, you could. You could throw away your detestable idols and stray away no more."

JEREMIAH 4:1 NLT

God's love for us is vast and deep, and He offers more than second chances! Even though some may never decide to choose Him—and He must deal with them as He sees fit—He continually offers us the chance to return to Him. What wonderful news this is for us!

If you are feeling like you are past redemption, take heart! Read through the book of Jeremiah and be reassured that God desires you. Use a highlighter to mark every time He offers redemption. As you do this, you will begin to see that He ultimately desires for you to be with Him.

Lord, I am amazed by Your love for me! Thank You for not giving up on me and for giving me second chances.

REJOICE! *evening*

Always be full of joy in the Lord. I say it again—rejoice!

PHILIPPIANS 4:4 NLT

Begin to count your blessings, and feel the weight lifting off your shoulders. Feel the freedom you have to enjoy your life. Enjoy your home and the comfort it brings. Enjoy your family, pets, and things you have. Allow yourself to fully feel the joy that comes with the first snow, the first warm breeze of spring, or the first rays of sun in the morning. There are so many wonderful things to enjoy even as you read this!

Life is complicated, yes. But it should never be allowed to rob you of the joy the Lord provides. "I say it again—rejoice!"

Lord, teach me Your ways and show me Your faithfulness, that I may be full of joy because of You. You created this earth to be enjoyed, and enjoy it I shall!

morning
LET GOD REIGN!

Oh, how great are God's riches and wisdom and knowledge! How impossible it is for us to understand his decisions and his ways! For who can know the LORD's thoughts? Who knows enough to give him advice? And who has given him so much that he needs to pay it back? For everything comes from him and exists by his power and is intended for his glory. All glory to him forever! Amen.

ROMANS 11:33–36 NLT

As you go about your day, rest in the assurance that God, not you, is in control. God understands every feeling you experience, and He can comfort you. God knows the best steps for you to take in life, and He is willing to guide you. He is above all and knows all, yet He is not out of reach.

Set your eyes firmly on the Lord, and He will care for you.

Lord, please guide me by Your wisdom and provide for me according to Your riches. I praise You because You are good!

evening
UNFAILING LOVE SURROUNDS US

Many sorrows come to the wicked, but unfailing love surrounds those who trust the LORD.

PSALM 32:10 NLT

No matter what you may be facing, let Psalm 32:10 be your anthem. Let this be the promise you hold close to your heart. Let it be a verse you recite to yourself as you fall asleep at night. "Many sorrows come to the wicked, but unfailing love surrounds those who trust the LORD."

I have this promise to hold on to. Lord, remember me. Remember how I put my trust in You and seek You day and night. Surround me with Your unfailing love, that I may walk through this life knowing that I am secure in Your hands. Amen.

morning
FOCUSING ON TODAY

Don't brag about tomorrow, since you don't know what the day will bring.
PROVERBS 27:1 NLT

We will find that we can be happier in life by simply taking each day as it comes. If we are not focused on our calendar of events, and instead decidedly focused on each moment of *this* day, we will have the ability to enjoy moments that otherwise would have passed us by. The hilarious thing a child just said that bubbles into laughter. A lunch date with a friend that encourages your soul. These are all moments we can revel in and enjoy, rather than thinking about the next thing on the list or schedule.

Today, let's keep our focus on only the events of *today*. We will find fulfillment, laughter, and a reduction in stress if we refuse to borrow the worries of tomorrow.

Lord, thank You for encouraging me to live life moment by moment.
Help me to recognize the blessings that abound in each day. Amen.

evening
AN EVER-FLOWING SPRING

"The LORD will guide you continually, giving you water when
you are dry and restoring your strength. You will be like a
well-watered garden, like an ever-flowing spring."
ISAIAH 58:11 NLT

This is one of those verses to keep close to your heart during a busy season. When it feels like your next day of rest is far off, this is a promise to cling to and draw strength from. Every day, as often as you can, make space for quiet moments with the Lord. A few moments can give you everything you need. Even as you fall asleep at night, this passage can be one you recite to bring you into a peaceful rest.

Lord, as a gentle rain brings life to the driest soil, so Your
very presence and love bring life to my soul. Amen.

morning
FINDING JOY

*And now, dear brothers and sisters, one final thing. Fix your thoughts on
what is true, and honorable, and right, and pure, and lovely, and admirable.
Think about things that are excellent and worthy of praise. Keep putting
into practice all you learned and received from me—everything you heard
from me and saw me doing. Then the God of peace will be with you.*

PHILIPPIANS 4:8–9 NLT

There is such a benefit to fixing your thoughts on things that are good, pleasing, and perfect. God was not being legalistic when he said to think on these things. He was giving us sound advice. He was showing us the path to peace. What makes your heart beat a little faster? What brings joy to your heart and a smile to your lips? What makes your eyes crinkle with laughter and your feet step a little lighter? Think about these things.

*O Lord, You delight in every detail of my life!
May I fully indulge in the joy of life today. Amen.*

evening
REMEMBER

*"In the future your children will ask you, 'What do these stones mean?'
Then you can tell them, 'They remind us that the Jordan River stopped
flowing when the Ark of the LORD's Covenant went across.' These stones
will stand as a memorial among the people of Israel forever."*

JOSHUA 4:6–7 NLT

What has God done for you? It is just as important for us to build memorials in our lives—memorials that declare the goodness of God.

There is no right way to remember what God has done. It can be through journaling or a photograph. It could be a vase sitting in your living room filled with little slips of paper full of the ways God has provided on a daily basis. Each of these ways is a means to an end, and that end is remembering the faithfulness of God.

*You have been so good to me, Lord! Remind me of the big and the
little things, that my faith in You may grow and my joy increase.*

morning
BEAUTIFULLY IMPERFECT

*Yet I am confident I will see the LORD's goodness
while I am here in the land of the living.*
PSALM 27:13 NLT

We are imperfect, so let's find some comfort in that. We can accept that we are broken and work from there. A lot of the time, we stress ourselves out by trying to be flawless. But when we put that type of obsessive striving aside, we can sort through the pieces with a clear head because we're not hindered by trying to do it "just right." There is freedom in giving ourselves permission to be imperfect.

*O God, I need You more than ever. I am broken into a
thousand pieces. I will find comfort in Your peace that passes
understanding, and in Your love that knows no limits.*

evening
DARE TO DREAM

I can do all things through Christ who strengthens me.
PHILIPPIANS 4:13 NKJV

God's Word says that we can do all things through Christ who gives us strength. *All* means *all*, right? So encourage the children in your life to dream big, and then follow their example.

We should all be able to believe BIG when it comes to the dreams and ambitions that God has placed within us. God wouldn't have placed them there if He weren't going to help us achieve them. So get back that childlike faith and start believing BIG.

Lord, help me to dream big and encourage others in their dreams. Amen.

morning
UNCONDITIONAL LOVE

*"For the LORD your God is living among you. He is a mighty savior.
He will take delight in you with gladness. With his love, he will calm
all your fears. He will rejoice over you with joyful songs."*
ZEPHANIAH 3:17 NLT

We love to dote on our kids—even the canine and feline ones. Well, guess what? That's exactly how God is. He is a doting parent too. If He had a "Daddy's Brag Book," our pictures would be in it! And just like I couldn't wait to buy Mollie Mae a new collar, God loves to give His children good gifts. The Bible says, "If you then, though you are evil, know how to give good gifts to your children, how much more will your Father in heaven give the Holy Spirit to those who ask him!" (Luke 11:13 NIV).

Father, thank You for loving me so much. Amen.

evening
WALK IN YOUR CALLING

*Therefore, since we are surrounded by such a great cloud of witnesses, let
us throw off everything that hinders and the sin that so easily entangles.
And let us run with perseverance the race marked out for us.*
HEBREWS 12:1 NIV

Whether you're called to be a firefighter or a teacher or a stay-at-home mom, you are important. Your life means something. And God called you to fulfill that special role, because He had a plan for your life from the time you were in your mother's womb. It's powerful to realize that you're doing exactly what you were born to do, and the devil knows this truth. That's why he will do everything he can to discourage you and get you to compare yourself with others and their callings, trying to convince you that your calling is not as important. Don't fall for his lies. Instead, thank God for your calling and walk in it with great enthusiasm and courage. Run your race. When you do, you'll enjoy the journey and every step toward that finish line will be purposeful.

*Father, I thank You for creating me for such a time as this. Help me
never to forget the importance of my calling, and help me to fulfill my
divine destiny. I love You, Lord. In the mighty name of Jesus, amen.*

morning
A LOVING FATHER

*For the LORD corrects those he loves, just as a
father corrects a child in whom he delights.*
PROVERBS 3:12 NLT

Children respond to correction best when it comes from a loving parent. A loving parent doesn't discipline a child because they are embarrassed about the behavior, but because they love the child and long for a better future. They want to protect their child from unnecessary pain and teach them the way they should go. Our Father corrects us because He delights in us. We can listen and respond to His correction, because we know, beyond a shadow of doubt, that everything He does springs from His deep, deep love for us.

*Father, You love me and You delight in me. I can hardly believe it's
true. When You are correcting me, help me to remember this blessed
truth and receive Your correction as a beloved child. Amen.*

evening
THE PATH TO GOD'S WILL

*All the paths of the LORD are faithfulness and truth to those
who comply with His covenant and His testimonies.*
PSALMS 25:10 NASB

God doesn't always give us a clear road map, but He does clearly ask us to keep His covenant and His testimonies. When we do so, our individual steps will become clearer, and we will find ourselves more and more in step with His will. As He guides us closer to our destination, we will find much joy in the journey.

*Lord, when I agonize over which way to take, help me to focus
on Your covenant and Your testimonies. Help me to trust You to
lead me on the paths You want me to take, knowing that when
I follow Your Word, I am always in Your will. Amen.*

morning
HE IS MORE THAN ABLE

Now all glory to God, who is able, through his mighty power at work within us, to accomplish infinitely more than we might ask or think. Glory to him in the church and in Christ Jesus through all generations forever and ever! Amen.
EPHESIANS 3:20–21 NLT

When we think of God, we tend to think about His abilities relative to our own. We don't even consider doing great things for Him, because we can't fathom how it could happen. Could you be unknowingly limiting God? Whether or not we recognize it, His mighty power, the Holy Spirit, is at work within us, doing more than we can imagine. Avail yourself of this power—let Him do through you things that you can't even begin to comprehend.

Father, I cannot even begin to comprehend Your majesty. Thank You for the Holy Spirit, working in and through me, to accomplish Your purposes through Christ and the Church. Amen.

evening
THE WORLD IS WATCHING

How great is the goodness you have stored up for those who fear you. You lavish it on those who come to you for protection, blessing them before the watching world.
PSALM 31:19 NLT

One of the ways God demonstrates His love to a hurting world is to lavish His love upon His children. When we whine and complain about little things, we diminish God's blessing to us before a watching world. It's important for us to respond appropriately to all of God's blessings and to demonstrate how deeply our heavenly Father loves us.

Father, You have blessed me abundantly. I confess that I sometimes miss those blessings and spend more time focusing on what is lacking than on what You have provided. Help me to be grateful before a watching world. Amen.

IT'S NOT ABOUT *morning* THE RULES

For the Kingdom of God is not a matter of what we eat or drink,
but of living a life of goodness and peace and joy in the Holy Spirit.
ROMANS 14:17 NLT

While there are some do's and don'ts, the Christian life is ultimately not about rules. In fact, the more rules we make for ourselves and others, the more vulnerable we are to creating our own version of the Gospel, just like the Pharisees did. We become ensnared in a legalistic way of life, bound to a man-made version of what not to do that leads us a long way from the abundant life God has planned for us. The rules are secondary to living the Christian life, which is about goodness, peace, and joy, available only through the Holy Spirit.

Holy Spirit, help me not to focus on rules. Instead, draw me to living a life
of goodness, peace, and joy, gifts I can only receive through You. Amen.

THE OLD, OLD *evening* STORY

I have inherited Your testimonies forever, for they are the joy of my heart.
PSALM 119:111 NASB

We weren't there when He parted the Red Sea and carried the Israelites out of captivity. We weren't with Moses when he received the Ten Commandments; nor were we with young David when he killed the giant. But as God's children, we have inherited these testimonies. These stories are a part of our legacy and give us a common connection with believers throughout the centuries—our brothers and sisters in Christ. Relish the stories of God; they are the joy of your heart.

Father, thank You for the testimony in scripture. I praise You for my
family legacy—thank You for sharing these sweet stories with me. I want
to pass them down to my loved ones and experience the joy of family
togetherness with all the believers throughout the ages. Amen.

morning
NEW EVERY MORNING

*This I recall to my mind, therefore I have hope. Through the LORD's
mercies we are not consumed, because His compassions fail not.
They are new every morning; great is Your faithfulness.*
LAMENTATIONS 3:21–23 NKJV

God's Word says we don't have to be consumed by regrets from the past or fears of the
future. Every morning, with the rising of the sun, comes a new measure of His mercy,
compassion, and faithfulness. So let your worrisome thoughts go and replace them
with hope. His mercy and compassion will never fail.

*Father, when I can't sleep, bring Your mercy and compassion to
my mind. Give me hope in Your faithfulness. Thank You for the
promise of the new morning, and help me to rest in You. Amen.*

evening
PLANTED BY THE WATER

*"But blessed are those who trust in the LORD and have made the
LORD their hope and confidence. They are like trees planted along
a riverbank, with roots that reach deep into the water. Such trees
are not bothered by the heat or worried by long months of drought.
Their leaves stay green, and they never stop producing fruit."*
JEREMIAH 17:7–8 NLT

Psalm 1 also paints a beautiful picture of what it means to stand steadfastly with
the Lord. Trees don't get to choose where they're planted; but we do, and we must
choose carefully. For maximum growth, we must plant ourselves near a source of
living water. . .close to the Body of Christ. We must immerse ourselves in prayer, feed
ourselves with God's Word, and be fertilized and challenged by the companionship
of other believers. When we do this, we can be assured that we will stay healthy and
never stop producing fruit.

*Father, help my roots to grow deep as I learn
more and more to depend on You. Amen.*

MY MORNING PRAYER
morning

*Let me hear Your faithfulness in the morning; for I trust in You;
teach me the way in which I should walk; for to You I lift up my soul.*
PSALM 143:8 NASB

No matter what our day holds, we can face it confidently by practicing this scripture. Let's look for God's loving-kindness and keep trusting Him no matter what. Ask Him to teach and lead us in the way He wants us to go. We have the privilege of offering up our souls (thoughts, emotions, and will) to Him anew each morning. Have a good day.

*Good morning, Lord. You are my loving Father, secure Refuge,
and trustworthy God. Deliver me from my enemies and show me
Your loving heart as I trust in You. Help me to please You today
in my decisions and goals, in my attitudes toward circumstances,
and in the way I respond to people around me. Amen.*

KNOWING CHRIST MEANS OBEYING HIM
evening

We know that we have come to know him if we keep his commands.
1 JOHN 2:3 NIV

How do Christians *know* Christ? By obeying His Word and living as He did (1 John 2:5–6). How do Christians *obey* Christ? By loving. Jesus said all the commands hang on these two: "Love the Lord your God with all your heart and with all your soul and with all your mind" and "Love your neighbor as yourself" (Matthew 22:37–40 NIV). God knows that life works best when we obey, and that means loving God and people.

*Father in heaven, thank You for bringing me to the cross of Christ,
where all my sins were forgiven and I received Your gift of new life
because I believed. As Your child, I want to live for You by being
obedient. It's the least I can do in gratitude for Your salvation.*

morning
IT'S ALIVE!

*If you look carefully into the perfect law that sets you free, and
if you do what it says. . .God will bless you for doing it.*
JAMES 1:25 NLT

What is currently your greatest need or concern? Find verses that deal with that issue
and write them out. Choose one to memorize. Every time that problem pesters you,
wield your sword (quote your verse) and ask God for help. Romans 10:13 promises
that when we call on the name of the Lord, we will be delivered (saved or rescued).

    In a few weeks, you will find the problem or temptation diminishing. When we
keep responding to the seed of God's Word and using it in our lives, it grows and bears
fruit even when we don't realize it.

*Dear Lord, thank You for being the Lover of my soul and for
speaking to me through Your written Word. Amen.*

evening
ETERNAL REWARDS

*Choosing rather to suffer affliction with the people of God than to enjoy
the passing pleasures of sin, esteeming the reproach of Christ greater
riches than the treasures in Egypt; for he looked to the reward.*
HEBREWS 11:25–26 NKJV

As Christians, we get to choose our focus and the goals we devote our lives to. While
eternal life is a free gift, not a reward, to everyone who believes in Christ, the Bible
also teaches that believers will receive rewards in heaven for being "good and faithful
servants" (Matthew 25:21).

*Lord, I want to remember that my life here is a temporary one so that
my choices will glorify You. Make me willing to give up human pleasures
in exchange for future joys at Your right hand forever. Amen.*

morning
CLOTHED

She is clothed with strength and dignity; she can laugh at the days to come.
PROVERBS 31:25 NIV

When you feel totally beaten down and think there is no way you can continue, all you need to do is ask for God's strength. He will clothe you in it to cover up all your vulnerability and brokenness.

No wonder the woman in this verse could laugh at the future. She knew that in God, she had limitless strength and a dignity that no one could take away. Nothing in her future—or yours—could change that.

Lord, thank You that I am clothed with strength and dignity.
Nothing on this earth can take away the dignity I have as
Your daughter or break the strength that You offer me.

evening
DO NOT FEAR

"Do not fear, for I am with you; do not be afraid, for I am
your God. I will strengthen you, I will also help you, I will
also uphold you with My righteous right hand."
ISAIAH 41:10 NASB

Stop looking anxiously around you at all the burdens, worries, and fears of your life. Instead, focus on your God. He promises to strengthen and help you. Nothing in this world is so overwhelming that you cannot overcome it with the almighty God's strength. And even when you feel that you have fallen with no strength to get up, He promises to hold you up with His hand.

Lord, help me to fully understand that You are with me, strengthening
me, helping me, and holding me in Your hands. Amen.

morning
TRUST AND LEAN

Trust in the LORD with all your heart and do not lean on your own understanding.
PROVERBS 3:5 NASB

How often do you lean on your own understanding and strength instead of God's? You are remarkably less capable of controlling your life than God is. Instead of trusting yourself—someone who doesn't know the future and certainly can't control it—lean on the all-powerful God who knows each step you will take. Relinquish all your anxious thoughts over to His control. Trusting God with your future is far more productive than worrying about it. So lean on Him and trust Him with *everything* in your heart. He will sustain you.

Lord, forgive me for not trusting You as I should. Forgive me for leaning on my own understanding instead of relying on Your infinite wisdom and strength. Thank You that these commands You give me are for my greatest benefit. Amen.

evening
ACKNOWLEDGE GOD

In all your ways acknowledge Him, and He will make your paths straight.
PROVERBS 3:6 NASB

When life feels mundane and meaningless, acknowledge that God has put you where you are for a reason and that He will not waste your time or your talents. Worship Him while you wait for the next step in life.

God promises that when you acknowledge Him in all your ways, He will make your paths straight. What a comfort that He will guide you and lead you on the path you should take.

Lord, I acknowledge that You are sovereign and loving in the circumstance that I am in right now. Continue to lead me down a straight path. Amen.

DAY 362

morning
HOPE-GIVER

*Now may the God of hope fill you with all joy and peace in believing,
so that you will abound in hope by the power of the Holy Spirit.*
ROMANS 15:13 NASB

You can hope for an eternity spent illumined by the light of your heavenly Father. You can hope for the time when God will wipe every tear from your eye. You can hope for the time when you will be reunited with all God's children who have gone before you. You can hope in a God who will never leave you and never forsake you through life on this earth and even through death. You can hope in a joyful welcome home at the end of this life. You can hope in the fact that God works everything according to His will for the good of His children. God truly is the God of hope.

Lord, fill me with the joy and peace that come with putting my hope in You.

evening
LOVE IN THE DARK

*I recall this to my mind, therefore I wait. The LORD's acts of
mercy indeed do not end, for His compassions do not fail. They
are new every morning; great is Your faithfulness.*
LAMENTATIONS 3:21–23 NASB

The author of these verses is suffering deeply. He is greatly afflicted and nearly without hope. But even in the deepest pit of despair, he has the experience to back up his claims that God's love has never ceased from his life. When you go through a dark period in your life, be encouraged by the testimony of this fellow child of God. God is not a fair-weather God who abandons you when the going gets rough. His love will find you and carry you through the darkest and most soul-wrenching of trials. You can have the same faith and unwavering confidence in His compassion that you have in the fact that the sun will rise in the morning. There is hope even in the darkest place.

*Lord, may I experience Your compassion in amazing ways so that
I too can have faith in Your love in the midst of trials. Amen.*

morning
WATCH EXPECTANTLY

*But as for me, I will be on the watch for the LORD; I will wait
for the God of my salvation. My God will hear me.*
MICAH 7:7 NASB

Wait for God. Too often we become impatient after we pray, wanting a quick fix or an obvious and direct answer. In this verse, we find that Micah was willing to wait for God to answer. While you wait, praise Him for what He is already doing in your life.

Your God will hear you. Be confident in this. God does not turn away from His children. He hears you and desires to give you good things. Next time you pray, be confident that the Most High God is listening.

*Lord, thank You that You hear every one of my prayers.
I wait expectantly to see in what ways You will answer me.*

evening
KNOWN AND LOVED

*I am the good shepherd, and I know My own and My own know Me, just as the
Father knows Me and I know the Father; and I lay down My life for the sheep.*
JOHN 10:14–15 NASB

Even though Christ knows the darkest and most secret parts of you, He still loves you. He doesn't love you because He can gain something from it. He doesn't love you on a surface, nonchalant level. He *laid down His life* for you. There is no greater love. He knows you better than anyone else does, and yet He loves you with a deeper, purer love than anyone else can give you. You are deeply known and deeply loved.

*Lord, I can't comprehend that You would love me in spite of all my
faults. Thank You for bestowing on me a love I don't deserve.*

morning
EARTHEN VESSELS

But we have this treasure in earthen containers, so that the extraordinary greatness of the power will be of God and not from ourselves.

2 CORINTHIANS 4:7 NASB

Maybe you balk at the thought of being weak. After all, self-sufficiency is a highly regarded trait in our world. But we all experience various times of weakness and brokenness. Instead of being ashamed of this, ask God to use it for His glory. Don't be afraid to admit your vulnerability to Him and ask Him to shine through it.

Carry the treasure He has bestowed on you with joy, rejoicing that He would choose you as a vessel through which to shine His glory.

*Lord, may I see my weaknesses not as something to be
ashamed of but as something to be thankful for as they
display Your glory all the more clearly. Amen.*

evening
ETERNAL PERSPECTIVE

Therefore we do not lose heart, but though our outer person is decaying, yet our inner person is being renewed day by day. For our momentary, light affliction is producing for us an eternal weight of glory far beyond all comparison, while we look not at the things which are seen, but at the things which are not seen; for the things which are seen are temporal, but the things which are not seen are eternal.

2 CORINTHIANS 4:16–18 NASB

It's easy to let your focus get distracted by the myriad issues confronting you on a daily basis. But this verse encourages you to look less at the things that are seen and more at the eternal things that are unseen. Commit to strengthening your relationship with God—that is what will last into eternity. When you have the right perspective, the difficulties of this world will truly seem momentary and light.

*Lord, give me an eternal perspective.
Focus my attention on eternal matters. Amen.*

morning
ROOTED AND GROUNDED

*And that you, being rooted and grounded in love, may be able to
comprehend with all the saints what is the width and length and
height and depth, and to know the love of Christ which surpasses
knowledge, that you may be filled to all the fullness of God.*
EPHESIANS 3:17–19 NASB

Pray that you would be filled up to all the fullness of God. Being filled up to the full-ness of God leaves no room for anything else. That God would desire to fill us up with Himself is awe-inspiring. Ask Him to do just that.

*Lord, ground me in Your love. Help me to comprehend Your overwhelming
love for me. Fill me up to overflowing with Your Spirit. Amen.*

evening
GIVE THANKS

I will give thanks to the LORD with all my heart; I will tell of all Your wonders.
PSALM 9:1 NASB

Consider the wonderful things God has done for you and the love and blessings He has bestowed on you. Remind yourself now of all His wonders. Reminisce about the work He has done in your life and the lives around you in the past year. Ground your mind now in an attitude of thanksgiving that will saturate the rest of your days.

*Lord, thank You for choosing and adopting me as one of Your children.
Thank You for all the material blessings You have freely given me. Thank
You for the people You have placed in my life to encourage me and stand by
me. Thank You that I live in a country where I can openly give You thanks
and speak of Your wonders. Thank You for Your faithfulness through my
life. Thank You for lavishing on me a love that is beyond comprehension.
Thank You that I have a steadfast hope in my salvation and an eternity
with You. Thank You that You will never leave or forsake me. Amen.*

SCRIPTURE INDEX